PS 173 .W46 C87 2000

Curry, Renee R., 1955-

White women writing white :
H.D., Elizabeth Bishop,
$62.50

WHITE WOMEN WRITING WHITE

**Recent Titles in
Contributions in Women's Studies**

Dissenting Women in Dickens's Novels: The Subversion of Domestic Ideology
Brenda Ayre

Deprivation and Power: The Emergence of Anorexia Nervosa in
Nineteenth-Century French Literature
Patricia A. McEachern

A History of Popular Women's Magazines in the United States, 1792–1995
Mary Ellen Zuckerman

Busybodies, Meddlers, and Snoops: The Female Hero in Contemporary
Women's Mysteries
Kimberly J. Dilley

Untying the Tongue: Gender, Power, and the Word
Linda Longmire and Lisa Merrill, editors

Scheherazade's Sisters: Trickster Heroines and Their Stories in World Literature
Marilyn Jurich

Gender and Genre in Gertrude Stein
Franziska Gygax

Rewriting the Word: American Women Writers and the Bible
Amy Benson Brown

Ethnicity and Gender in the Barsetshire Novels of Angela Thirkell
Penelope Fritzer

Women of Courage: Jewish and Italian Immigrant Women in New York
Rose Laub Coser, Laura S. Anker, and Andrew J. Perrin

Contemporary Irish Women Poets: Some Male Perspectives
Alexander G. Gonzalez

Queer Poetics: Five Modernist Women Writers
Mary E. Galvin

WHITE WOMEN WRITING WHITE

H.D., Elizabeth Bishop, Sylvia Plath, and Whiteness

Renée R. Curry

Contributions in Women's Studies, Number 175

GREENWOOD PRESS
Westport, Connecticut • London

Library of Congress Cataloging-in-Publication Data

Curry, Renée R., 1955–
    White women writing white : H.D., Elizabeth Bishop, Sylvia Plath, and whiteness / Renée R. Curry.
       p. cm.—(Contributions in women's studies, ISSN 0147–104X ; no. 175)
    Includes bibliographical references and index.
    ISBN 0–313–31019–X (alk. paper)
    1. American poetry—White authors—History and criticism.
2. Whites in literature. 3. H.D. (Hilda Doolittle), 1886–1961—Criticism and interpretation. 4. Bishop, Elizabeth, 1911–1979—Criticism and interpretation. 5. Women and literature—United States—History—20th century. 6. American poetry—Women authors—History and criticism. 7. American poetry—20th century—History and criticism. 8. Plath, Sylvia—Criticism and interpretation.
9. Whites—United States—Race identity. 10. Race awareness in literature. 11. White women in literature. I. Title. II. Series.
PS173.W46C87 2000
811'.5099287—dc21   99–21706

British Library Cataloguing in Publication Data is available.

Copyright © 2000 by Renée R. Curry

All rights reserved. No portion of this book may be reproduced, by any process or technique, without the express written consent of the publisher.

Library of Congress Catalog Card Number: 99–21706
ISBN: 0–313–31019–X
ISSN: 0147–104X

First published in 2000

Greenwood Press, 88 Post Road West, Westport, CT 06881
An imprint of Greenwood Publishing Group, Inc.
www.greenwood.com

Printed in the United States of America

The paper used in this book complies with the Permanent Paper Standard issued by the National Information Standards Organization (Z39.48–1984).

10 9 8 7 6 5 4 3 2

62.50

Copyright Acknowledgments

The author and publisher gratefully acknowledge permission for use of the following material:

From Richard Dyer, *White* (Routledge, 1997). Reprinted with permission.

From H.D., *Collected Poems: 1912–1944*, edited by Louis L. Martz (New Directions, 1983). Copyright © 1982 by The Estate of Hilda Doolittle. Reprinted by permission of New Directions Publishing Corp. and Carcanet Press Limited.

From H.D., *Helen in Egypt* (New Directions, 1961). Copyright © 1961 by Norman Holmes Pearson. Reprinted by permission of New Directions Publishing Corp. and Carcanet Press Limited.

From H.D., *Hermetic Definition* (New Directions, 1972). Copyright © 1972 by Norman Holmes Pearson. Reprinted by permission of New Directions Publishing Corp. and Carcanet Press Limited.

From H.D., *Trilogy* (New Directions, 1973). Copyright © 1944, 1945, 1946 by Oxford University Press, renewed 1973 by Norman Holmes Pearson. Reprinted by permission of New Directions Publishing Corp. and Carcanet Press Limited.

Excerpts from *The Complete Poems 1927–1979* by Elizabeth Bishop. Copyright © 1979, 1983 by Alice Helen Methfessel. Reprinted by permission of Farrar, Straus & Giroux, Inc.

Excerpts from "The Arrival of the Bee Box," "Cut," "Daddy," "The Swarm," and "Wintering" from *Ariel* by Sylvia Plath. Copyright © 1963 by Ted Hughes. Copyright renewed. Reprinted by permission of HarperCollins Publishers, Inc.

Experpt from "Fever 103" from *Ariel* by Sylvia Plath. Copyright © 1963 by Ted Hughes. Reprinted by permission of HarperCollins Publishers, Inc. "Fever 103" originally appeared in *Poetry Magazine*.

Excerpts from "The Rivals" and "Tulips" from *Ariel* by Sylvia Plath. Copyright © 1962 by Ted Hughes. Copyright renewed. Reprinted by permission of HarperCollins Publishers, Inc.

"Fulbright Scholars," "Perfect Light," "18 Rugby Street," and "You Hated Spain" from *Birthday Letters* by Ted Hughes. Published and reprinted by permission of Faber and Faber Ltd.

From *Collected Poems* by Sylvia Plath. Published and reprinted by permission of Faber and Faber Ltd.

Excerpts from "Face Lift," "The Other," "Electra on Azalea Path," "Whiteness I Remember," "Conversation Among the Ruins," "Winter Landscape, With Rooks," "Pursuit," "Tale of a Tub," and "Soliloquy of the Solipsist" from *The Collected Poems of Sylvia Plath*, edited by Ted Hughes. Copyright © 1960, 1965, 1971, 1981 by the Estate of Sylvia Plath. Editorial material copyright © 1981 by Ted Hughes. Reprinted by permission of HarperCollins Publishers, Inc.

"Moonrise" from *The Colossus and Other Poems* by Sylvia Plath. Copyright © 1960 by Sylvia Plath. Reprinted by permission of Alfred A. Knopf Inc.

Excerpts from "Love Letter" and "The Surgeon at 2:00 A.M." from *Crossing the Water* by Sylvia Plath. Copyright © 1962 by Ted Hughes. Reprinted by permission of HarperCollins Publishers, Inc.

Excerpts from "In Plaster" and "Magi" from *Crossing the Water* by Sylvia Plath. Copyright © 1971 by Ted Hughes. Reprinted by permission of HarperCollins Publishers, Inc.

From *The Journals of Sylvia Plath* by Ted Hughes, ed. Copyright © 1982 by Ted Hughes as Executor of the Estate of Sylvia Plath. Used by permission of Doubleday, a division of Random House, Inc.

Excerpt from "Thalidomide" from *Winter Trees* by Sylvia Plath. Copyright © 1963 by Ted Hughes. Copyright renewed. Reprinted by permission of HarperCollins Publishers, Inc.

I dedicate this book to
Mei Debra Lan Qin Curry,
Debi Curry, and Bill Brigham,
the people who teach me daily
about love.

Contents

	Acknowledgments	xi
Chapter 1	Introduction: "A Poetics of Presumption"	1
Chapter 2	"Minute Granules on a White Thread": H.D. and a Masterful Whiteness	21
Chapter 3	"A Sort of Inheritance; White": Elizabeth Bishop and Selective Self-Reflection on Whiteness	75
Chapter 4	"White: It Is a Complexion of the Mind": The Enactment of Whiteness in Sylvia Plath's Poetry	123
	Conclusion	169
	Bibliography	171
	Index	179

Acknowledgments

I must first acknowledge and thank my parents, Harry and Carole Curry, for my life, my talents, and my perspectives. Devin and Curt Hood, my niece and nephew, keep me humble through every project. They are the best people to laugh with on the face of the planet. Without Patricia Dyer, who cares for and loves my daughter while I write, and without Kaleena Renée Llorente, baby-sitter *extraordinaire*, I would not have been able to put these words on paper. Of course, there is also Ben, the Labrador who warms my feet every moment I sit at the computer.

The finest people with whom I have had the pleasure of critiquing, thinking, collaborating, and debating the issues in *White Women Writing White* include its earliest readers Terry Allison and Sherri Williams Foster. In addition to those readers, Dawn Formo and Susie Lan Cassel have provided immeasurable insight and support throughout the project. My colleagues and friends in the History Program at California State University, San Marcos, Peter Arnade, Patty Seleski, and Jill Watts, generously walked me through the complicated historical aspects of whiteness. David Avalos, Steven Gould Axelrod, Elizabeth Colwill, Catherine Cucinella, Sharon Elise, Victoria Fabry, Joni Foster, Don Funes, Merryl Goldberg, Vicki Golich, Tamara Rodgers Hopton, Cathryn Bradeen Knox, Andrea Liss, Regina Eisenbach Llorente, Theresa Nesbitt, Deborah Small, Gabriella Sonntag, Carlos von Son, and Pat Worden have been the most collegial of partners in this intellectual endeavor. No descriptors can reveal the variety of ways these people have helped me.

I must acknowledge and thank all the extraordinary teachers from whom I have learned the significance of literary study: Theresa Coletti, Stephen Dobyns, Burton Hatlen, Constance Hunting, Joyce Kornblatt, Nancy McKnight, Stanley Plumly, Kenneth Rosen, Martha Nell Smith, Steve Trechter, Chase Twitchell, Marie Urbanski, Joseph Wittreich, and David Wyatt. I owe sincere appreciation to Toni Morrison for writing *Playing in the Dark*. I am also infinitely grateful to H.D., Elizabeth Bishop, and Sylvia Plath for writing the poetry that taught me how to read.

I prize the financial assistance I received from the 1994 and 1995 California State University Faculty Development Grants, and the 1997 sabbatical awarded me by California State University, San Marcos (CSUSM). CSUSM has more than adequately encouraged and enabled this project through to completion. I am also thankful for the discussions that occurred about whiteness at the American Literature Association Symposium on Women Poets in the Americas, Cancun, Mexico, 1995 (Jacqueline Brogan, coordinator); National Poetry Foundation Conference on Poets of the 1950s, Orono, Maine, 1996 (Burton Hatlen, coordinator); the First International Elizabeth Bishop Conference, Worcester, Massachusetts, 1997 (Laura Menides, coordinator); and the CSUSM Faculty Center Research Discussion on Whiteness, 1998 (Vicki Golich, coordinator). These conversations transformed my thinking. Last, but not least, I thank my editors George Butler and Elizabeth Meagher, and Audrey Klein, all of Greenwood Press, for recognizing the value of *White Women Writing White*.

An especial acknowledgment also goes out to Caitlin and Laurel Brigham.

Chapter 1

Introduction: "A Poetics of Presumption"

WHITE PEOPLE DO NOT SEE THEMSELVES AS WHITE

"White people do not see themselves as White" (Katz and Ivey in Helms 50). This finding initiates and undergirds the premise of *White Women Writing White*: White women who write do so as white women, from within ideological, social, economical, political, and psychological frameworks of whiteness; yet simultaneously they reveal limited, if any, conceptual relationship to the conditions of whiteness or to the effects that whiteness has on the written product. To name H.D., Elizabeth Bishop, and Sylvia Plath as white and to pursue interpretation of their writings as white writings is to become engaged with positionality and authorship. Asserting a positionality has become a "significant aspect of our critical behavior," according to Michael Awkward. He also contends, rightly, that

> sincere responses to the injunction, "Critic, position thyself," are seen by many as among the most effectively moral and significant gestures of our current age, protecting us from, among other sins, fictions of critical objectivity that marred previous interpretive regimes. (4)

Although I do not address the writers under discussion in *White Women Writing White* as critics, I do address their positionality in order to respond to a current cultural imperative as well as to an old, unheeded invitation by Bishop. She asked that we "see" more clearly into the perhaps "barbaric," "indecent," and "cruel" past of her authorship. In a conversation with poetry critic Anne Stevenson that took place years ago, Bishop said,

Surely there is an element of mortal panic and fear underlying all works of art?. . . I think we are still barbarians, barbarians who commit a hundred indecencies and cruelties every day of our lives, as just possibly future ages may be able to see. But I think we should be gay in spite of it, sometimes even giddy—to make life endurable and keep ourselves "new, tender, quick." (Lensing 58)

This charge toward giddiness in the face of suspected daily barbarism constitutes what George Lensing and Thomas Travisano refer to as her "tough stoicism" and her "obdurate self-control" (Lensing 58); I recognize this posture as signifier of the excess of ease that comes with whiteness.

In this book I analyze the act of writing white as participation in a poetic discourse of presumption regarding racial positionality. Loosely delineated, writing white constitutes writing authored from an acknowledged or unacknowledged white perspective; writing that implies or explicitly delivers the concept of "whiteness" to a text; writing that remains "ignorant" regarding white racial politics internal to and external to the text; and/or writing that employs the word "white" to maintain ideological systems of mastery and dichotomy in the text. This book examines poetry texts in particular because scholars and philosophers have long associated poets and poetry with prophecy, wisdom, sages, and muses

David Perkins, in *A History of Modern Poetry*, reminds us that we inherited from William Wordsworth's Romantic tradition an assumption that poetry was to be "uplifting" (140) and filled with *grands mots*. The Modernists struggled with great effort against such tendencies. In their stead, "colloquialisms and informality" have become widespread (Jeffries 34).

James Olney finds that a certain quality exists in all languages to which we give the name of poetry:

It is a question not of *being* strange but of *making* strange . . . the great poets do see differently from the rest of us: they see farther and deeper into language and the human condition, and their vision will always, necessarily seem strange. (93)

Olney reserves the status of poetry for that language delivered by a poet, a person able to "see" differently.

Roy Harvey Pearce claims particular territory for the American poet:

The American poet, in his dedication to the idea of the dignity of man, has had as his abiding task the reconciliation of the impulse to freedom and the impulse to community, as the use of language in poetry may help bring it about. (5–6)

This impulse to freedom and community comes under scrutiny when discussion of women poets enters the scene: Alicia Ostriker argues that women poets use a "major strategy—revisionist mythmaking—as a means of exploring and attempting to transform the self and the culture" (*Stealing* 11), and Jan Montefiore summarizes an aesthetic apparent only in women's poetry: "Poetry is, primarily, the stuff of experience rendered into speech; a woman's poems are the authentic speech of her life and being" (3).

Poets reportedly commune with and see beyond the reality of this temporal world. Issues such as the way poets deal with the worldly constructions of race and their positionality regarding race enable us to view the encumbered humanness of our poets, their limitations, their inabilities to imagine a place, a schema beyond this world and its own ideologies:

> Poets, who we would like to think are enrichers of our reality, have in this regard often participated in its impoverishment. . . . The power relationships which exist in white language appear as a matter of course in white poetry. The white poet claims the power to describe the "bad object," to set it outside his own discursive empire, to maintain the poetic as a white project. (Nielsen 12)

White Women Writing White asks why it is that people who spend their lives nudging the walls of their imaginations cannot penetrate, indeed cannot even recognize, the confines of their whiteness. Alexis de Tocqueville forewarned Americans in the 1840s, as Walter W. Stafford reminds us in the 1990s, that

> the most formidable of all the ills that threaten the future of the Union arises from the presence of a black population upon its territory; and in contemplating the cause of the present embarrassments, or the future dangers of the United States, the observer is invariably led to this as a primary fact. (114)

Stafford interprets de Tocqueville to mean "that any imagination for the future in the United States has to deal with racism, particularly that against Blacks" (114). Each of the poetic imaginations under discussion in this book "deals" with a heritage of racism throughout her poetry.

THE MOVE FROM ENGLISHNESS TO AMERICAN WHITENESS

To further the discussion of whiteness and its particular effect on twentieth-century U.S. white women writing poetry, I must first discuss briefly the developmental history of conceiving and constructing a white race.[1] In the United States, race identity constitutes the most immovable category of human existence, unaffected by class, education, wealth, or achievement. In *The Invention of the White Race*, Theodore Allen suggests that to understand the development of the white race as a construct, we must first understand exactly what was peculiar about the "Peculiar Institution"—that "system based on the lifetime, hereditary, chattel bond-servitude of African-Americans" (1, 233). Allen argues that a "dissatisfaction" triggered this peculiarity, a dissatisfaction that occurred in the United

States among Englishmen near the end of the eighteenth century. Before this time, the Englishmen felt they knew themselves:

> They had known "who they were" in the seventeenth century and during most of the eighteenth century: they were Englishmen. Something happened to their "need to know" that they were Englishmen, and they found a new identity as "white" Americans. (Allen 10)

Allen discusses this identity as the political and arbitrary construction of a race. He also points out that such constructions were not without precedent: In colonial Hispanic America, royal certificates of whiteness could be purchased; in the late nineteenth century, a Portuguese emigrant to Guyana would not be considered white, whereas that same emigrant would be white in the United States; and, as recently as the early twentieth century in the United States, having less than 100 percent white genealogical lineage constituted a person of color (27). The mere idea that a certificate of a "buyable" whiteness or of a "whitening" dependent upon geography reveals whiteness as an artificial, albeit successfully marketed, site of desire.

The move from English to American whiteness did not eradicate Englishness. Rather this marker became absorbed along with ideas about what it meant to be civilized and to be Christian into "the dislocating dazzle of whiteness" (Gilroy 9). What exactly caused this absorption at this time? Allen refers to a dissatisfaction among Englishmen, but such restlessness hardly seems grounds enough to substantiate the extreme elevation of whiteness that occurred in the United States.

In *Race in North America: Origin and Evolution of a Worldview*, Audrey Smedley argues for a more specific combination of occurrences that gradually precipitated the set and inflexible racial classification system peculiar to the United States: Science classified human groups as unique life forms; an inegalitarian cultural ethos spurred rankings of these human groups; the dominant culture believed that human physical attributes revealed inner workings; this same culture ranked these inner workings according to behavioral and moral criteria; and finally, the dominant culture purported that these differences were created by God and thereby remained irrefutable and unchangeable. These occurrences evolved into the classification of "race" as the word entered the English language late in the eighteenth-century United States. Smedley draws particular attention to the innateness of race as a new and distinct way of classifying peoples (27, 39).

Concerns about definitions of race, whiteness, and blackness are not confined to academic studies. In a recent newspaper article in the *Los Angeles Times*, Robert Lee Hotz reports that the U.S. federal government has been researching race for over 200 hundred years: "[W]hen it comes to juggling legal concepts of race, federal judges all the way up to the U.S. Supreme Court have had an easier time defining what a white person is *not*, than defining what one is" (A14).

THE DEVELOPMENT OF A WHITE DISCOURSE

Although many languages—Spanish, Portuguese, Italian, French, German, Dutch, and English—exhibit race and racist classifications (Smedley 16), conceptions of racism vary among languages. Smedley argues that in North America, race ideology, and thereby racist discourse, became necessary as a means to justify North American slavery. Slavery existed long before conceptions of racism, but the need to continue slavery in North America contributed to a need to develop a strict sense of racial difference. The resulting essentialism remains the most fundamental issue to racism and its discourse in the United States.

With the definition and construction of race as a marker of essential difference in place, the effort to associate dark skin-color and the language of blackness with the negative connotations of savagery, evil, and filth ensued. As well, whiteness as a color, and as a race, connoted (and still connotes) the positive: beauty, purity, innocence, and perfection (Smedley 107). In discourse, however, the word "white," as used to refer to race, unobtrusively slips away from the language, and "white" as mere signifier of beauty and perfection remains. The word "black" maintains references both to race and to negativity. Such slippage and usage in language enable the creation of the Other in discourse. The white race remains unnamed because it constitutes the given, the normal. Only the Other, that which must be named as abnormal, as marginal, that which must be watched, policed, and noted both in the world and in discourse need be mentioned.

Because of such slippage in language, twentieth-century white people rarely comprehend whiteness without reference to the Other. In *The Social Construction of Whiteness: White Women, Race Matters*, Ruth Frankenberg finds that

> Whiteness and Americanness seemed comprehensible to many only by reference to the Others excluded from these categories. . . . [O]ne effect of colonial discourse is the production of an unmarked, apparently autonomous white/Western self, in contrast with the marked, Other racial and cultural categories with which the racially and culturally dominant category is coconstructed. (17)

One of the white mythologies that Robyn Wiegman discusses is that of America as an identity that portends to unify racial differences:

> But where races emphasizes the polarity of difference as its reigning epistemic logic, "America" offers the singularity of identity as its triumphant resolution, a resolution that incorporates the fragmented excesses of social scripting into a narrative of continuity and unification. (174)

This unmarked white, American skin, a skin without a name, signifies a permission to remain oblivious to "colossal unseen dimensions" of dominance and privilege (McIntosh 18). Once again, "White people do not see themselves as White" (Katz and Ivey in Helms 50).

THE WHITENESS AND THE MALENESS OF WHITENESS

When the rare white person first recognizes his or her lack of understanding of whiteness, a number of feelings and reactions arise that Houston Baker and Dana Nelson, both literary critics, warn against as "guilty and self-indulgent confessionals" (Nelson xii) regarding white treatment of the Other. This reactionary discourse only continues the dominance of the white culture in that white apologies further promote the white conscience as solely important to writing. This white conscience, in purging itself, repeats the white story of racism and perpetuates the definition of the white race as that which reacts to people of color. Whiteness thereby becomes elusive: It shifts from "no culture" to "normal culture" to "bad culture" and back again (Frankenberg 202–203). Whiteness must be probed beyond its emptiness and normalcy, beyond its relationship to the Other, beauty, innocence, and perfection. White scholars must look into the specter of whiteness and see where its hauntings begin, see what it warns of, what it threatens, and also view whether its horrors, like ghosts, may ever be laid to rest. To probe the white race means finally to write, and to right, white, not to reverse the binary opposition between black and white nor to create a bad culture, but to construct a complex, self-conscious human whiteness in language.

When white scholars discuss racism and the elusive idea of whiteness, another presumption enters the conversation; they presume as their subjects white persons, white male ideology, and white male oppressive constructs. White women have slipped out of many conversations regarding racism and regarding the elusivity (and exclusivity) of whiteness. White women scholars are currently discussing this absence, noting the "critical omission of 'race' from much of white feminist criticism" (Loomba 5). *White Women Writing White* resituates white women into the conversation of a developing and clearly maintained whiteness. As Diane Fowlkes points out, "Centering *white* women presents a problem in that such a focus reinforces the racial privilege that white women enjoy, consciously or unconsciously" (2). However, the whiteness of these women has all too infrequently evaded attention. This refocusing does center white women again, but it does so to highlight that which has been previously ignored. Although white women have argued against their exclusion from the white male world's glories, they have hardly argued for inclusion in white male nightmares. In the case of claiming whiteness, invisibility has served as a beneficial mask that enables and furthers white women's irresponsibility. At this point, it becomes important to mention, as does Ania Loomba in her essay "The Color of Patriarchy," Lynda Boose's fear. If we call white women scholars irresponsible, we enter the realm of "the contestatory model of scholarship" which "turns the literary profession into a shoot 'em out at the You're-Not-O.K. Corral" (Loomba 19). Boose argues for "familial supportiveness"; Loomba argues that the familial has often been a place of exclusion. As scholars, white women can and should contest each other's ideas, especially those having to do with exclusionary practices. Such practices keep humanity chained and keep our intelligence thwarted. Loomba reminds us that we can look forward to "a fuller, if more heterogeneous and problematic, understanding of women ... central to all cultural and historical processes" (33). Such a relocation calls for white women to reconsider their participation, culturally and historically, in the maintenance of racism and conferred dominance. This project does not necessarily mean that we look for denied truths (Wiegman 35) and stop at that point. Rather, we may use the discoveries of this project as vehicles for seeing the present anew and hoping for a new and wiser future.

WHITE WOMEN POETS: IGNORANT INHERITORS OF COLONIALISM

I explore the work of poets H.D., Elizabeth Bishop, and Sylvia Plath as work written by white women. In this discussion, I do not wish to design a unitary purpose, a unitary lack, a white unitary resolution, or a sameness because, as Awkward reminds us,

> What critics of the American borders especially cannot lose sight of is that regardless of our origins, neither we nor the artists whose work we examine exist as reflections of untainted "whiteness," "blackness," "asianess," "maleness," "gaiety," or "femaleness." We are all, to some degree, formed by the cultural crisscrossings of race, gender, class, sexuality, and religion that serve, I believe, to determine much of the nature of our lives in a contemporary American "meeting ground" characterized by unprecedented access to the images, perspectives, and behaviors of locational others. (14)

I suggest a complicated positionality of white women writers, different from one another, but similar in their near-blindness to aspects of their whiteness—its privileges and limitations—and to the ways in which their language uses typical white markers of difference regarding people of color. This position bolsters their unspeakable power and their invincible presence.

In his book, *White*, Richard Dyer vehemently claims that he does not believe "real racists" lurk behind white people who are struggling with their empowered heritages. He asserts,

> I did not invent racist thought, it is part of the cultural non-consciousness that we all inhabit. One must take responsibility for it, but that is not the same as being responsible, that is, to blame for it. (7)

In this spirit, I am suggesting that we read H.D., Bishop, and Plath as ignorant, but not innocent, inheritors and perpetuators of colonialism (Frankenberg 171, 182). White women not only inherit racism, but they also fall heir to a language of denial related to that racism—a denial deeply encoded to protect us from the knowledge of wrongs perpetrated years before. In *Beyond the Pale*, Vron Ware insists on one particular piece of veiled history as continuing to taint white women's and African-American women's ongoing ability to work together in feminism. Although the early women's rights movement developed out of and alongside antislavery campaigns,

> many younger white women who became involved in the movement for women's suffrage in the second half of the nineteenth century had become convinced that their rights should come before those of former slaves, and that women's interests would only be hindered by being linked to the demands of black people. At the heart of this belief was the fear that white women needed protection from black men. (Ware 201)

The unspeakableness of this fear signifies the shame still felt by white women. However, I refuse to abide by absolutist definitions of white privilege that steep the conversation in issues of race and class alone. Such definitions ultimately enforce a familiar type of self-loathing while ignoring the multiple hierarchies that frame white women's lives and literatures. By such a refusal, I want to point out a complexity that cannot be reduced or transcended.

H.D., Bishop, and Plath each sprang from privileged backgrounds and enjoyed privileged lives at various points with wealth, status, class, and career recognition. However, in terms of sexual orientation, gender roles, and/or reputation, they each experienced underprivileged status and life situations that caused them grave social and emotional difficulties. To categorize and overlook these difficulties as mere privileged sufferings thwarts the complex problems that whiteness affords for white people as well as for the world and the discourse over which white people exert their mastery. Binary oppositions such as "privileged" and "underprivileged" bind us in a supposed natural or simple order of the day when many more complicated structures of domination interact with one another.

It will seem to some readers that feminism is under attack in this book, simply by virtue of marking the whiteness of important women poets. These three white women poets are ones to whom many white feminist scholars have devoted years of research. What I propose here threatens to negate or to call into question some of that research. Worse, it threatens to relocate these poets closer to the men from which much of feminist scholarship has distinguished them. In short, *White Women Writing White* seems disloyal. I propose that we can only read it as disloyal if, in fact, feminism is white.

Wiegman courageously outlines the imperatives to braving claims of disloyalty to feminism, especially disloyalty that occurs while in the pursuit of feminist scholarship. She claims that change will result only from "drawing into the orbit of feminist inquiry a host of questions about the structure of white supremacy on which hierarchies among women have dwelled" (45). I concur with all of Wiegman's suggestions regarding this disloyalty, and I reiterate them here as a supportive nod in her direction and as a prelude to the difficult work that may lay ahead for white feminists reading this work. Wiegman asks readers to be brave enough to interrogate the feminist idea of one "sisterhood" as a "phantom collectivity," as a "myth of integration" (179) not for the mere sake of being contestatory, but to make themselves wiser as feminists. She asks that we question such myths in order to

reframe the implicit assumptions of loyalty and alliance that so often accompany feminism's modern and postmodern deployments. This allegiance has in the past been pressed forward as a covert, at time overt, demand, and it has been this demand that many women, especially "women of color," have routinely resisted. (183)

Posing these questions allows us as feminists to process the inner workings of feminism: We may ask "what," "how," "why," and "at what cost" feminism has come to know what it knows (Wiegman 185). We do not yet know whether feminism can hold up under such scrutiny. Once we further unveil its myth of innocence in relationship to racism and elitism, "feminism faces a future unwritten by a methodological guarantee" (Wiegman 187). (Women of color have been unveiling this myth far longer than have white women.) *White Women Writing White* participates knowingly in this threat. The book does not aim to admit to racism for the mere sake of participating in a "there I've said it" type of scholarship. It does not claim some hierarchical moral ground by being one of the first to make such claims. Such goals would simply play into what Wiegman describes as furtherance of the "integrationist dream":

The desire to get race—and the critique of feminism's racism—off of *us* reiterates the integrationist dream, casting in this case white women as the heroic interlopers and reshapers of feminism's historical reinscriptions of white supremacy. (189)

This book aims to make visible the invisible and to initiate discussion among feminists about how to and whether to continue feminist scholarship once its whiteness becomes more clear. Other feminists have said feminism is white. This book merely whitens already white women poets for the purpose of enabling more of us to hear and to see the continuing racist implications of ignoring the power of whiteness. In order to proceed, Wiegman suggests, and I agree, that white women, and those positioning themselves as white, must "figure disloyalty as something more than renunciation (or mythic repair)" (193); we must be willing to admit to failures, monolithic failures that harmed and continue to harm women. These admissions "may be the very conditions that return us to it once again" (Wiegman 201). But the "it" to which we return will not be same. We will have been disloyal to that inadequate feminism, and as a result, it will fade as a destination because we already achieved some of it and found it wanting. As Wiegman concludes,

Every destination, in other words, becomes inadequate with our arrival, just as the historic shape of our arrival transforms the destination into an emblem of our own contingent historicity. (202)

White Women Writing White is not a final response, nor an initial response, to the role that whiteness has played in feminism. This book provides evidence of whiteness that already has influenced the destiny of current feminist poetics, and it threatens to prove unjustifiable any continuance of a scholarship that supports this inadequately white way.

POETICS OF PRESUMPTION

White poets fortify and protect themselves in literature by writing a poetics of presumption. Supported by positionality, politics, and phraseology, white writers presume they will be thought of as white by their readership, and when they refer to other white people, they rarely, if ever, designate them as white. White writers both knowingly and unknowingly adopt a white positionality profoundly marked by (1) essentialist or Romantic racist language; (2) saying while not saying; (3) elusive mastery signifiers; and (4) color evasion/color blindness. All of these markers contribute to a positionality of camouflage. White writers maintain a practiced and determined ignorance regarding white politics infiltrating a text as well as an overdetermined predilection for prioritizing color aesthetics over color politics. White writers employ phraseology that (1) equates the word "white" with all that connotes the positive and the word "black" with all that connotes the negative; (2) employs dialect to signify difference and Otherness; (3) exhibits fixed stereotypes of people of color; and (4) engages in comparative analyses that establish the color white as the most hierarchically desirable color. By outlining some of the workings of white discourse, I do not want to prescribe a recipe, a test, nor a definitive list by which critics and readers may survey white writing attributes. Rather, I wish to provide a suggestive way to identify and to read through white presumptions for the purpose of understanding the impact on white women writers of their own whiteness and also the impact on poetry of white women's whiteness. The potential benefits to such a study include a better understanding of how racism affects white people and an understanding of how changes in racist attitudes might affect white lives in terms of

> access to the ideas and talents of others whose realities are different, relief from responsibility for the welfare of others who have been dependent subjects, freedom from the anxiety that the oppressed will rise up in anger against us, and freedom from crippling guilt regarding racism. (Crowfoot and Chesler 213)

This book aims to bridge the understandings it purports regarding poetry to those important in the lived world. Thus, often the text intermingles findings from social sciences with those in humanities, thereby expressing the ideology that society and literature impact each other and that scholarship in each discipline may equally inform each other.

A poetics of presumption regarding whiteness may have at some point sturdied the need that whites had to feel powerful and masterful. At this time, a presumptive poetics steeped in racism

> produces false fears in Whites and allows these fears to control where they live, where they go to school, where they travel, where they work, with whom they socialize, where they play, and whom they love and marry. Whites develop unhealthy mechanisms, such as denial, false justification, projection, disassociation, and transference of blame, to deal with their fears about minorities. (Fernandez 164)

These mechanisms play out in poetry as well as in behavior.

Essentialist Racism

Essentialist racism assumes that racial differences stem from nature and that these givens of nature prove evident, immovable, and noticeable to everyone—everyone who matters:

> [P]recisely because it proposed race as a significant axis of difference, essentialist racism remains the benchmark against which other discourses on race are articulated. In other words, the articulation and deployment of essentialist racism approximately five hundred years ago marks the moment when, so to speak, *Race was made into a difference* and simultaneously into a rationale for racial inequality. (Frankenberg 139)

A positionality steeped in the belief of essential difference informs our words about race. A white position in literature may often only be glimpsed by discerning a remote reflection from the language on the page. We must look into the mirror of the differentiation marker. To read white, we must reflect upon black, red, brown, and yellow—the words marked *different*. We best know whether a writer is white by the naming of other races on the page. Whiteness is presumed by its absence in language.

In her poem "Twelfth Morning; or What You Will," Bishop delivers a natural veil of whiteness through which a black boy will be viewed:

> Like a first coat of whitewash when it's wet,
> the thin gray mist lets everything show through:
> the black boy Balthazar, a fence, a horse,
> a foundered house
>   (*Complete Poems* 110)

In terms of essentialist racism, either Bishop writes with a rare and provocative self-awareness about her own whiteness when she admits to whiteness as a "natural" veil through which "everything" must pass into view, or this poem flaunts a perfect example of essentialist racism with its presumption of whiteness as the essential given and blackness as the essential difference to be viewed through whiteness. This black boy, referred to as a part of "everything," must "naturally" be viewed through at least a thin coat of whiteness. A thick coat may have obliterated him completely. In this poem, Bishop participates in maintaining whiteness as that attribute of mastery that "lets," allows, and permits all other matter to exist.

Romantic Racism

Romantic racism also says nothing overt about whiteness; rather, in its attempt to draw attention to race and color, it equates people of color with the exotic. This perspective stems from white fear expressed as awe; this discourse produces "structures which describe the black, often in admiring tones, as an unconstrained libido acting out the sexual and social fantasies of the white subconscious" (Nielsen 11). Romantic racism also promotes the idea that people of color suffer from a nothingness, an inauthenticity, and that they experience a significant relationship to nature. In their "naturalness," they simultaneously prove themselves less civilized, less intelligent—simply there. As markers in a text, people of color signify nothing to the white figure's everything.

Saying While Not Saying

Proclaiming one's position as a white writer often emerges as a discourse hint of saying while not saying. Like Kenneth Warren in *Black and White Strangers: Race and American Literary Realism*, I assert that even when writings do not appear to address issues of whiteness or race, concerns about whiteness and race design, interrupt, and affect the structure of the text (10). An example in literature, as noted by Frankenberg, is the delivery of an all-white neighborhood to the narrative. This construction speaks of whiteness and racism because "the very existence of a neighborhood whose residents are all white bespeaks a history of racist restructuring of that community" (Frankenberg 47). Although such a setting provides a place for the unfolding of a plot, ostensibly not even dealing with racism, clearly the imagination crafting such a setting has been profoundly influenced by a monolithic whiteness or secured by this same monolith.

Elusive Mastery Signifiers

Whiteness can be written into a text explicitly, but more commonly, various elusive mastery signifiers, such as the undesignated but presumed all-white neighborhood previously mentioned, point out its presence and position as masterful designer and observer of the world. Frankenberg recognizes whiteness as a "location of structural advantage," a "standpoint," a set of "cultural practices that are usually unmarked and unnamed" (1). Although still permitting a fugitive presence on the page, naming these signifiers advances the reader's ability to identify a white positionality that prides itself on its invisible omniscience.

In lyric 2 of "Red Rose and a Beggar," although she does not overtly address issues of race, H.D. signifies mastery in her presumptions of ownership, possession, and invisibility as well as in her right to occupy someone else's mind for the sheer purpose of discerning a supposed equality:

> you are my whole estate;
> I would hide in your mind
> as a child hides in an attic,
>
> what would I find there?
> religion or magic—both? neither?
> one or the other? together, matched,
>
> mated, exactly the same,
> equal in power, together yet separate,
> your eyes' amber.
>   (*Hermetic Definition*, "Red Rose" 4)

The "I" of the poem operates from a structural advantage. She has the power to enter another mind; she has the power to feign childlikeness; she has the power to sleuth; and, ultimately, she has the power to proclaim equality. The mastery of these actions implies a practiced entitlement to power and intrusion.

Although this poem seems topically to have little to do with racism, at the level of poetic discourse, H.D. marks the poem with whiteness. Naming mastery discourse as a signifier of white positionality serves to unsettle whiteness from its unmarked place of dominance. Naming whiteness both admits to the existence of a perfected camouflage and encourages the reader's eye to discern it. Even to speak of whiteness resituates white people in the discourse of race and racism.

Power and Color Evasion/Color Blindness

Whiteness also makes its position evident in poetic discourse through power and color evasion. The language of evasion exudes from a closed sensual being—closed to the usual human sensations as described by eighteenth-century French author Crèvecoeur: "Their ears by habit are become deaf, their hearts are hardened; they neither see, hear, nor feel for the woes of their poor slaves, from whose painful labors all their wealth proceeds" (quoted in Nielsen 7). This evasion results from the construction of a white self "innocent of racism," a white self trained not to see or to acknowledge color in order to maintain a "polite language of race" (Frankenberg 142–143, 188). This color blindness directly descends from the nineteenth-century slave owners' realization that in order to continue the project of enslavement, they had to develop a sense of selective perception—"the obliteration from one's daily experience of any consciousness of the slaves' human qualities" (Smedley 144). This selective perception, this color blindness, this politeness, although it feigns to benefit the person of color by not rekindling issues of racism, also serves to keep the white person from claiming association with the masterful, dominating race and from dismantling ongoing racist institutions.

In white women's poetry, color blindness reveals itself in a "we are all the same" strategy. Plath's "Whiteness I Remember" employs a "non-Heraldic," "off-white" stallion which invites being read as a metaphor for her experience as a "rider" of whiteness. The end of the poem overtly remarks upon the ultimate sameness of all colors—as long as they spin out white:

>   Resoluteness
> Simplified me: a rider, riding
> Hung out over hazard, over hooves
> Loud on earth's bedrock. Almost thrown, not
> Thrown: fear, wisdom, at one: all colors
> Spinning to still in his one whiteness.
>   (*Collected Poems* 102)

The poem, when read with a eye to white discourse, also signals the dizzying blindness suffered from too long a ride aback of whiteness and the color blindness that all too frequently whitens other colors in its persistent attempt to impose sameness. This white rider endures hazards and hooves and makes noise sound to the depths of earth's bedrock. This white rider survives being thrown to attain the knowledge that whiteness, meaning allness, provides the ultimate answer for all.

Ignorance

Ignorance dominates the political structure of white discourse. As previously noted, when white women write, they often fail to mention their

Introduction

whiteness as a part of perspective or as a limiting device regarding their point of view. Frankenberg asserts, "Something other than a simple denial, a straightforward failure to take note of race and cultural difference, is clearly going on here" (154). Eve Sedgwick reminds us that ignorance, although often sentimentally equated with passive innocence, in fact has an active foundation:

> [A] particular ignorance is a product of, implies, and itself structures and enforces a particular knowledge.... Insofar as ignorance is ignorance *of* a knowledge (a knowledge that may itself, it goes without saying, be seen as either "true" or "false" under some other regime of truth), these ignorances, far from being pieces of the originary dark, are produced by and correspond to particular knowledges and circulate as part of particular regimes of truth. (104)

Particular truths, therefore, create particular ignorances. By ignorantly refusing to name and undo its own innocence, white discourse thereby silently screams its collusion in perpetuating racist discourse.

As a world traveler and as a member of the Modernist intelligentsia, H.D. knows the particulars of Western colonialism's heritage. Yet, in lyric 16 of "Red Rose and a Beggar," the "I" ignorantly and willfully strings Asian seeds along a white thread with concern only for whether she might need to protect her finger:

> Sesame
> seed,
> string
> minute granules
> on a white thread
> or red,
> will they split
> on my needle?
> do I need a thimble?
> sesame
> seed
> from South Asia,
> that is far away,
> what comes between?
> hemp—seed,
> *fleur de chauvre,*
> from India?
> that is the *hachish superieur*
> of dream;
> is it better to string
> poppy-seeds?
>   (*Hermetic Definition*, "Red Rose" 18)

The "I" does not feel anything toward the splitting of the seeds, seeds clearly not intended to endure this type of piercing; one of her primary concerns lays with her finger and its potential to redden the white. She needs protection from the needle with the white thread as do the other seeds. Ignorantly, H.D. reissues the language of racist discourse in these images to the purpose not of interrogating such imagery, but rather to an aesthetic end. Keeping oneself innocent of racism enables one to write with racially fraught vocabulary and yet to ignore its implications.

Aesthetics

White writers often sacrifice knowledge of politics and social realities for an aesthetic occasion. When discussing Modernist poet William Carlos Williams's relationship to jazz and the African American, Aldon Lynn Nielsen notes that "Williams wants the energy and freedom of jazz for his own, to make a beautiful thing of words torn from blank blackness" (82). Williams does not admit the politics of early twentieth-century jazz, jazz clubs, and the black community into his poem. He masterfully controls the particularities of blackness and beauty for his own aesthetic purposes.

Connotations

In terms of phraseology, the word "white" has been synonymous with freedom. "White discourse has long held that the ideal human status is to be free, white and twenty-one" (Nielsen 142), but people of color have other dreams—not dreams that signify Other dreams, but dreams that add to a plurality of dreams in a global society. White discourse offers no acknowledgment of the particular happiness, the freedom nor the humanity of the Other. "The free Negro contradicted the white image of those who by their very racial definition were not entitled to freedom" (Smedley 222). "White" connotes a "tradition of civility" (Bhabha 149). "White" also equates with Christian, progress, perfection, and perfectibility, an association embarked upon when the Native Americans were presumed not progressive enough to head into the future (Allen 80; Smedley 281). "The act of Christianizing the heathen is 'the noblest Work, that was undertaken among the Children of men'—'children of men' clearly excluding the African slave. The 'black' slave is an 'opportunity,' a 'trial,' a 'creature'" (Nelson 27). Last, but not least, "white" and "black" together conjure occult images and practices in texts.

Dialect

White people participate in life, and white characters participate in literature. White discourse, although it may employ the figure of the person of color in the text, will rarely allow that figure to take a significant action or to speak. If people of color do speak, a white writer often constructs a dialect to signify this voice as the voice of the Other. Importantly, Nielsen makes the distinction, "Dialects do not signify speech; they signify otherness manifesting itself in speech" (55). Dialect serves as a reminder of the normality of whiteness and the difference of nonwhites—people who allegedly need nonstandard graphic representation on the page to signify existence and disruption.

In "Songs for a Colored Singer," Bishop tries her hand both at structuring a simplicity of language that she associates with blacks as well as at designing a few dialectical phrases:

> I say, "LeRoy, just how much are we owing?
> Something I can't comprehend,
> the more we got the more we spend...."
> He only answers, "Let's get going."
> LeRoy, you're earning too much money now.
> (*Complete Poems* 47)

Although the poem devotes eight stanzas to the plight of the wife and the good-for-nothing LeRoy, the sense of these people as people remains vague, inhuman, and Other. The dialect and the simple language provides a stutter to the poem and an emblem of difference when placed among Bishop's other poems. The white presumption here is that Bishop would deign to know the plight of such people well enough to use them as subject matter, complete with decorous language.

Stereotypes

Finally, white discourse presumes to depict people of color in particular repetitive stereotypical ways to reinforce such imagery in the reader's mind. "For it is between the edict of Englishness and the assault of the dark unruly spaces of the earth, through an act of repetition, that the colonial text emerges uncertainly" (Bhabha 149). These stereotypes include, but are not limited to, the black aspirant to whiteness (Nielsen 53), the eternal child, the uncontrollable Other, the lazy man, the doomed woman, the exotic woman, and the laughing character.

The black person as laughing character arises both in life situations and in literature. Poet Carl Sandburg finds "laughter to be innate to the black man" (Nielsen 35). In Bishop's "Twelfth Morning; or What You Will," the black boy Balthazar happily sings the end of the poem. In *Rac-ing Justice, En-gendering Power*, Toni Morrison writes,

> It is the laughter, the chuckle, that invites and precedes any discussion of association with a black person. For whites who require it, it is the gesture of accommodation and obedience needed to open discussion with a black person and certainly to continue it. (xiii)

Whites want to preserve the happy-go-lucky black person because they feel less threatened in the face of a stereotype than in confrontation with an angry reality.

RENDERING LIMP THE ALL-KNOWING WHITE READINGS AND WRITINGS

Ironically, African Americans have written the accumulating, but still minute, body of work regarding the white woman as writer, reader, and viewer of the black text. Mark Reid wants to render limp the blind, all-knowing readings often practiced by white readers (380). Barbara Smith rails against that specialized "lack of knowing" practiced by the white woman, suggesting that she read with a sense of her privilege, not as a favor to black women, but as a favor to herself (168). When white critic Minrose Gwin suggests that white women learn to read themselves in black women's texts as white Other ("A Theory" 22), Barbara Christian insists upon reading as a white *woman*, refusing to turn the strongest connection into a form of Otherness (49). In *Playing in the Dark*, Morrison asks why scholarly studies of whiteness and the impulse toward mastery have not been pursued by white people.

The occasional white woman scholar has taken up these issues to find that indeed white women have disregarded the humanity of Other women both in life and in writing:

[W]hite women in life and literature see black women as a color, as servants, as children, as adjuncts, as sexual competition, as dark sides of their own sexual selves—as black Other. They beat black women, nurture them, sentimentalize them, despise them—but they seldom see them as individuals with selves commensurate to their own. (Gwin, *Black and White* 5).

White women's discourse often takes great pains to reshape a reality that empowers them. Even lifting the pen empowers them to a degree. In the past, however, this empowerment has written them into a male world—a world frequently more desirable than that of sorority with women of color. By entering farther and farther into that male world, white women have excluded women of color from their world, have excluded themselves from participating in a world wide with Other women, and have created an immense expanse of difference.

If white women writers want to further feminism in literature, these writers must begin the work of shifting their gazes from interrogation of oppression to interrogation of privilege; they must recognize, denounce, and/or enact their access to power and authority; they must forfeit the idea that patriarchy serves as all women's primary oppressor; and they must admit their ignorant collusion in oppression.

LET THE BORDER OF WHITE IDENTITY BE MALLEABLE

Even with a shift in attention by white women writers, a perfect harmony of trust, forgiveness, and resolution will not be possible. Furthermore, even with that hope in mind, white women cannot be so responsible as to take over the entire effort. "As with all human activity, the cultural practices of white people in the United States in the late twentieth century must be viewed as contingent, historically produced, and transformable through collective and individual human endeavor" (Frankenberg 233). Change will occur. We can initiate this change by attending to current ideologies and writing acts that support continuance of a white poetics that recognizes and accounts for presumption.

White Women Writing White lifts blinders for a moment to shed a stark light on whiteness. This illumination can lead to a glimpse of the mind of mastery and clues to its construction. Understanding the complexities of race as construction will help us to begin the process of dismantling.

NOTE

1. The work of Aldon Lynn Nielsen, Audrey Smedley, Paul Gilroy, and Theodore Allen, along with entries from the *Oxford English Dictionary*, enables the construction of the following approximate chronology of race's entry into white ideology and discourse:

890	—"Black" referring to dark-skinned peoples enters English writing in L. Aelfred's *Baeda*.
1000	—"Brown" referring to brown-skinned peoples enters English writing in Caedmon.
Late 15th Century	—Structuring of a racial worldview coincides with colonial expansion of Western European nations.
16th Century	—Europeans conceptualize racism.
	—Race as a mode of classifying human beings in language appears in Spanish, Portuguese, Italian, French, German, Dutch, and English.
1549	—"Race" referring to a generation of people enters English writing.
1587	—"Red" referring to North American Indians enters English writing in Golding's *DeMornay*.
17th Century	—Epistemological shift from a study of similitude and resemblance to a study of difference and identity occurs in Europe.
	—In the U.S. colonies, Native Americans and Africans are seen as different based on moral conditions.
	—White oppressors begin to count black Africans not as humans, but as exchange objects.
	—Usage of the term "white" arises as Europeans begin to see themselves in opposition to the black slave.

	—Lexical shift of "red" and "tawny" from adjectives describing the native to nouns defining the Indians occurs in the U.S. colonies.
1600	"Race" referring to a tribe, nation, or people regarded as of common stock enters English writing.
1604	—"White" referring to an "ethnic type" enters English writing in D'Acosta's *History of the Indies*.
1671	—"White" referring to a "white man" enters English writing in Charante's *Customs Tafiletta*.
18th Century	—Race is used as a means of categorizing inherently unequal human populations in the English language.
1787	—"Yellow" referring to skin color of Asiatic peoples enters English in *Asiatick Reasearches*.
19th Century	—Race supersedes class as a dimension of social differentiation.
	—Race is used as a social device to transform the freed black population of United States into a subordinate human caste.
1852	—"Black" referring to the negro race enters English writing in T. Hughes's *Ludlow's History of the United States*.
1940s	—Distinction is made between sociological race and biological race.
1960s	—Recognition in the United States of racism as an evil in itself coincides with the civil rights movement.

Chapter 2

"Minute Granules on a White Thread": H.D. and a Masterful Whiteness

Poet H.D. (Hilda Doolittle) was born in 1886 in Pennsylvania to Charles Leander Doolittle and Helen Wolle Doolittle. Educated at Bryn Mawr, she became close friends with young white poets Ezra Pound and William Carlos Williams. Her early published poetry (1913) compelled the Imagist movement. She continued writing experimental poetry throughout her long life. H.D. also wrote novels, acted in a film with famed African-American Paul Robeson, and underwent psychoanalysis with Sigmund Freud. She spent most of her adult life in the company of her daughter, Perdita, and her lesbian lover, Bryher, who was a dedicated patron of the arts. H.D. died in Zurich, Switzerland in 1961 of complications resulting from a stroke.

H.D.'s poetry composes racially inscribed noise. Wai Chee Dimock characterizes such noise as an "apt analogy" for describing what readers bring to the "hearing" of a text:

> Noise includes all those circumstances that complicate readers' relations to a text: circumstances that, filling their heads and ringing in their ears, make them uninnocent readers, who encroach on the text with assumptions, expectations, convictions. Noise includes all those circumstances that so quicken the pulse, so sensitize the interpretive faculties, as to call forth unexpected nuances from words composed long ago. An effect of historical change, noise is a necessary feature of a reader's meaning-making process. (1063)

When twenty-first-century readers read the whiteness in H.D.'s texts, they read hints of racial mastery that were not signified similarly to the poet. Dimock reminds us that "'inferential and associative relations' of any text always exceed anything imagined by the author" (1066). This chapter argues that when reading with an eye toward positionality, readers will note expressions of whiteness in H.D.'s poetry that reflect poignantly on H.D.'s ideology and imagination. H.D. grounds her work (often unknowingly) in presumption of a whiteness equivalent to and inseparable from a positively masterful existence. H.D. recognizes, interrogates, and struggles with this presumption only to succumb to its invincible allure each time she confronts it.

For H.D., poetry, like all art, has the ultimate power: the power to convey brilliant thought into the world. H.D. conveys certain aspects of her effulgence to the world via expressions of whiteness. In *Notes on Thought and Vision* (1919), H.D. correlates her artistic vision with that of Leonardo da Vinci; both celebrate the perfection of whiteness. According to H.D., da Vinci became most artistically overwhelmed and inspired when faced with images such as "a child with yellow hair that fell or stood up in tight whorls." H.D. asserts that "the child's hair acted on him directly" (26–27). In this example, H.D. points to a characterizing detail of whiteness—the yellow hair—as capable of transforming the artist's vision of the world. H.D. comprehends da Vinci's artistic vision through his veneration of whiteness. Aldon Lynn Nielsen claims that maintaining "the poetic project as a white project" remains uppermost in the imaginations of white poets (12). By reiterating blond-haired boys as ideal and transformative, H.D. participates in maintenance of a white poetic; however, I argue that her participation in this preservation project varies throughout her literary career.

The poem most commonly discussed in terms of H.D.'s lived relationship to racial issues is "Red Roses for Bronze." Susan Stanford Friedman claims that "highly coded, erotic undertones" related to H.D.'s attraction for black actor Paul Robeson ("Modernism" 100) play out in this poem. Friedman further describes the 1931 poem as a "tribute to the 'bronze god' she loves, but with whom she refuses a casual affair" ("Modernism" 100). H.D. and Robeson acted together in the 1930 film *Borderline*. Bryher had served as a patron to Robeson and his wife Essie, a situation that Friedman suggests the Robesons came to dislike over time ("Modernism" 102). Although Friedman discusses this poem and "Hermetic Definition," as well as *HERmione*, a novel by H.D., in terms of H.D.'s and Bryher's thoughts, behaviors, and feelings toward blacks, at no time does Friedman look at the works in regard to interactions with Robeson in terms of the poet's own whiteness.

Robeson's bronze beauty provided an addition to H.D.'s fairly circumscribed sense of beauty as white and female. In *The Wise Sappho* (1919), H.D. specifies that part of Sappho's significance can be defined in terms of her whiteness and its connection to perfection: "The under-lip curls out in the white face, she has twisted her two eyes unevenly, the brows break the perfect line of the white forehead" (59). H.D.'s imagination reproduces perfection in terms of white women and bronze men. Although H.D. pictures her muse as "'a creature of ebony strung with wild poppies or an image of ivory'" (King 162) no record exists of H.D. having attempted any type of relationship with Essie Robeson as either friend or potential living muse. Although H.D. comfortably participates in exoticizing a black woman for the purpose of art, she demonstrated no real-life interest in black women.

H.D.'s white poetic also shapes such poems as lyric 43 in *Tribute to the Angels* (1945). Adelaide Morris reads the poems of this 1945 text through alchemical formulas and transactions as well as through dream visions that cause, in H.D.'s terms, "a vibration that we cannot name" (291–292). Albert Gelpi describes the poems of *Tribute to the Angels* as epiphanic peace poems (327). Although these readings do explore important aspects of H.D.'s interest in medieval chemistry and in the psychoanalysis of war, the poems of this book also invite interpretations informed by the late twentieth-century understandings of racial markings in texts. H.D.'s unnamable "vibrations" and her epiphanies often melt into or resolve due to her sense of whiteness as a foundation of perfection:

> And the point in the spectrum
> where all lights become one,
>
> is white and white is not no-colour,
> as we were told as children,
>
> but all-colour;
>   (*Collected Poems* 573)

The perfection that H.D. reveals in this poem reflects Richard Dyer's sense that "[t]o be white is to be at once of the white race and 'honourable' and 'squaredealing'" (65). Lyric 43 designates a moment of reverie in which H.D. reminds herself that whiteness constitutes the entirety of being, the purity of being, and the cleansing of being. Even though the whiteness in the poem constitutes an aesthetic attribute, when H.D.'s imagination fastens onto whiteness, a soothing, consoling sensation takes over that renews the self and supplies it with the energy to commence anew. To attain whiteness is to attain allness and perfection. Renewals occur for H.D. (and the "we" she assumes) after having reaffirmed the "all-colour," accommodating aspects of whiteness. Dyer claims that the color white symbolically relays superior morality and importance and that it often resonates its connotations in "relation to white-skinned peoples" (70). White often signifies perfection in H.D.'s poetic spectrum. In particular, it signifies the perfection of white people.

Yet, something much more complicated occurs in the poetry, especially as H.D. employs Greek figures and Greek culture to exemplify and destabilize white incomparability. Many previous scholars have examined H.D.'s artistic relationship to the ancient Greek world. Although Rachel Blau DuPlessis makes claims for H.D.'s attention to "versions of the female in Greek culture" (*H.D.: The Career* 19), she does not address the presumed whiteness of the female Greeks. Elizabeth Dodd also analyzes H.D.'s concern with the Greeks, but her work compares H.D.'s interest in Greece with that of other Modernists (33). Cassandra Laity observes that "H.D. emphasizes 'sameness' or the breakdown of gender difference in her 'Greek' landscapes which frequently celebrate the sister-bond" (60), but "sameness" and the "sister-bond" prove particularly problematic in discussions of whiteness. Glenn Hughes situates H.D.'s interest in the Greeks in a wider literary context:

English poetry since the Renaissance has leaned heavily on the Greeks, in both form and spirit, but seldom has it given evidence of such authentic kinship as in the poems of H.D. With her it is much more than a mere employment of themes culled from the inexhaustible Greek mythology; it is more than a following of Greek unities or an acceptance of the Greek conception of tragedy. It is rather something suggestive of a mystical affinity, or, to the fanciful mind, a reincarnation. (112)

As Hughes would have it, H.D. embodies what it means to be Greek. This embodiment becomes suspect when entering the debates regarding the racial markings of ancient Greek bodies—many of which were black.

In "Creating a Women's Mythology," Friedman also takes up H.D.'s interest in revising Greek mythology. She claims that H.D.'s poetry, especially *Helen in Egypt*, strives to create a "women's mythology" comparable to men's mythology. Friedman claims that H.D.'s mythology works with the same cultural background and the same aims of attaining vision and selfhood. To accomplish this feat, H.D. "resurrects matriarchal values" by recuperating "the desecrated Goddess (Isis-Aphrodite-Astarte-Asset, etc.) to her original position of veneration" ("Creating" 375). Friedman fails to note that "the desecrated Goddess" names a complex site having as much or more to do race than with gender. Significant evidence exists to suggest, for instance, that the goddess Isis was black:

The worship of the goddess Isis, deeply rooted among Egyptians and Ethiopians, developed into a cult that spread from northeast Africa throughout the Greco-Roman world. Isis was worshipped by many peoples under a variety of names, but it was the Ethiopians and Egyptians who, according to Apuleius, called the deity by her true name, Queen Isis. (Snowden 97)

The recuperation of an Afroasiatic goddess confounds any readings of H.D. and her revision of "women's mythology." H.D. not only revises Greek mythology, she also revives the Ancient model of Greece as colonized by Egypt. In other words, H.D. reconfigures the peoples of Greece as black peoples.

H.D.'s figuration of black Greece is not as radical as it first might seem. Historians have debated for centuries the "true" origins and racial make-up of ancient Greeks. In *Black Athena*, Martin Bernal clarifies the existence of two models of Greece, an Aryan model and an Ancient model. The Aryan model, "developed only during the first half of the 20th century," constructs a European Greece. The Ancient model defines a Greece, colonized by Egypt and Phoenicia around 1500 B.C. The Aryan model perceives Greece as white. The Ancient model perceives Greece as part of Egypt and Africa; therefore, we, in the twenty-first-century, would recognize these people as black (1).

An extreme Aryan model was highly popularized in the 1920s and 1930s, a time when H.D. was deeply involved in Greek studies. According to this model, an "unreported" northern invasion overwhelmed the "Pre-Hellenic culture" (Bernal 2). This model denies Egyptian, African, and Phoenician influences on Greece. According to Bernal, even previous to the twentieth century, people were gradually turning away from the Ancient model:

For 18th- and 19th-century Romantics and racists it was simply intolerable for Greece, which was seen not merely as the epitome of Europe but also as its pure childhood, to have been the result of the mixture of native Europeans and colonizing Africans and Semites. (2)

Thus, for the last two centuries, the African ancestry of Greece has been denied to varying degrees.

In *Before Color Prejudice*, Frank M. Snowden, Jr., maintains that the ancient Greeks would have recognized a Greek by virtue of a shared culture, not merely a shared skin color (92). However, this seeming openness must be read as it specifically addresses the issue of skin color, for as Bernal claims, the "nationalist" ancient Greeks

despised other peoples and some, like Aristotle, even put this on a theoretical plane by claiming a Hellenic superiority based on the geographical situation of Greece. It was a feeling qualified by the very real respect many Greek writers had for foreign cultures, particularly those of Egypt, Phoenicia and Mesopotamia. (28)

In attempting to revive this exact type of respect, not only for foreign culture, but also for past cultures, H.D. suggests that writing must be a "sacred" thing. Gary Burnett discusses H.D.'s sense of the sacred as that associated with historical contextualization of art:

H.D.'s "sacredness," far from being the static Hellenistic anachronism both Williams and many of her subsequent critics claim it to be, directly attempts to inhabit the present world responsibly, to "paint it to-day" in an art informed by a tradition rather than by an avant-garde thrust cutting it off from the past. (56)

H.D. attempts to write Greece responsibly into her texts, which means that her Greek figures resonate with contention about the origins of Western civilization. Yet, H.D. also writes a powerful and dominant whiteness into her texts as well.

Some scholars might argue that to analyze H.D.'s work from within a late twentieth-century framework and understanding of textual racial markings is unfair. However, Dimock makes it clear that "any effort to periodize absolutely, to put a text into a discrete slice of the past, must do violence to its continuous moving and meshing" (1065). Even though H.D.'s thoughts about racism and the role of whiteness would have been culturally determined by the information available and events experienced during the first half of the twentieth century, her work has thrived beyond that point and, therefore, may (and must) be read with an eye toward current race theories and their impact on literature and authorship.

In attempting to uncover H.D.'s racial sensibilities, some scholars have made lofty claims for the radical political awareness of H.D.'s work as it regards Otherness. Friedman relates such elevated awareness to H.D.'s own position as outsider. She claims that H.D. was not only an expatriate, but that she was fundamentally "exiled" from "all kinds of convention":

> She felt different as the only girl to survive in a family of five brothers; she felt different as a Moravian in a predominantly Christian world for whom the Moravians were an exotic sect; she felt different as a woman nearly six feet tall; she felt different as a woman who "had two loves separate," as she wrote, who was, in other words, bisexual; she felt different as mother of a child whose parentage she had to hide; she felt different as an artist in a materialistic world. ("Exile" 33)

H.D. felt different in all of these regards. However, race is arguably the most determinate attribute of difference in the late twentieth century. With regards to race, H.D. does not occupy the outside position.

Friedman makes further claims regarding H.D.'s affinity with Others. In her essay, "Modernism of the 'Scattered Remnant,'" Friedman curiously offers H.D.'s knowledge of people involved with the Harlem Renaissance as evidence of her "fully progressive modernism" (94). According to Friedman, H.D.'s

> personal experience with the Harlem Renaissance played a key role in deepening and broadening her early feminism into a fully progressive modernism based in an identification with all the people who exist as "the scattered remnant" at the fringes of culture. ("Modernism" 94)

Just what were these "personal experiences" with the Harlem Renaissance? Friedman tells us that H.D. knew white people (Carl Van Vechten and Nancy Cunard) who knew black people in Harlem, and that even though H.D. never visited Harlem, nor the United States for that matter, during the period of the Harlem Renaissance, H.D. had been reading about the issues ("Modernism" 96).

Friedman wants desperately to align H.D. along the "fringes of culture" and to redeem her from Barbara Guest's characterization of the poet as living out "an unquestioning, old-fashioned conservatism common to many late nineteenth-century upper-middle class Americans" ("Modernism" 93). Friedman even situates H.D. as especially given to tolerance and openness because she was a Moravian, a particular form of Christanity usually dated as beginning in 1722.[1] DuPlessis also argues that H.D. claims a position of Otherness by declaring "the uncontained self," "her visions," her "lesbian/bisexual[ity]," and her "maternity ... as mother and as daughter" (*H.D.: The Career* 34). Friedman and DuPlessis never discuss the H.D. who is white, dominant, and Other from those who are non-white. H.D.'s whiteness remains invisible and unclaimed. DuPlessis does note that to write from Otherness requires certain recognitions of bodiliness on H.D.'s part, but recognition of whiteness is not part of this poet's bodily awareness. She asserts, "To write from Otherness implies ... that a woman's physical experience, her body itself, allows her access to special spiritual and intellectual insights" (*H.D.: The Career* 39). H.D. associates such spiritual insights with the whiteness of Christ in *Notes on Thought and Vision:* "He [Christ] was the white hyacinth of Sparta and the narcissus of the islands.... Christ was the grapes that hung against the sun-lit walls of that mountain garden Nazareth" (53). Dyer argues that it poses no great surprise when associations are made between spiritual enlightenment, Christ, the human body, and whiteness because "[t]he supreme embodiment of Western humanity is Christ, whose whitening in Christian iconography was such that his 'hair and his beard were given the colour of sunshine, the brightness of the light above'" (118). H.D. may claim a position of Otherness, an outsiderness, and a sense of ostracism that endows her with special insight, but in reality, H.D.'s whiteness negates a difference that lacks. H.D.'s difference inexplicably confers a gain of likeness with Christ and his "light" of superiority.

H.D.'s poetry does not proffer politically progressive readings of the sort that Friedman wants to be there, nor does it invite the apolitical or avoidance politics suggested by Guest. H.D.'s poetry, when read, not with an eye to alterity, but with attention to H.D.'s recognition and understanding of her position as a white woman, situates whiteness as an undebatable and incomparable expression of beauty and perfection. Paradoxically, the poetry also intimates the unspeakable Afroasiatic heritage, including the black bodiliness, embedded in white Western civilization.

SEA GARDEN

H.D.'s early poems published in *Sea Garden*, the ones which constitute the bulk of H.D.'s reputation as an Imagist, have signified many correlations to many scholars. Friedman reads the poems of *Sea Garden*, first published in 1916, as "modern pastorals" that "exteriorize" H.D.'s imagination ("Exile" 30). Laity names English poet Algernon Charles Swinburne as the master influence on *Sea Garden*, especially with regard to her "conception of the dual Romantic landscapes" in the poetry (62). DuPlessis finds unconventional inversions of power in the flowers of *Sea Garden*: "These flowers of the sea gardens are of a harsh surprising beauty, slashed, torn, dashed yet still triumphant and powerful, despite being wounded, hardened, tested by exposure" (*H.D.: The Career* 12). Friedman, Laity, and DuPlessis interpret the poetry with potency and clarity; however, Zara Bruzzi's research offers the greatest insight in terms of rendering visible the meaning of whiteness in H.D.'s work.

Bruzzi locates the origins of *Sea Garden* in two texts: Balzac's *Seraphita*, and a collection of archaic Greek lyrics, *The Homeric Hymns* (99). *Seraphita* proves most important to this study. In particular, H.D. uses *Seraphita*'s associations with "angelic metamorphoses" and "Platonic perfection" to design the white landscape of *Sea Garden*. "*Seraphita* begins with a vivid description of an ostensibly real locale, centered upon a Norwegian fjord" (Bruzzi 99). Fjords, created by powerful white, moving glaciers, are the natural wonders of *Seraphita*. The image of the fjord and its looming mountains prove central, according to Bruzzi, to both Ezra Pound's and H.D.'s early texts (100). H.D.'s imagination grasps this white Norwegian image and delivers it repeatedly, embedded with associations of power, purity, and hierarchy, to pages of poetry:

> Great, bright portal,
> shelf of rock,
> rocks fitted in long ledges,
> rocks fitted to dark, to silver granite,
> to lighter rock—
> clean cut, white against white
>   (*Collected Poems*, "Cliff Temple" 26)

When looking up from the fjord toward the cliffs, H.D. describes an ascending brilliance that transforms rock to rock from darkness, to silver, to an ultimate whiteness. Bruzzi argues that this repetitive and "ecstatic scramble towards the vertiginous heights of a cliff or mountain" is emblematic of a spiritual epiphany for H.D. (100–101). In terms of racial markings, this text's clamber toward whiteness also signals the social and cultural construction of whiteness and white peoples as powerful, pure, superior, and aesthetically beautiful.

Throughout her poetry, H.D. attributes aesthetic beauty to whiteness. Although H.D. may not have consciously inscribed racial connotations into the language she chose for *Sea Garden*, and although literary scholars predominantly have only become sensitive to the racial implications of the word "white" since Toni Morrison's *Playing in the Dark* (1992), H.D.'s early poetry reveals much about the poetic imagination's relationship to the skin that houses its author. Some scholars will contend that it places an undue burden on H.D.'s texts to interpret them via the current political and racial landscape. However, Dimock warns that limiting contextualization to the mere moment of literary production minimizes the potential meanings of the works:

> [T]he meaning of a text is assumed to be the property of the historical period in which it originated; coextensive with that period, it remains undisturbed by anything beyond.... To historicize in this sense, then, is to impute meanings to a text by situating it among events in the same slice of time. This synchronic model hardly acknowledges that the hermeneutical horizon of the text might extend beyond the moment of composition, that future circumstances might bring other possibilities for meaning. (1060–1061)

H.D. understood the representation of knowledge as porous. Her interest in palimpsests evidences this understanding. DuPlessis reminds us that even the palimpsest[2] signified that after all the layers of textualizing, "there is always something not fully decipherable" (*H.D.: The Career* 56). Although the later poetry more determinedly expresses H.D.'s whiteness as racial, at the time of *Sea Garden*, H.D. did not intend, nor would she be capable of deciphering, all the white mastery now so apparent in her work.

Dimock argues that this lack of fixed meanings occurs because words signify different meanings across time:

> The behavior of words across time—their tendency to undergo subtle or even striking modifications—has long been the province of historical linguistics. The ceaseless passage of time touches language on many registers (syntactic, phonological, morphological), but what is most noticeable is the changes in the webs of meaning surrounding individual words. These semantic webs, broadening, contracting, acquiring new overtones and inflections, bear witness to the advent and retreat of social norms. As time alters the fabric of human association, it also alters the fabric of linguistic usage, the reputable or deployable nuances of words that make possible that association. (1060)

When looking into H.D.'s imagination via her poetry, we find desire for an ultimately white, and thereby perfect, world. Other colors exist on her imaginative palette, but they exist only to highlight the importance of whiteness as an aesthetic imperative in the imaginary landscape.

In *Sea Garden*, white statues and white violets decorate the landscape. In speaking of a cliff statue in "The Contest," H.D. designs a direct association between mightiness and whiteness:

> You stand rigid and mighty—
> granite and the ore in rocks;
> a great band clasps your forehead
> and its heavy twists of gold.
>
> You are white—a limb of cypress
> bent under a weight of snow.
> (*Collected Poems* 12)

Bruzzi argues that the gold, white, and silver colors of this poem and others represent Balzac's Venus or H.D.'s interest in alchemy or Moravianism (102–103). I read the alignment that occurs between might, whiteness, and splendor as significant to rendering the meaning of this poem.

Although she is fond of describing statuary, and one could argue that these cliff gods or rock statues may in fact be white in color, H.D., nonetheless, elects to endow the image with the language of might and splendor. This splendor, Dyer argues, signifies an always already bestowed virtuousness:

In Western tradition, white is beautiful because it is the colour of virtue. This remarkable equation relates to a particular definition of goodness. All lists of the moral connotations of white as symbol in Western culture are the same: purity, spirituality, transcendence, cleanliness, virtue, simplicity, chastity. (72)

The alignment of might, whiteness, and splendor in "The Contest" permits access to the racial composition of H.D.'s imagination. H.D. imagines an impeccable equivalence between whiteness, power, and beauty.

In "Sea Violet," H.D. designates white as the most desirable color in nature:

> The white violet
> is scented on its stalk,
> the sea violet
> fragile as agate,
> lies fronting all the wind
> among the torn shells
> on the sand-bank.
>
> The greater blue violets
> flutter on the hill,
> but who would change for these
> who would change for these
> one root of the white sort?
> (*Collected Poems* 25–26)

By posing a question, this poem concedes a suspicion that someone might deem the blue violets "greater," but it furthers the interrogation by asking who would "change," meaning exchange, one small root of the white sort in return for the blue one? In this version of H.D.'s aesthetic, white is not exchangeable. The undebatable value of whiteness far outstrips in nature the value of any other color.

In this poem, H.D. proposes a hierarchy in nature atop of which whiteness reigns supreme and irreplaceable. Bruzzi again turns to *Seraphita* for explication of H.D.'s relationship to flowers, and she finds that the flowers symbolize "the angelic condition itself" (102). H.D.'s white violets are pure, untouched, elevated, and angelic; they emit an essential and undebatable desirability. By designing a white violet essentially more desirable than one of another color, H.D.'s early twentieth-century poem engages late twentieth-century debates regarding essentialist racism (Frankenberg 11). Essentialist racism permits one to assume that racial differences stem from nature and that these givens of nature prove evident, immovable, and noticeable to everyone who matters.

Throughout *Sea Garden*, H.D. also writes comparative juxtapositions such as "white against white," and formal comparative structures such as "whiter than the in-rush of your own white surf." These comparative structures suggest that whiteness cannot justifiably be evaluated nor comprehended unless posed against variations of itself. In "The Cliff Temple," H.D. uses a comparative whiteness to describe a cliff's cleanliness:

> Great, bright portal,
> shelf of rock,
> rocks fitted in long ledges,
> rocks fitted to dark, to silver granite,
> to lighter rock—
> clean cut, white against white.
>   (*Collected Poems* 26)

The stanza begins in greatness and ends in whiteness. As the eye travels from the great rock, it notices a slight transformation to darkness, to silver, to lighter rock, and then ultimately to the "clean cut" white rock against white. This whiteness is far more superlative than mere whiteness. Dyer argues that "really white unattainable whiteness" (78) designates an artist seeking an ideal. H.D. structures this poem in a movement from greatness to unattainable whiteness because "[t]he very idea of a best and of striving towards it accords with the aspirational structure of whiteness" (Dyer 80). When H.D.'s imagination depicts aspiration, the resulting image is typically white and typically posed in comparative relief against a white backdrop.

In "Sea Gods," H.D. again uses a comparison in order to situate whiteness. In a stanza that describes various types and colors of violets—gold, red, deep-purple—she ends with a stanza that compares the white violet to an even whiter surf:

> We bring the hyacinth-violet,
> sweet, bare, chill to the touch—
> and violets whiter than the in-rush
> of your own white surf.
> (*Collected Poems* 30)

H.D. assumes that since splendid gifts of nature occur in white—white violets and white surf—then whiteness, in and of itself, must be one of the superlative gifts in the world. Furthermore, the only way, or the best way, to please a gift recipient is to offer him or her something whiter than that which they already own. Whiteness, thereby, constitutes the quintessential gift.

H.D. further expresses a position of whiteness in her poetry by her uses of blackness. In "Storm," H.D. depicts raindrops as black and as a deadening burden to the "live" white branches:

> You crash over the trees,
> you crack the live branch—
> the branch is white,
> the green crushed,
> each leaf is rent like split wood.
>
> You burden the trees
> with black drops,
> you swirl and crash—
> (*Collected Poems* 36)

Metaphorically and imaginatively, black burdens whiteness. The nature setting affords H.D. the opportunity to again promote an essentialist argument: as in nature, so among people. Storm residue is black, and it burdens the white branches; small as these drops are, they wreak havoc on the white branches, cracking them and breaking them. The color scheme in this poem speaks of an imagination that polarizes whiteness and blackness by associating whiteness with living branches and blackness with killing storms. In H.D.'s sense of the binary relationship between whiteness and blackness, blackness poses the threat to white life.

Friedman claims,

> While the sprinkling of unnamed shores and temples, daemons and dryads in *Sea Garden* evokes Greece, the landscape of the volume is never anchored in human geography, because, as Guest suggests, the "country" is imaginary and symbolic. ("Exile" 40)

I suggest instead that H.D. anchors *Sea Garden* in imagery which portrays the human geography of racial understanding as it exists in the white imagination.

HYMEN

The poems of *Hymen*, published in 1921, resonate with the social, cultural, and personal events compelling H.D.'s self-reflection on whiteness during this time. Beginning in this decade, a number of legal cases came before the Supreme Court of the United States to construe and define the "white person" (Lopez 2). The Court had to establish race by law and determine whether to measure race "by skin color, facial features, national origin, language, culture, ancestry, the speculations of scientists, popular opinion, or some combination of these factors" (Lopez 2). These cases had been going on since the Civil War but had reached a peak level in the 1920s (Lopez 3).

In the arts, performances of blackface by both whites and blacks "reenacted the subordination of African Americans" in the 1920s. As well, "Urmyths of racechange surfaced to interrogate, subvert, or topple racial stereotypes" (Gubar, *Racechanges* 99). Blackface was so popular in Broadway musicals in the 1920s that it inspired the 1922 song, "It's Getting Dark on Old Broadway" (Gubar, *Racechanges* 114).

Personally, H.D. experienced some of the most significant changes in her life between 1919 and 1921. She met Bryher, survived double pneumonia, gave birth to Perdita, separated from her husband Richard Aldington, lost her brother and father to the war in France, traveled to Greece, had the "writing-on-the-wall" experience at Corfu,[3] and attempted to live in the United States (California and New York) for the last time. A. Kingsley Weatherhead suggests that H.D.'s poetry of this period "may be a means of mitigating and exercising grief" (28), while Friedman emphasizes that this period concretized H.D.'s determination to tell her story "in different historical settings—especially ancient Greece, Rome, and Egypt, where each locale symbolized a specific ambiance" ("Exile" 43). The predominant ambiance of *Hymen* has to do with connection and disturbance to connection. *Hymen* resonates with allusions to both the membranous connective qualities of the anatomical hymen as well as the connective attributes related to Hymen, the god of marriage in classical mythology. The other hymen, the thin white film that veils women's vaginal openings and signifies their purity, serves as an apt metaphor for the invisible (because unspeakable) white covering that guarantees the value of white women.

In *Hymen*, H.D. uses comparative juxtapositions similar to those employed in *Sea Garden* such as "white on white," "snow on snow," and "snow on whitest buds of myrrh" to emphasize the extreme purity of whiteness. In this text, she also creates similes to explicate the multiple ways of precisely depicting whiteness: "white as hare," "white as ash," and "white as forked lightning." In addition to these techniques, H.D. also produces a layering effect that propagates and propounds the whiteness to such a hyperbolic extent that the integrity of whiteness becomes questionable. This method reflects the fear of racechange.

White gladiolus, children outlined in white, melting snow, and pale, ivory-like gold supply the title of the poem/play "Hymen" with manifold overlays of whiteness as H.D. sets the stage for a veiled figure—a bride—"swathed in folds of diaphanous white" to enter. As the bride makes her entrance into the poem, the choral Strophe, phobic about the potential for racechange, address her fairness:

> But of her
> Who can say if she is fair?
> Bound with fillet,
> Bound with myrtle
> Underneath her flowing veil,
> Only the soft length
> (Beneath her dress)
> Of saffron shoe is bright
> As a great lily-heart
> In its white loveliness.
>   (*Collected Poems* 105)

The chorus assert that no one can determine the "fairness" of the bride. Although "fair" has many connotations, in this instance, the chorus scrutinize the bride for "fairness" in terms of both freedom from bodily blemish and character imperfection. "Fairness" also connotes light-skinned. The chorus remain skeptical of the bride's fairness because she cannot be seen clearly: she is bound by ribbons, fettered with white fragrant flowers, and only her ivory-white shoes show from beneath her dress. The Strophe complain that a plethora of white adornments do not bequeath fairness and purity onto the bride herself. In the poem/play "Hymen," H.D. clearly provides an opportunity for white coverings to be made conspicuous and to be questioned.

The Antistrophe of the poem/play presume upon their own credibility to assure the Strophe that the bride is fair. The Antistrophe know her purity because they whitened her themselves:

> We can say that she is fair.
> We bleached the fillet.
> Brought the myrtle;
> To us the task was set
> Of knotting the fine threads of silk:
> We fastened the veil,
> And over the white foot
> Drew on the painted shoe
> Steeped in Illyrian crocus.
>   (*Collected Poems* 106)

The Antistrophe, in a somewhat humorous, naïve, or ironic tone, suggest that they know the bride is fair because they have decorated her to appear so. They have tied her hair with a bleached fillet; they have brought with them the myrtle, with its white fragrant flowers emblematic of love; and they have fastened her veil over the white foot. In this section, H.D. suggests that whiteness is vouchsafed by those who produce it and commodify it.

The Strophe, however, will not be bamboozled. They revise and reiterate their question:

> But of her,
> Who can say if she is fair?
> For her head is covered over
> With her mantle
> White on white,
> Snow on whiter amaranth,
> Snow on hoar-frost,
> Snow on snow,
> Snow on whitest buds of myrrh.
>   (*Collected Poems* 106)

The Strophe point out that the interrogation, detection, and measurement of the lady's fairness folds in on itself because the Antistrophe (mis)use emblems of whiteness to evaluate the fairness of whiteness. More to the point, the Strophe charge the Antistrophe with promoting the fairness of a whiteness that cannot be seen.

The Antistrophe reply again that they must be trusted, for they "know" her underneath:

> But of her,
> We can say that she is fair;
> For we know underneath
> All the wanness,
> All the heat
> (In her blanched face)
> Of desire
> Is caught in her eyes as fire
> In the dark center leaf
> Of the white Syrian iris.
>   (*Collected Poems* 106)

The Antistrophe concede that the bride's face might be so pale as to be deemed imperfect, but they insist that her eyes tell the true tale of a desire as pure and unique as that housed in the center of the "white Syrian iris." H.D. suggests in this poem that whiteness is a layered system of protective masks that cannot be shed even to verify the purity of the body that it covers. As she makes clear through the Antistrophe, one is often forced to trust the definers and producers of whiteness that the product—the fair, pure, unblemished, species—exists beneath its wrappings.

In another poem, "Simathea," H.D. submits that whiteness may occasionally displease. To represent the fading perfection of whiteness, H.D. employs similes rather than the comparative degree or the layering effect to diminish the whiteness:

> (Ah when he comes,
> stumbling across my sill,
> will he find me still,
> fragrant as the white privet,
> or as above,
> polished in wet and sun,
> worried of wild beaks,
> and of the whelps' teeth—
> worried of flesh,
> left to bleach under the sun,
> white as ash bled of heat,
> white as hail blazing in sheet-lightning,
> white as forked lightning
> rending the sleet?)
>   (*Collected Poems* 116)

The similes that correlate whiteness with negativity—"white as ash bled of heat," "white as hail-blazing in sheet-lightning," and "white as forked lightning"—depict whiteness as associated with natural destruction such as death and the power of lightning. Thus, the fading whiteness of a female beauty, once fragrant as the European shrub with the small white flowers, threatens to become a whiteness associated with natural decay and devastation. As in "Hymen," H.D. situates whiteness as a particular, yet indefinable, commodity, one that women must acquire and maintain (in its original state) in order to preserve their desirability to men.

Hymen also houses a poem entitled "White World." Donna Hollenberg rightly reads the whiteness of this world as "an alternative, 'white' emotional state, linked with restored integrity and lesbian love" (82–83). Hollenberg claims more generally that H.D. uses "white" to describe intactness. The poem opens with a powerful declaration of possession: "The whole white world is ours," and it continues to describe a colorful landscape:

> The whole white world is ours,
> and the world, purple with rose-bays,
> bays, bush on bush,
> group, thicket, hedge and tree,
> dark islands in a sea
> of grey-green olive or wild white-olive,

>   cut with the sudden cypress shaft,
>   in clusters, two or three,
>   or with one slender, single cypress-tree.
>   (*Collected Poems* 134)

The grammar of this stanza is crucial to understanding H.D.'s sense of whiteness in this poem. The particular grammatical crux occurs in the first three lines. While it seems clear that "is" acts as the verb of the first line, it is not clear whether "the world" of the second line has a new verb ("bays"—of the third line) or whether the "and" of the second line simply means "as is." If "bays" is the verb associated with "the world" of the second line, then the stanza designs two worlds: one white world separate from a purple world that howls forlornly, resonating from bush to thicket to cypress shafts.

If the "and" of the second line means "as is," then the poem reads, "The whole white world is ours, / as is the world purple with rose-bays." The second reading seems more apt; however, in either reading the white world exudes superiority and desirability. If the purple world bays forlornly, then it fails to comfort its inhabitants and proves the white world that joins "each to each in happiness complete" more alluring. Likewise, if the white world is "ours" in the initial line, and H.D. adds "the world, purple with rose-bays," then the white world proves a powerful assimilator of multicolored and multi-inhabited worlds.

H.D.'s description of Sappho's poetic worlds sheds light on the association H.D. makes between the white world and superiority. In *The Wise Sappho*, H.D. describes the power of Sappho's poetry in terms of its whiteness:

> [I]t is not warmth we look for in these poems, not fire nor sunlight, not heat in the ordinary sense, diffused, and comforting (nor is it light, day or dawn or light of sun-setting), but another element containing all these, magnetic, vibrant; not the lightning as it falls from the thunder cloud, yet lightning in a sense: *white* [italics mine] unhuman element, containing fire and light and warmth, yet in its essence differing from all these, as if the brittle crescent moon gave heat to us, or some splendid scintillating star turned warm suddenly in our hand like a jewel, sent by the beloved.
>
> I think of the words of Sappho as these colours, or states rather, transcending colour yet containing (as great heat the compass of the spectrum) all colour. (57–58)

In this illuminating passage, H.D. proclaims whiteness as a state and an essence, a container of all color. By situating whiteness as the ultimate container, she designs an elusive mastery signifier. Whiteness equates with a masterful ability to accommodate. White, an inhuman element, a container larger than all the essences it contains, is magnetic and vibrant—and H.D. assumes all are drawn to it. To H.D., the whiteness of the white world and its magnetic and assimilative attributes make poetry and life complete.

In "Egypt," the white world has been deceived. H.D. takes a chastising tone in this poem. She berates Egypt for its cheating ways, its "guile" and its "craft":

> Egypt had cheated us,
> for Egypt took
> through guile and craft
> our treasure and our hope,
>   (*Collected Poems* 140)

Angela DiPace Fritz claims that this poem centers on the very spiritual concerns that will create *Helen in Egypt*, H.D.'s book-length poem published in 1961. She sees amid the corruption of Egypt, a rebirth for Helen and for Greece (37). Hollenberg reads the poem as a countervailing argument against "the nineteenth-century aesthetes' depiction of love between women as decadent and sinister" (84). Neither of these readings, however, address the fact that this poem begins by rebuking Egypt and ends by re-birthing Hellas. Neither reading explains why H.D. refers to Egypt as the "White poison flower we loved / and the black spike." The coordination of whiteness and blackness as ways of describing Egypt directs us to read the poem with an eye toward the racial implications of the historic transformation of Egypt into Greece.

In light of the Supreme Court cases going on during the late 1950s and early 1960s, which attempt to define the "white person" sometimes by virtue of heritage and origin, the poem particularly invites a reading that discerns how Egypt could be both white flower and black spike. In "Egypt," H.D. reminds us of the dubious heritage of white Western civilization. In the poem, she deftly implies that Egypt had cheated the Western successors of Greece by taking the greatest treasure—the whiteness of its people—through the guile of miscegenation. She furthers this perception with sexual suggestiveness by describing the naïve Greeks as so enamored of Egyptian knowledge, that they figuratively "sipped" it from a "black spike" and passed it on to others. The phallic black spike thus sires many Greek offspring. The "us," the Westerners, feel blinded and poisoned by the black spike of Egypt. At the end of the poem, however, H.D. suggests that through the "grey eyes" and the "face grown grey" that have resulted from these unions a new hope will be reborn: the hope of Hellas.

Bernal reminds us that

> after the rise of black slavery and racism, European thinkers were concerned to keep black Africans as far as possible from European civilization. Where men and women in the Middle Ages and the Renaissance were uncertain about the colour of the Egyptians, the Egyptophil Masons tended to see them as white. Next, the Hellenomaniacs of the early 19th century began to doubt their whiteness and to deny that the Egyptians had been civilized. It was only at the end of the 19th century, when

Egypt had been entirely stripped of its philosophic reputation, that its African affinities could be re-established. (30)

H.D. asserts that in spite of Egypt's presumed blackness and presumed lack of philosophical gifts, Greece's superior reputation will not be long sullied by alliances, filial or philosophical. Whiteness will prevail.

RED ROSES FOR BRONZE

The decade that passed between *Hymen* and *Red Roses for Bronze* (1931) witnessed a complex ambivalence in H.D. regarding the presumed privileges of occupying a white body. In 1929, H.D. arrogantly asserts her love for the skin she's in:

"We" differentiate one from the other only by the shell and as the shell is MY shell and as I have made this particular shell for my own particular line of defense, I can't see what I could or should want with anybody's shell but my own. (Quoted in Arthur 68)

Yet, after meeting Robeson and working with him throughout the making of the film *Borderline* (1930), H.D. writes an entire book of poetry, *Red Roses for Bronze*, that endeavors to negotiate the many cultural and personal dispositions that conflate into the topic we call "race." Dodd calls this book "a transitional book" that anticipates the expansive power of *Helen in Egypt* and *Hermetic Definition*. DiPace Fritz reads this book as "the pursuit of a transcendent self" (50). Gelpi claims that *Red Roses for Bronze* "showed the poet in an agitated and uncertain state about herself and her work" (318). Louis Martz reads these poems as desperate and restricted: "*Red Roses for Bronze*, shows no development: the Greek mask is still holding, even more tightly, and, despite some excellent sequences, . . . the struggle for expression is almost desperate in places" (90). Although many interpretations of this book focus on H.D.'s fantasies about Robeson, her uncertainties, and her pursuit of a more stable self, no one emphasizes the profusion of references to whiteness.

Red Roses for Bronze not only provides an outlet for H.D.'s fantasies about Robeson and his blackness, it also renders a terrain on which H.D. can forge a connection to her own whiteness. This book of poems offers a challenge to the hierarchical white aesthetic by contemplating whether whiteness may ever prove as powerful an aesthetic as love. *Red Roses for Bronze* reveals H.D.'s struggle to represent a changing and vulnerable whiteness.

Although Hollenberg reads the central theme of the book as "[i]ncipient emotional and artistic paralysis" (92), the entire book can be read as an intricate emotional movement that chronicles the process of a white woman dealing with her unrequited love for a black man. The opening poem, "Red Roses for Bronze," contemplates reforming the living black man, the lover in her fantasies, into a sculpture, thereby fashioning a figure easier to "stroke" and to love. "Myrtle Bough" suggests the possibility of a transformation that sheds the armor of race and love, but only to reveal an underlying sameness, a glorious "ivory" interior. In "Choros Sequence," the white lover suggests that she might forego her whiteness and her "luminous throne" for one smile from her lover's face. "Halcyon" expresses fear of rejection due to her "disagreeable color." "Songs from Cypress" proclaims an inability to understand preferences based on color. "White Rose" declares a fatigue with the burden of whiteness. "Calliope" offers a warning to the white spirit to curtail its pride and its sense of exemption from "lower thought." "All Mountains" elevates this particular love above the "white love" of the islands below and suggests that a loftier love abides in the "upper air" and "mountain trees." "Triplex" reifies assimilation inside the white "I." "Epitaph" ultimately acknowledges that the love she desires may be "illicit."

Friedman reads the racial markings of "Red Roses for Bronze" as a reversal of " 'the implicit rape fantasies of . . . the black man-white woman script'" (quoted in Edmunds 158). Reading the poem for racial markings less particular but more poignant than the rape fantasies provides an interesting immersion into the emotions associated with white mastery. Posing as a sculptress creating a bronze figure of a man, H.D. suggests, albeit tentatively, in Section I that a recast of her love in bronze "might" gain her some peace:

> if I might ease my fingers and my brain
> with stroke,
> stroke,
> stroke,
> stroke,
> stroke at—something (stone, marble, intent,
> stable, materialized)
> peace,
> even magic sleep
> might come again.
>   (*Collected Poems* 211)

This section suggests that upon casting the beloved in bronze, the sculptress/lover would be able to have him sexually, and then finally, she might attain the sleep that would quell her obsession. In reading the poem with an eye toward white mastery, it is clear that H.D. wants to mitigate the power of the living black figure and figuratively enslave him in art. The fourfold repetition of the lines "If I might" underscores H.D.'s sense that the hypothetical premise frames a prodigious desire. The desire of a white woman for a black man poses one set of social and cultural problems; that the sculptress of this poem threatens to control a black man's freedom to choose his own sexual partners poses another. Furthermore, she indicates that the exact and only facial gesture to be preserved would be "the slight mocking, slightly cynical smile." She wants to control even his countenance.

Marilyn Arthur reads the bronze sculpture as "the artifact, the created, the passive adored and static other, imprisoned in bronze, voiceless, and with a hollow interior" (76). Although the figuring of Robeson as a bronze sculpture unquestionably resonates with white mastery, H.D. has made a significant change since 1919 when she aligned herself with Leonardo da Vinci via his inspirational blond-haired boys. Now the black body of Robeson inspires her to artistic vision: "your dark hair / catches the light / in serpent curves, / here, / there" (*Collected Poems* 213). Although participation in maintenance of a white poetic project is still in full force, her artistic vision has widened. Unfortunately, in the same moment that she envisions the black body as an invigorating figure equivalent to the blond-haired boy, she also protects herself from imagining supra-cultural possibilities by employing a stereotypical analogy—a black man's hair as serpent curves—which continues a racist alignment between Satan and dark peoples. Dyer claims that this ambivalence is inevitable in white people: "White power . . . reproduces itself regardless of intention, power differences and goodwill, and overwhelmingly because it is not seen as whiteness, but as normal" (10). Whiteness as masterful sign and blackness as diminished one are so thoroughly embedded in H.D.'s imagination that even when a powerful exterior inspiration, such as Robeson, affects her, her imagination impairs its potential to invent a new language.

Throughout the rest of the poem, H.D. addresses her extraordinary jealousy and hatred of other women to whom he might be attracted. To prove the power of her love, she designs a graphically destructive image of the lengths to which her jealousy might compel her:

> such is my jealousy
> (that I discreetly veil
> with just my smile)
> that I would clear so fiery a space
> that no mere woman's love could long endure;
> and I would set your bronze head in its place.
>   (*Collected Poems* 215)

The sculptress admits that she would situate the decapitated head of the sculpture within a pyre so fierce that no "mere" woman's love could approach it. She proceeds to describe how she would tend the fire-surrounded head:

> about the base,
> my roses would endure,
> while others,

>   those, for instance,
>   she might proffer,
>   standing by the stair,
>   or any tentative offers of white flowers
>   or others lesser purple at the leaf,
>   must fall and sift and pale
>   in (O so short a space)
>   to ashes and a little heap of dust.
>   (*Collected Poems* 215)

This culmination asserts, in terms of masterful whiteness, that only she, the sculptress, would have the power to tend the fiery bronze head. Her flowers would survive beyond those brought by any other woman (in particular, those brought by the "she" who stands "by the stair"). Most important, her flowers would be better and last longer than "white flowers." Since the poems of *Sea Garden*, white flowers have been for H.D. the superlative gifts in nature. Here H.D. flaunts custody of a supreme ideal when she establishes herself as possessor of a flower more enduring and spectacular than white flowers. The poem, thereby, ends in an insolent image of white dominance.

In "Myrtle Bough," H.D. uses mythic Greek personages to mask multiple race, class, and gender transformations of lovers. The interracial fantasy with Robeson continues to hover over the poem. In the poem, H.D. offers possibilities of love between a "man and a maid," "two maids," or two "pages." The entire poem resonates with the relationship between Harmodius and Aristogiton, two Athenian youths of the sixth century B.C., renowned for their great friendship.

"Myrtle Bough" invites an interpretation of its whiteness through the title. That the fragrant myrtle flower is white and situated on the strongest branch of its shrub correlates the strength and potency of love with the naturalness and purity of whiteness. Throughout the poem, demands for recognition of a "Love, beyond men and women" occur, which require that the figures of the poem shed their various "armours." Upon the shedding of these armours, real cores are revealed, and these core substances are pure and white. Harmodious has "immaculate strength." Narcissus, having "stripped off" her "weight of chastened, burnished armour," reveals an "ivory" ankle. Once these armours have been cast aside, the "sleeping ivory," blue-eyed loved one can arise and take flight "with white wings and wings of gold / across bright skies." The transformation of a loved one requires, in H.D.'s poetic imagination, a recuperation of a presumed core whiteness. Love, although inexplicable to men and women, clearly endures as a high-flying, white- and gold-winged creature obvious "to all eyes" by the end of the poem.

In "Choros Sequence," the speaker/lover discusses the level of sacrifice she would make to secure her lover. The greatest sacrifice she can make is that of her whiteness: "I would forgo / my snowfields for your sun." In the ideal world that she imagines, she would dramatically step away from her whiteness and into the lover's smile and touch:

> I, mistress of the oft-imperiled zone,
> translucent,
> wrought of many colours,
> step
> ardent yet temperate
> from my luminous throne;
> he smiles
> and all the effrontery of my race
> rises to meet his smiling, cynical face,
> and all my effrontery and all my wiles
> blanch and wither
> beside his enchanting smiles;
> and all the gold woven about my veil
> and all the pearls, entwined
> for their sorcery,
> fail
> beside the devouring embers
> of his touch
>   (*Colected Poems* 258)

Dyer writes that in art white women are depicted as more than white; often these representations are translucent "in ways that may deny their fleshliness altogether, allow it to coexist in a kind of disavowel" (115). For the lover in this poem to disavow her flesh and her whiteness highlights her acknowledgment of its power. Even as she steps away from "her luminous throne," she maintains a singular white characteristic:

> I pale
> beside him
> who has vine and plant for dower,
> I but a white rose,
> one white rose
> in flower
>   (*Collected Poems* 259)

H.D. makes it clear in the poem that a white person cannot even willingly shed his or her entire whiteness. At least one white flower, a reminder of the power of the whole, will remain.

"Halcyon" depicts a moment embedded in fear of rejection. In Section VI of this poem, the lover faces the fact that her love has become "impatient," "unkind," "bitter," "crude," and "cruel" because of her "colour": "you don't find / this colour agrees with you" (*Collected Poems* 274). Although ostensibly talking about the color of her dress in the poem, she mentions the dress only in parenthesis thereby framing it as a less significant part of the entire color question. The poem proceeds to portray endless quarrels, accusations, departures, crying, and shouting until the final section. In Section X, the final quarrel, the rejected lover comforts herself with images of whiteness:

> we quarrel again—
> don't talk—dismiss happiness,
> unhappiness, pain, bliss,
> even thought—
>
> what's left?
> incomparable beyond belief,
> white stones,
> immaculate sand
>   (*Collected Poems* 277)

The return to whiteness following rejection quells pain, memory, and thought. H.D. associates the halcyon, the mythical bird that denotes calm, peace, tranquillity, and prosperity, with immaculate whiteness. In "Chronos Sequence," the lover suggested that she might forfeit her whiteness in order to be with the beloved. "Halcyon" amends this notion, however, by recognizing that such sacrifices are only made because a return to whiteness "incomparable beyond belief" is possible. H.D. asserts that whiteness is not endowed nor dispensable. Whiteness, for white people, is always already there.

"Songs from Cyprus" reflects a palimpsest of past Cyprus history, current Cyprus history, and the race issues central to *Red Roses for Bronze*. The element of Cyprus's past history relevant to the poem is its multiple occupants since 1450 B.C. H.D. employs Cyprus as a site signifying both limitless ability to be possessed as well as a site exemplifying boundless resistance to long-term possession. Records of Cyprus's history begin with Egyptian occupation and chronicle centuries of various and simultaneous settlements. Arcadia took over about 1400 B.C., followed by the Phoenicians, Assyrians, Egyptians, and Persians. For numerous centuries thereafter, Cyprus passed hands among Persians, Greeks, Egyptians, Venetians, and Turks until British rule began in 1879.

At the time H.D. authored *Red Roses for Bronze*, the 1931 riots in Cyprus had broken out to demonstrate against British rule, which resulted in further British constraints. In Section VI of "Songs from Cyprus," H.D. figures Cyprus as a loveless place because peace has been lacking there for so long. She discusses her failure to understand the age old struggles for hierarchy, possession, and power through images of color:

> I do not understand
> the ways that seek white lilies for one love,
> (casting aside the darker
> scarred with fire)
> and for another, red.
>   (*Collected Poems* 280)

In this poem, H.D. truly attempts to discern the compelling characteristics that determine all types of forbidden choices, but she admits through the "I" of the poem, that she cannot understand why some seek white people to love, some seek dark, and others seek red. For her, Cyprus provides a metaphor for all ongoing cultural, political, and racial struggles to possess and to dominate Otherness. She concludes the poem with a warning:

> All flowers are hers
> who rules the immensurate seas,
> in Cyprus, purple and white lilies tall;
> how were it other?
> there is no escape
> from her who nurtures,
> who imperils all.
>   (*Collected Poems* 281)

H.D. warns that the songs emerging from Cyprus, like the songs of the mythological Sirens, are particularly composed to lure those who want to dominate Others. This poem exhorts that Others who provide sustenance for white desire to dominate, simultaneously signify the neediness and vulnerability of white mastery. Whiteness needs Others. White control thus becomes imperiled by its own need to have its superiority nurtured.

This poem designates an epiphanic moment for H.D., a moment when she realizes that her desire for Paul Robeson is not the genuine issue. She actually wants him to desire her, but Robeson (as Cyprus) can only nurture H.D.'s desire to have him. He does not desire her; therefore, he (Cyprus) imperils her ability to fully master the situation. Read as an ideology of survival and mastery, this poem houses evidence that H.D. finds whiteness to be a core aesthetic, one that begins and ends all discussions of love, beauty, and peoples coming together. Whiteness stands in this poem as that racial marker that remains inexchangeable, and for the first time, H.D. comprehends and represents the particular loss that intransmutable whiteness ensures.

In "White Rose," H.D. expresses a weariness with whiteness. She cautions the white rose to be wary of its dalliances with conceit and to be mindful of beauty's limitations:

> white rose,
> white rose,
> beware,
> beauty is beauty
> but not, not so rare
> and not so bountiful
> that it may spare
> a moment
> to revile
> Love
>   (*Collected Poems* 285)

From experience, the speaker counsels that although the white rose may constitute beauty incarnate in some eyes, more powerful forces exist—such as love. After the revelations of "Songs from Cyprus," H.D. warns against white privilege and its presumed exemptions. She asserts in "White Rose," that, tragically, white dominance may exempt one from the privilege of loving and being loved.

H.D. reiterates the disadvantages of white mastery in "Calliope." She calls out to the "spirit, white":

> beware,
> too soon, too soon
> you think yourself exempt
> from all our lower thought,
> our lesser magic,
> Love's exquisite revel;
> grow not too soon, too bold,
> return
> *(Collected Poems* 287)

As muse of heroic poetry, Calliope figures in this poem as the overseer and protector of poetry's heroes and heroines. The warnings of the poem ostensibly emerge from Calliope's wisdom, and in this poem, she prophesies a need to move beyond the color of the flesh and into the realm of love.

"Songs from Cyprus," "White Rose," and "Calliope" evince an ideological shift in the racial markings of H.D.'s poetry, a shift toward a humble whiteness. Just such a sense of humility surfaces in "All Mountains":

> Let Phoebus keep the market,
> let white Love
> claim all the islands
> of seaport or river
> would I contend with these?
> nay,
> I would rather pity him, my brother,
> pity white passionate Love
> *(Collected Poems* 290)

H.D. associates the desire for "white passionate Love" with Phoebus, the sun god. Dyer reminds us that whiteness has been associated with the celestial and with light from above since the twelfth century (119). In this regard, H.D. writes nothing unusual. However, her declaration that Phoebus (white Love) be permitted to "keep" possession of all its lowly islands does emit an atypical tone of disdain for white love. The speaker avers that she pities white passionate Love, as associated with Phoebus's sunny, yet paltry, islands, because it must continuously lay passive to the "promptings" and the "restlessness" of the seas. It appears at first glance that a remarkable shift in the expression of whiteness occurs in this poem. This white love seems tainted and less desirable than another type.

However, the culmination of the poem reveals a telling moment of inescapable white mastery. After declaring that white passionate Love is, at best, pitiable, the speaker does not look to another "color" for love. Instead she patronizingly asks Zeus to respect these infantile lovers while granting an elevated love:

> Ah Zeus,
> ennoble,
> shelter these
> thy children,
> but give me the islands of the upper air,
> all mountains
> and the towering mountain trees.
>   (*Collected Poems* 290)

DiPace Fritz claims that in "All Mountains," H.D. "seeks a rarefied existence—'give me the islands of the upper air.' She wishes to dwell apart and worship in 'secret altars,' surrounded by snow" (62). In diminishing the power of white love, H.D. cannot imagine looking to another color of love; she still wants the love to be white, but she wants it transformed into a higher version of white.

Annalee Newitz describes such transformations of whiteness as proof that white people "are capable of generating images of a whiteness which is marked, imperfect and disempowered" (133), but she also argues that white artists typically only reveal imperfect whiteness when it appears primitive, lower-class, and representative of "white trash" (134). Ultimately, the transformed, separate, lowly whiteness must be kept separate from the "real" whiteness. This need for separation explains why the speaker in "All Mountains" would ask Zeus to raise her love above the pitiable white Love of the islands. Dyer informs us that both the Aryan and the Causasian models of whiteness share a sense of "soul-elevation" and beauty that originates from the whiteness of the mountains (21). H.D. suggests in her poem a return to the original whiteness, the whiteness of the mountains.

Yet another meditation on her proposed relationship with Robeson, "All Mountains" reveals H.D.'s desire for a relationship between a white woman and a black man significantly different from the pitiable white loves of the world. In calling to a higher power to confer that difference, she discloses her need for the difference to signify hierarchically, and, if at all possible, she wants the new love to express itself more purely like the oxygen of the "upper air," and more loftily like the "towering trees." In other words, she wants a miscegenetic relationship, but one deemed by the gods to be whiter than white.

In "Triplex," H.D. revises the female self. She becomes a complex system of women—all with different racial markings:

> Let them not hate in me,
> these three;
> Maid
> of the luminous grey-eyes,
> mistress
> of honey and marble implacable white thighs
> and Goddess,
> chaste Daughter of Zeus,
> most beautiful in the skies.
> *(Collected Poems* 291)

The Maid with grey eyes represents the miscegentic union between Egyptians and Greeks that H.D. first mentioned in her poem "Egypt." The Mistress is a white woman in view of her "white thighs." The Goddess, daughter of Zeus, is most likely black. Zeus, deemed Ethiopian, and succeeded by black children, was referred to in early literature as black-faced and dark-faced (Snowden 94). "Triplex" reveals a moment in which H.D. prays for the power to resist warring among other women, ostensibly for the male figure. This poem reconsiders the extraordinary jealousy and hatred expressed toward other women in "Red Roses for Bronze" by situating women of differing races as constituents of one woman. Ultimately, however, H.D. does not offer the three women an unrestrained existence in which to "grow side by side." A singular "me" embodies the women, signifying H.D.'s ability to imagine a world of equality only insofar as it culminates in assimilation into a predominant culture.

The penultimate poem of *Red Roses for Bronze,* "Epitaph," commemorates H.D.'s coming to terms with the difficulties of interracial love as well as the death of possibility. She, the white woman, has been rejected by the black man. Throughout the entire book, she has revealed the emotional process of coming to terms not only with this rejection but with a love that is culturally scorned. The poetry displays various ways in which she has internalized just such contempt. The only gesture left is to suggest an epitaph for the love that white woman could never incite. In fact, she authors multiple epitaphs that reveal her situation through a variety of perspectives:

> So I may say,
> "I died of living,
> having lived one hour"

The self's version of the situation is that although it was a short-lived and emotionally chaotic fantasy, it was worth the risk involved. Others have a different point of view:

> so they may say,
> "she died soliciting
> illicit fervour"
> (*Collected Poems* 299)

H.D. comprehends that one person's sense of having lived may prove to be someone else's model of unsanctioned passion. Even though H.D. tries desperately to understand the white body as undesirable, she cannot escape the social and cultural constructions that endow her white body with privilege, advantage, and allure. H.D. does enact the process of recognizing and battling one's own white body and its power, and this act signifies an important turn for white women. Dyer informs us that white women represented in literature are often capable of acknowledging and criticizing the negative aspects of white enterprise, but mostly they do nothing to change it. "Doing nothing . . . provides the basis for the complex construction of a particular white femininity" (186–187). H.D. does something. She diligently chronicles the humbling process of being undesirable to a black man while maintaining a respect for her own desires toward him. Rather than doing nothing, H.D. makes art to represent, question, and rebel against a situation about which nothing may be done.

TRILOGY

H.D. published the three long poems of *Trilogy* separately: "Walls Do Not Fall" in 1944, "Tribute to the Angels" in 1945, and "Flowering of the Rod" in 1946. All three poems were published posthumously as *Trilogy* in 1973. These intricately layered poems, palimpsests, represent reactions to the bombings of World War II (Martz 93); they reconstruct and revise the lives of Christ's mother, Mary, and the other Mary, Mary Magdalene (Chisholm, "Autoheterography" 99); and they narrate social and cultural histories through fleshly bodies (Edmunds 4). For the purposes of interpreting the racial markings of this text, Chisholm's work on how repression affects the cultural and historical memories of peoples in *Trilogy* ("Autoheterography" 100) proves particularly useful, as does Morris's work on "projection," the final stage of alchemical transmutation. According to Morris, the alcehmical belief that to change a substance was "simply a matter of altering its 'form'" (118–119) guides "nearly every image in *Trilogy*" (119). H.D.'s reiteration of this process throughout the poems signifies her desire for a universalizing form, a transcendent body beyond constructs such as race and gender that could be designed through ritualized transformations. Intriguingly, however, no matter how intricately H.D. weaves the ritualized transmutation processes throughout the poems, *Trilogy* ends with images engulfed in the whiteness of a silently falling snow. For H.D., universal transcendence and transformation result in assimilation under the emblem of whiteness.

H.D. structures "Walls Do Not Fall," like the two sibling poems in *Trilogy*, in forty-three lyric sections. The overall thematic of this poem is exposure of the marvels, material and spiritual, uncovered in the ruins caused by the bombings. As Edmunds points out, H.D. narrates each lyric from varying "I" perspectives that aid her in reaffirming the concept of metamorphosis: The narrator "speaks in turn as mollusk, lover, worm, poet, religious initiate, dreamer, witness, ram, lamb, beggar, lunatic and prophet" (34). Edmunds claims that this malleable "I" serves her well because it allows her the opportunity for continual rebirth (34); I add that the ever-changing "I" affords H.D. an opportunity to promote the idea of "I" as a universal representative, capable of representing all subjects, all races. Although she seeks to transform the connotations of "I" as a gesture toward recognition and naming of Others, the "I," ironically maintains a degree of confinement that erases variability.

As demonstrated in *Red Roses for Bronze*, H.D. does have a sense of humility about the extent to which she will be successful in achieving the transmutations, especially transformations regarding race, through poetry. In lyric 8 of "Walls Do Not Fall," she reveals the useless and pathetic trap of inexpression to which poets may succumb:

> poets are useless,
>
> more than that,
> we, authentic relic,
>
> bearers of the secret wisdom,
> living remnant
>
> of the inner band
> of the sanctuaries' initiate,
>
> are not only 'non-utilitarian,'
> we are 'pathetic':
>
> this is the new heresy;
> but if you do not even understand what words say,
>
> how can you expect to pass judgement
> on what words conceal?
>   (*Collected Poems*, "Walls Do Not Fall" 517)

She reminds herself and the readers that words will conceal and resist not only on the surface of the work, but also in the silences, white space, and cultural noise of the text. Although this poem does not, on the surface, discuss the horrors of World War II's racial genocide, what the poem cannot say alludes directly to this issue.

By lyric 38, H.D. expresses frustration with the struggles and failures of humans, including herself, to understand the historical issues that compel people, as well as the psychological issues that drive us, to behave as we do.

She questions what new knowledge she can gain by again entertaining the parallels between the past and the present. Throughout the first four couplets, the poem does not reveal the exact issue causing frustration; it generalizes about historical parallels and psychic affinities, but the poem does not claim a particular issue as catalyst for the search. As the poem moves toward chronicling and compounding the particular methods of study that have been employed regarding this subject, it becomes clearer that the issue under discussion is racial differentiation:

> my mind (yours),
> your way of thought (mine),
>
> each has its peculiar intricate map,
> threads weave over and under
>
> the jungle-growth
> of biological aptitudes,
>
> inherited tendencies,
> the intellectual effort
>
> of the whole race,
> its tide and ebb
> (*Collected Poems*, "Walls Do Not Fall" 539)

Biology, genetic inheritance, and intelligence are three of the key scientific guideposts by which racial differentiation has been made for the past 150 years. Since the late nineteenth century, statistical measurements of biological data have been used to determine the biological aptitudes of various races. Audrey Smedley claims

Such seemingly objective techniques, regardless of the accuracy or integrity of the date, produced a kind of typological thinking about races and racial differences that was to characterize most of anthropology until long after World War II. (261)

H.D. toys with this method as a possibility for differentiating among races.

Another common method for determining racial differentiation is based on inherited tendencies as first presented by Sir Francis Galton in 1869:

Arguing that there is a physiological basis for psychological traits, he invented techniques for measuring what he thought was intelligence, along with the bell-shaped curve for demonstrating its "normal distribution." . . . These are still basic models for twentieth century psychology. (Smedley 266)

According to Galton, various skills, talents, and personality traits are inherited and passed along through families and races.

H.D. discusses these methods as part of the ebb and flow of information regarding how to differentiate among races. Like biological measurements and inheritance factors, intellectual effort and performance signified racial limitations. In the early twentieth century, Americans developed and utilized intelligence tests "on a large scale," which became universally used to measure racial differences and to justify inequities of racial treatment (Smedley 267).

In lyric 38, H.D. suggests an alternative to these methods. She allows that each mind has its own "peculiar" "personal approach" and that the differences are actually "minute" and "particular." She prompts us to look to nature for depictions of similar differences. First she says to look toward the uniqueness of "vein-paths on any leaf," and then she proposes that we look to the individuality of "every snow-flake" that "has" its "star" and its inclusive shape: that of the color spectrum. H.D.'s closing representation signifies an elevation of the white snowflake as an accommodating natural image capable of taking on a shape that houses all colors. Alicia Ostriker claims that in this poem H.D. says that "we each have our own truth, equally valuable, which we must learn to see. Hints, clues, texts, sacred images which have survived from the shattered past abound, and yet none is a substitute for our own act of engaged perception" ("No Rule" 347–348). H.D.'s engaged perception is a masterful white perception. For all her intentions to sidestep the age-old theories of racial differentiation, she ultimately reifies whiteness as the most natural of universalizing factors.

"Tribute to the Angels," the second poem of *Trilogy*, has predominantly been interpreted through white feminist perspectives that discuss H.D.'s interrogations of patriarchy. DuPlessis, for instance, claims that H.D. displaces patriarchal forces by recentering the figures of Mary and Mary Magdalene in history and lore, while also concerning herself with the possibilities of transforming patriarchy (*H.D.: The Career* 94). Gubar suggests that H.D. establishes a "a new language" aimed at recovering the "feminine" as a primary force in history ("Echoing Spell" 72). I offer a reading that accounts differently for the "Marys" and the refusal to name "colours" in the poem. In "Tribute to the Angels," H.D. once again attempts to transcend issues of racial differentiation and again finds herself celebrating whiteness in the form of the "Lady of the Snow."

In lyric 9, H.D. first questions the color of the "jewel" in the bowl. This bowl is the alchemist's bowl, capable of nurturing transformations. Hollenberg claims that by refusing to name the color of the jewel, H.D. enacts a return to "life's source," a pre-naming, pre-childbirth experience (131). Hollenberg's sense of the transformation emphasizes a "feat of memory"; my sense of the transformation emphasizes the initial question posed in the poem. H.D. asks five questions of the jewel that address color, offerings, love, parents, and desire. As soon as she spots the jewel in the bowl, her first question addresses color. H.D. makes it clear that we have been culturally constructed to notice the color of subjects before we notice anything else.

In lyric 13, she pursues the questions of the jewel's color and ultimately determines that no name exists to describe it:

> "What is the jewel colour?"
> green-white, opalescent,
>
> with under-layer of changing blue,
> with rose-vein; a white agate
>
> with a pulse uncooled that beats yet,
> faint blue-violet
>   (*Collected Poems*, "Tribute to the Angels" 554)

DuPlessis sees the jewel as suggestive of a "milk-filled breast" as well as of an "anti-bomb: an implosion which shows the same colours and vibrancy as an actual explosion, but to opposite intent" (*H.D.: The Career* 92). I read the jewel as a chalcedony and a racial marker. It bears a milky, opalescent outer layer that contains veins of other colors. In terms of racial markings, the jewel that the speaker of the poem reluctantly discusses is a form of whiteness that accommodates Other colors. The significant point for H.D. is that no matter how unique a substance she attempts to present, the language constructs the same old white, assimilative paradigm.

In lyric 14, H.D.'s "I" understands the power of language to whiten and to assimilate its subject's qualities, thus she declares a personal moratorium on speaking and thinking about naming the jewel. She prefers instead to look at it:

> I do not want to name it,
> I want to watch its faint
>
> heart-beat, pulse-beat
> as it quivers, I do not want
>
> to talk about it,
> I want to minimize thought,
>
> concentrate on it
> till I shrink,
>
> dematerialize
> and am drawn into it.
>   (*Collected Poems*, "Tribute to the Angels" 555)

Gubar reads in this lyric a journey on H.D.'s part toward a "noncoercive vocabulary, a new language that will consecrate what has been desecrated by her culture" ("Echoing Spell" 73). More specifically, Gubar claims that H.D. wants to recover the "jewels" of feminine culture that have been diminished by patriarchy ("Echoing Spell" 73). I think H.D. makes an issue of the jewel's color in relationship to naming because she wants us to read the issue at hand as more specific than male/female dilemmas or any binary problems. The "I" in this poem suggests not a recovery of something that has been forsaken, but rather a "shrinking" and "dematerilaization" of the self so that entry into Otherness will become possible.

This courageous absorption into Otherness threatens the white psyche and brings on dream visions that manifest in an apparition of Our Lady of the Snow. In lyric 32, the menace (even though chosen) of being assimilated into Otherness stimulates a vision of whiteness that will assert its superiority and perfection:

> For I can say truthfully,
> her veils were *white as snow,*
>
> *so as no fuller on earth*
> *can white them;* I can say
>
> she looked beautiful, she looked lovely
>   (*Collected Poems,* "Tribute to the Angels" 566)

DiPace Fritz claims that the Lady in these lyrics symbolizes the purity and significance of the goddess for H.D. (130). Martz reads a "joyous, teasing mood" in these lyrics which use the white language of Christ's transfiguration (98). Gubar suggests that the Lady is not simply one goddess, but is instead "Persephone, the *Sanctus Spiritus, Santa Sophia,* Venus, Isis, and Mary, but most importantly the female spirit liberated from precisely these mystifications" ("Echoing Spell" 74). Because the Lady appears without her child, Hollenberg argues that she is "No mere 'symbolic figure' of traditional female values such as 'peace, charity, chastity,' that have been privatized and devalued or channeled to serve male interests" (132). DuPlessis offers that "Because Mary carries a book, not a baby, . . . H.D. offers the possibility that Mary is not a conduit for One whom she bore, but is herself the One: the goddess is God" (*H.D.: The Career* 93). Whether she symbolizes purity, transfigures Christ, represents all women in one, defies "feminizing" signifiers, or becomes God, the issue still remains that the Lady's veils were whiter than any other whiteness on earth, that the whiteness signifies her beauty and loveliness, and that this white Lady can assimilate and represent all other women. Even though H.D. has struggled to redefine Mary as a whole being even without her maternal signifier, the child, she has not revised Mary's whiteness.

Just as in her early poem, "Sea Violet," in which white violets are pure, untouched, elevated, and angelic and in which they exude an essential and undebatable desirability, the Lady of "Tribute to Angels" emanates similar essentializing characteristics. Again H.D. participates in an essentialist racism (Frankenberg 11) that supports the assumption that were an impeccable representative of the female gender to appear, she would, naturally, appear not only as white and in white, but also as white beyond comparison and competition.

In lyric 40, H.D. revisits the language she has used to describe the Lady and suggests that the language will not allow her to designate the Lady properly:

> what I wanted to indicate was
> a new phase, a new distinction of colour;
>
> I wanted to say, I did say
> there was no sheen, no reflection,
>
> no shadow; when I said white,
> I did not mean sculptor's or painter's white,
>
> nor porcelain; dim-white could
> not suggest it, for when
>
> is fresh-fallen snow (or snow
> in the act of falling) dim?
>
> Yet even now, we stumble, we are lost—
> what can we say?
>
> she was not impalpable like a ghost,
> she was not awe-inspiring like a Spirit,
>
> she was not even over-whelming
> like an Angel.
>   (*Collected Poems*, "Tribute to the Angels" 572)

No matter how H.D. tries to steer the language away from the implied mastery of whiteness, she cannot. She recognizes that whiteness cannot be dimmed, cannot be made ordinary because, as she will determine in the final lyric of this section, white is "all-colour." White is assimilative by its very definition.

Lyric 43 delivers a complicatedly resigned celebration of all-inclusive whiteness to the culmination of the book:

> And the point in the spectrum
> where all lights become one,
>
> is white and white is not no-colour,
> as we were told as children,
>
> but all-colour;
> where the flames mingle
>
> and the wings meet, when we gain
> the arc of perfection,
>
> we are satisfied, we are happy,
> we begin again
>   (*Collected Poems*, "Tribute to the Angels" 573)

Whiteness inspires an allness associated with happiness and with new beginnings. As we witnessed in *Red Roses for Bronze*, H.D. dauntlessly proceeds through the mire of determining, redefining, recognizing, dimming, and silencing whiteness, but she cannot exit the social and cultural constructions that urge her toward the resurrection of a masterful whiteness to redeem the complications of the poem.

The third poem of *Trilogy*, "Flowering of the Rod," has been read as an alchemical attempt to dismantle the "familiar racist and misogynist reading of the Scriptures that dismisses Kaspar as a dark heathen and Mary Magdalene as a devil-ridden harlot, making both peripheral to the real story" (Morris 121). Although H.D. again pursues her project of attempting to dismantle racist narratives through these two figures—Kaspar, one of the Magi, and Mary Magdalene—she ultimately recuperates an all-encompassing whiteness to reaffirm the essential naturalness of white mastery. The snow that repetitively blankets this poem exemplifies the representation of essential white mastery: "remember the snow / on Hermon" (lyric 1); "I go...into the snow" (lyric 2); "we must fly, / like the snow-geese of the Arctic circle" (lyric 3); "the wave...vanishes like snow on the equator" (lyric 4); "And the snow fell on Hermon" (lyric 36); "the snow fell on the almond trees" (lyric 36); "and the snow fell / silently...silently" (lyric 36); "And as the snow fell on Hebron" (lyric 37); and *"snow falls on the desert"* (lyric 37). Ostriker observes correctly that repetition in H.D. becomes "an objective correlative for the spiritual power of metamorphosis and rebirth which the poet in her poem is attempting to recover and is recommending to us" ("No Rule" 349). Through repetition of "snow" in "Flowering of the Rod," H.D. recovers whiteness and recommends to readers the ubiquity of this silent and invisible master.

DiPace Fritz argues that in lyrics 36 to 41, H.D. presents the transfiguration of Christ on Mount Hebron, complete with its white raiment, to recall the Scriptural mountain quest toward redemption. I argue that H.D. also writes these redemptive lyrics "sacredly," which she describes as an accurate and responsible contextualization of the present within the past (Burnett 56). H.D. writes a blanketing whiteness into "Flowering of the Rod" because post–World War II racial sentiments demand that whiteness be presented as predominant. In lyric 37, the omnipresence of whiteness both envelops the landscape and conflates the particulars of the terrain into one minute unit:

> And as the snow fell on Hebron,
> the desert blossomed as it had always done;
>
> over-night, a million-million tiny plants
> broke from the sand,
>
> and a million-million little grass-stalks
> each put out a tiny flower,

> they were so small, you could hardly
> visualize them separately,
>
> so it came to be said,
> *snow falls on the desert*
> (*Collected Poems*, "Red Roses for Bronze" 605)

The "million-million" individual flowers are so small in comparison to the enwrapping snow, that their individuality becomes a moot point. In terms of white racial markings, H.D.'s lyric clarifies that no matter how many resurgences of variance occur, whiteness will prevail: "it had happened before, / it would happen again" (*Collected Poems*, "Red Roses for Bronze" 606).

HELEN IN EGYPT

Helen in Egypt, the epic poem that H.D. wrote between 1952 and 1955, chronicles the trajectory of a particular interrogation into the origins of Western civilization: How did Helen of Troy get to Egypt? Three sections—"Pallinode," "Leuke," and "Eidolon"—constitute the text, and each of the first two sections divides into seven books. "Eidolon" contains only six books. H.D. writes each book in three-line stanzas. Stesichorus, a lyric poet and contemporary of Sappho's, first posed the hypothesis that Helen left Troy for Egypt. Euripedes followed up on this tale, and H.D. revises the account with special attention to redemption of the hated Helen and to the question of an Afroasiatic Egypt's role in Western civilization. *H.D.* implies that Helen had black ancestors.

Some Modernists, fascinated with archaeological findings that established the factual existence of Troy, wrote revisions of this history (Roessel 38). Although archaeological investigation did establish the actuality of Troy, such excavations "did not do much for the existence of Helen" (Roessel 38). By the time of *Helen in Egypt*, Troy has been quarried frequently for literary value, resulting in multiple and varied representations of this "bedrock of Western civilization" (Benstock 165). Shari Benstock and Michael Wood argue that "no coherent picture emerges from its multiplicities and contradictions," and Wood concludes that "there is not . . . one single Troy" (Benstock 165). For H.D.'s purposes, the many Troys provide the perfect grounding for situating Helen as "everywoman."

H.D.'s assumption that one white woman, made infamous by white men, could represent all women is profoundly patriarchal and profoundly white in its nescience toward other cultures, other histories, other literatures, and other women. Furthermore, her construction of an "'apologia' or defense of Helen and, by extension, all women" (Friedman, "Creating" 376) also presupposes that all women long for such redemption. The epic proportions of *Helen in Egypt* more aptly clarify H.D.'s personal need to resurrect women's innocence and to venerate physical beauty. In an article, "The Cinema and the Classics," H.D. declares the significance of and the threat that beauty such as Helen's poses, and she also justifies moments of vindictiveness wielded by the beautiful:

And beauty, among other things, is reality, and beauty once in so many hundred years, raises a wan head, suddenly decides to avenge itself for all the slights that it has negligently accepted, sometimes through weariness, sometimes through sheer omnipotence, sometimes through cynicism or through boredom . . . once in so often, beauty herself, Helen above Troy, rises triumphant and denounces the world for a season and then retires. (32)

H.D. wrote this defense of beauty before *Red Roses for Bronze* and *Trilogy*, before her realizations, limited as they are, about the constraints of white embodiment. By the time she wrote *Helen in Egypt*, H.D. appeared to understand that further reification of Helen's beauty has racist implications. H.D.'s poem, thus, complicates the matter by restoring to white women a sense of blamelessness regarding their beauty's negative power and simultaneously instating another unnamable strength, a strength interior to beauty:

> it was not that she was beautiful,
> true, she stood on the Walls,
>
> taut and indifferent
> as the arrows fell;
> it was not that she was beautiful,
>
> there were others,
> in spite of the legend,
> as gracious, as tall
>   (*Helen in Egypt*, "Eidolon" 251–252)

H.D. suggests that Helen exudes an unnamable strength that is not beauty, and she situates this potency as originating from Helen's black heritage, a heritage Helen knows intuitively and emotionally rather than intellectually. This knowledge occasionally manifests itself to Helen from "the depth of her racial inheritance" (*Helen in Egypt*, "Pallinode" 13). Although H.D. arguably restores an Afroasiatic racial authenticity to Helen, Susan Edmunds correctly notes that the restoration occurs in the service of Freudian concepts that link white women and people of color to an "unconscious" primitiveness (11). Helen's discernibly white body, with hands "whiter than bone" (*Helen in Egypt*, "Leuke" 125), is the dominant outer body that has appropriated, as its unconscious, a primitive Afroasiatic woman.

H.D.'s captivation with this idea stemmed not only from Freud, but also from Robert Graves's *The White Goddess*. This white goddess inhabits a "principal" body that is white in color. This body also houses two other goddesses who are red and black: "the red goddess of love and battle" and "the black goddess of death and divination" (70). Graves's white goddess and Freud's primitive unconscious provide frameworks by which H.D. constructs her all-inclusive Helen. Betsy Erkkila aptly points out the political problems with reading such work as feminist. White women insist on highlighting the polarization between patriarchy and women as the significant work to be performed by feminists without attending to ways in which white women enact mastery over women of color (*Wicked Sisters* 3). By figuring Helen as a conflation of Graves's white goddess and as housing an Afroasiatic intuition, H.D. establishes a site of masterful whiteness in her heroine.

Any allusions to the possibility of Afroasiatic Egyptian influences on Greece and, therefore, on Western civilization ignite contentious debates among historians, anthropologists, and African Studies scholars of various disciplines. When reading *Helen in Egypt*, Benstock vividly observes Egypt "through the charred remains of Troy, site of the *failure* of the West to discover its origins, to uncover the beginnings of its own story" (166). Benstock supports her discernment that H.D. both wanted to acknowledge the possibility of Afroasiatic influences and fully understood the threat of the supposition by pointing to the moment in the poem when Theseus warns Helen not to entangle "Greek creative thought" in the "ancient Nile." This warning acknowledges H.D.'s awareness that certain forces might determinedly suppress Egypt's role in Western civilization.

Dianne Chisholm also argues that H.D. looks to "pre-Hel(l)enic" sources, namely Egypt, to bring Helen fully into being:

With Helen we trace the origins of her representation—that is, the classical representation of woman—to an earlier source than that of ancient Greece, back to *The Book of the Dead*; in the process of re-reading and remembering the textual body of Helen, we reenact the writing task of the Egyptian mythographer Thoth. ("Autoheterography" 101)

Thoth, the Egyptian god of wisdom and author of the Egyptian Hermetic Books, provides a partial answer to Helen's and Achilles's questions regarding her heritage: she is both Egyptian and Greek. Helen vehemently asserts that Thoth has a viable answer but that few will acknowledge its validity. Helen knows that most people will look only to Troy for answers about Helen and will, therefore, only know a fragment about her. As well, she acknowledges that neither source, Troy or Egypt, alone imparts the complexity of Helen nor of Western civilization's origins. Only a balancing of "the inevitable weight / of feather with feather" (*Helen in Egypt*, "Pallinode" 82) can divulge the full story.

The full story, according to H.D., intimates a significant black racial ancestry for Helen, for Achilles, and for Western civilization. Bernal argues that "Egyptian civilization was fundamentally African" and can "usefully" be called "black" (242). Robert S. Boynton tells us that this type of claim by Bernal enrages many classicists, especially those such as Mary Lefkowitz, who "view Bernal as disingenuously giving support to those who believe Greece stole its riches from Africa" (Boynton 44). Bernal argues that Greece was invaded in 1730 B.C. by the Hyksos, "a multicultural but predominantly Egypto-Semitic tribe" (quoted in Boynton 45), who thoroughly rooted their Afroasiatic culture, philosophies, and genes within Greek being. Lefkowitz ardently refutes claims of Egyptian influence on Greece:

[A]rchaeology does not provide any support for an invasion of Greece by Egyptians in the second millennium. Such information as we have suggests instead that settlers came to Egypt from Greece. (22)

As evidence, Lefkowitz sites the existence of Greek frescoes in Egypt during Hyksos rule, which suggests that "an 'invasion,' whatever form it may have taken, went from Greece to Egypt, rather than in the other direction" (22). Although H.D. would not have been privy to the fervor of this late twentieth-century debate, Bernal advises us that such discussions have been going on for many centuries (1).

Some scholars assert that the Afroasiatic Egyptian influence on Greece has been ritualistically denied as Western civilization has grown to pride itself on its whiteness. Bernal differentiates between two models of thinking about the role of Egypt in Western civilization: the Aryan model that views Greece as "essentially European" and the Ancient model that views Greece as Egyptian and Semitic (1). Lefkowitz argues that such models prove dubious not only because of the differentiation but because even should substantial proof emerge that Egypt, and thereby Africa, determinedly influenced Greek civilization, these Africans were not black. The "Africa" to which this era refers singularly constitutes the north coast:

The native population of the North were the ancestors of the modern Berbers; they are shown in Egyptian art with light hair and facial coloring. Their land was colonized by Phoenicians, Greeks, and finally by Romans. For that reason it is unlikely that most natives of what was called "Africa" in antiquity, that is North Africa, were "black" in the modern sense of the word. (Lefkowitz 32)

Other scholars disagree with Lefkowitz's African color scheme. Snowden claims that "Ethiopians became the yardstick by which classical antiquity measured colored peoples" (7). He sites a familiar classical color scheme: "Ethiopians, the blackest; Indians, less sunburned; Egyptians, mildly dark; and the Mauri (Moors)" (7). L. Bugner informs us that "'when the Greeks and the peoples of the Roman Empire wanted to represent a far-off, prestigious but different land, they used black as the sign of differentiation" (quoted in Pieterse 23). H.D.'s *Helen in Egypt* does not demonstrate an absolute allegiance with either side of the Greek origin debate. Instead, she enacts, through Helen's transformable body, and through the palimpsest structure of the poem, the various possible Helens, Troys, Egypts, and Western civilizations to illustrate the unfathomable prohibitions that regulate inquiry into whiteness.

It would be invaluable to understand H.D.'s exact disposition regarding the early twentieth-century debates about the origins of Greek civilization. Bernal claims that an "'[e]xtreme' Aryan Model . . . flourished during the twin peaks of anti-Semitism in the 1890s and again in the 1920s and 30s" (2). H.D., an earnest student of Greece throughout her life, would have been well aware of this sentiment. As well, during the time she actually composed *Helen in Egypt*, numerous uprisings occurred in the then present-day Egypt: "1952 began with the January 26 mob uprising and burning of Cairo after Egyptians refused to cooperate with a British plan to occupy the city" (Edmunds 96). Bryher writes to H.D. about her distress over the Egyptians' behavior: "[T]he Egyptians were as difficult as they could possibly be" (quoted in Edmunds 96–97). From this correspondence, Edmunds presumes that H.D. (perhaps not as zealously as Bryher) prefers a passive, nonresistant Egypt, especially non-resistant to white rule (97). H.D. attempts to portray a Greece with multiple and complex European and Afroasiatic characteristics, although she inevitably squelches most perceived threats to white mastery. As she made perfectly clear in *Red Roses for Bronze*, and as she reiterates in *Helen in Egypt*, H.D. only entertains the dismantling of whiteness when it threatens to shield one from love.

In "Pallinode," Helen informs Achilles that his excessive association with the whiteness and warrior status of the Myrmidons will embody him in an iron structure impenetrable to love:

> the body honoured
> by the Grecian host
> was but an iron casement,
>
> it was God's plan
> to melt the icy fortress of the soul,
> and free the man
>   (*Helen in Egypt*, "Pallinode" 9–10)

She positions herself as redeemer sent to make a "new Mortal" of this man by lessening his icy white fortress. As the initial consequence of shedding his honored, white glory, Achilles experiences himself as physically impaired. Loss of white armor equates with loss of physiological capabilities.

Helen wants Achilles to shed this whiteness both so that he will be less shielded against love and so that he will be open to understanding who she really is, information that transforms who he really is. In order for such foundational acknowledgment to occur, H.D. indicates that "this Helen is not to be recognized by earthly splendour nor this Achilles by accoutrements of valour" (*Helen in Egypt*, "Pallinode" 7). A transformation of typical signifiers marking Helen and Achilles occurs, and for Helen, this transformation includes admission of her Egyptian heritage. She knows her Egyptian self, not through the intellect, but through intuitive and emotional wisdom (*Helen in Egypt*, "Pallinode" 13). In relaying the weight of this wisdom to Achilles, she associates it with the remembrance of his mother, Isis/Thetis. She notes a mere moment of vulnerability in Achilles when she mentions his mother, but Helen concludes that Achilles could not yet comprehend the significance of her revelations about her Egyptian heritage and his mother's.

What Helen wants to impart to Achilles, as gently as possible, is that in Hermetic Texts, Thoth was the father of Isis (Bernal 139), and if indeed Thoth was Egyptian, a subject much debated, then Isis/Thetis may well lay claim to blackness. Chisholm concurs:

Helen's earliest memories of racial and biological prehistory (as recalled by the hieroglyphic writing on her own psychical, transhistorical walls) refer to an age of Egyptian culture predating that of Moses and the Monothesitic Sun King. She learns that she descends from the age of Isis. ("Autoheterography" 102)

Helen remains concerned about Achilles's inability to understand her because not knowing Helen of Egypt means that "he / knew not yet, Helen of Sparta, / knew not Helen of Troy, / knew not Helena, hated of Greece" (*Helen in Egypt*, "Pallinode" *14).* Ultimately, if Achilles does not understand that his own mother is Egyptian, he does not know himself to have a black heritage.

Helen finally employs a dramatic measure to force Achilles's comprehension of her relationship to Egypt—she blackens her face:

> I drew out a blackened stick,
> but he snatched it,
> he flung it back
>   (*Helen in Egypt*, "Pallinode" 16)

Helen's gesture threatens and horrifies Achilles to such an extent that he finally poses the exact questions Helen prodded toward: "'who are we? who are you? / where is this desolate coast? / who am I? Am I a ghost?'" (*Helen in Egypt*, "Pallinode" 16). Although Helen has finally provoked him into acknowledging a lack of perception about himself and his racial ancestry, by Book Three she is second-guessing her intentions and his power over her.

Edmunds suggests that in Book Two Helen fears an actual racial conversion (120): "as if God made the picture / and matched it / with a living hieroglyph" (*Helen in Egypt*, "Pallinode" 23), and that Achilles really saw her as black:

> in the dark, I must have looked
> an inked-in shadow; but with his anger,
> that ember, I became
>
> what his accusation made me
> (*Helen in Egypt*, "Pallinode" 23)

This fear compels Helen to speak with Achilles in Hellenic terms even though she would rather claim the oracular language of Thoth. She too partially fears her black ancestry.

She must balance her desire to reconnect fully with Egypt with the possibility of losing Achilles. He lures her into discussing the Battle of Troy again. She cannot bear his distance, but neither can she bear regurgitating their Greek history. She contemplates whether she would be happier alone.

Achilles prompts her one too many times to discuss again the Trojan War:

> Must we argue over again,
> the reason that brought us here?
> Was the Fall of Troy the reason?
> (*Helen in Egypt*, "Pallinode" 37)

Confused for a moment, Helen ponders whether the Egypt they now occupy is actually a place of exile, but with a start she remembers that Egypt is in fact her home, her source, her beginnings. Furthermore, she realizes that she again must do something drastic to remind Achilles why they currently reside in Egypt. Once again, she blackens her skin to signify their Egyptian heritage:

> I drew out a blackened stick,
> to darken my arms,
> to disguise my features
> (*Helen in Egypt*, "Pallinode" 38)

Through repetition, H.D. makes the point that skin color is the predominant marker of racial heritage and that white skin affords forgetfulness, while black skin triggers suppressed memory and associations.

For Helen, however, the question becomes what to do once reconciliation with the past has occurred. In the early books, she seems to want to forget Greece for Egypt, forget her whiteness for her blackness, just as she had forgotten Egypt for Greece. By Book Six of "Pallinode," however, Helen recognizes that "it is through her Greek identity that she understands" and that her Egyptian identity affords her the wisdom to accept "what she does not understand" (*Helen in Egypt*, "Pallinode" 80). Thus, she wants to bring the two pieces of her identity together. As racially progressive as such an amalgamation might first appear, Dyer makes the point that the choice to be "various" and to incorporate Otherness into the self has only been a right of white peoples (49). Helen's whiteness is never really at stake. As long as she looks white, she will always maintain the power, the privileges, and the constraints of white embodiment.

In "Leuke," the second section of *Helen in Egypt*, H.D. signifies Helen's bodily whiteness as ideal and unquestionable through comparative analysis. Paris says to Helen: "your hand was whiter than bone; / as you clenched your fist, / the knuckles shone, ivory" (*Helen in Egypt*, "Leuke" 125). She is whiter than the structure, the bones, that holds her body together. Frankenberg recognizes such gestures as those that locate whiteness as that viewpoint of "structural advantage," as "a standpoint" (1). Helen's whiteness issues from deep within her body. She is white to the bone, and with the help of this white structure, she walks with privilege through the world. H.D.'s fantastical movements of Helen from Greece to Egypt to Leuke and Egypt again metaphorically represent the inherent permissions granted the white body to course through worlds (geographical and spiritual) with ease. In "Leuke," whiteness is a position regulated at the level of bone structure, and it reverberates throughout the flesh, and throughout the island.

In Book Three, the apparition of Aphrodite appears to Paris to offer him a substitute for Helen. The substitute she offers is "Leuke, the white island." H.D. writes, "*It is as if she were offering Paris the most beautiful woman in the world—only this time, it is l'*isle blanche" (*Helen in Egypt*, "Leuke" 136). The only apt substitute for Helen, the epitome of white women, would be an entire island named for its whiteness. Paris needs a substitute because by the end of Book Three, Helen will leave him.

After leaving Paris, Helen finds another lover, Theseus. As Theseus gazes at her, he declares that she seems phantomlike and capable of traveling with the snow:

> How did you get here, Helen,
> do you know,
> blown by the wind, the snow?
>
> Come here, come near;
> are you a phantom
> will you disappear?
>   (*Helen in Egypt*, "Leuke" 147)

His implication that Helen appears camouflaged by the snow not only attests to Helen's whiteness, but also asserts the naturalness of her whiteness.

Even though Helen has sought out a new lover, she cannot forget Paris. She speaks to Theseus of Paris in terms of ultimate perfection, and that perfection she describes as white. She depicts Paris as

> whiter than snow,
>
> whiter than the white drift of sand
> that lies like ground shells
> (*Helen in Egypt*, "Leuke" 160–161)

Helen illustrates Paris's significance in terms of escalating whiteness. As well, she expresses rapture and love through accentuating layers of whiteness. H.D. grammatically produces this swell of whiteness through comparative analyses. White is always compared to something white, but is immeasurably whiter: "whiter than frost," "whiter than snow," and "whiter than the white drift of sand." When looking for language that represents perfection, H.D. again turns to images of unattainable whiteness.

As a result of remembering and retelling Paris's white perfection, Helen reignites her feelings for him, and she feels drained. To quiet herself, Helen meditates. H.D. situates this meditation against a backdrop of whiteness to represent the impeccably soothing nature of silence:

> I breathe quietly,
> I lie quietly as the snow,
>
> drifted outside; how did I find
> the threshold? Marble and snow
> were one; is this a snow-palace?
>
> does the ember glow
> in the heart of the snow?
> yes—I drifted here
> (*Helen in Egypt*, "Leuke" 174–175)

DiPace Fritz argues that the reiteration of snow in "Leuke" suggests the tempering of Helen's passionate nature (169–170). I add that H.D. tempers Helen's passion with a blanket of whiteness. Helen must be reminded that she is white and, therefore, impeccable. Like the essential white mastery signified by the snow that blankets "Flowering of the Rod," this snow represents the reverential command and unity one must have with and over nature in order to mediate one's internal voice. H.D. informs us that this internal voice can take on numerous personae, but significantly in Book Six, the voice "takes us back to Egypt but in a Greek mode" (*Helen in Egypt*, "Leuke" 178). Being one with the snow affords Helen enough power, comfort, and serenity to permit the emergence of her Egyptian past again. Snow, in this instance, reflects the fortitude and magnanimity associated with white people. In other words, H.D. wants Helen to recognize and appreciate her black heritage, but above all, she must not forget that she is primarily white.

"Eidolon," the last section of *Helen in Egypt*, "records that slow process of synthesizing dual selves in the search for wholeness" (Friedman, "Creating" 379). Friedman reads the duality issues as having to do with "Helen the hated" and "Helen at peace"; the Helen of patriarchy and the Helen of feminism ("Creating" 379). With an eye toward white positionality, I read "Eidolon" as Helen's progress toward uniting her Greek and Egyptian selves.

Part of Helen's decision has to do with choosing Paris or Achilles. In "Leuke," Helen leaves Paris to be with Theseus and there realizes most fully the white perfection of Paris. While she has been away, Paris has had some epiphanies of his own. H.D. writes,

> Even before she left him to find Theseus, Paris had been apprehensive, perhaps not so much fearing the loss of Helen to Achilles, but of her final translation to the transcendent plane, the fragrance of "Egyptian incense wafted through infinite corridors." (*Helen in Egypt*, "Eidolon" 213)

Paris "smells" the Egyptian in Helen. His apprehension makes it easier for Helen to choose between the two. Although Achilles is not thoroughly enamored of his and Helen's Egyptian heritage, Helen perceives him as less perfect in his whiteness than is Paris.

As Friedman points out, Helen must painfully reconcile numerous identities. Friedman meticulously names each identity, ranging from "Helen, daughter of Zeus and child of worldly Sparta" to "Helen of Leuke, alone, yet also together with Achilles and the child Euphorion" ("Creating" 390). Helen's quest, as Friedman reads it, is to reconcile her roles as "daughter, wife, mother, lover, and person alone" ("Creating" 390). The quest, as I read it, equally chronicles Helen's identification with her racial heritage as well as her ability to persuade Achilles to accept their Egyptian ancestry.

Three times in "Eidolon," Achilles entertains questions about his mother's race. In the first two instances, the racial question triggers an inquisition into her sexual activity, and in the third instance he fears that her weaknesses as a mother may be related to her mixed ancestry. In Book Three, he asks, "Did her eyes slant in the old way?/was she Greek or Egyptian?/had some Phoenician sailor wrought her?" (*Helen in Egypt*, "Eidolon" 245). Achilles reveals an embedded stereotypical association that links Thetis's blackness with an intense sexual drive and a promiscuity. At the moment Achilles ponders her ancestry, questions about her sexual activities arise.

At the end of Book Three, Achilles again expresses a paranoia about his mother's having "cheated," and again he associates her betrayal with her mixed ancestry:

> Did her eyes slant in the old way?
> Was she Greek or Egyptian?
> (*Helen in Egypt*, "Eidolon" 253)

Achilles has moved beyond his denial in "Pallinode" of Helen's, Isis/Thetis's, and his own blackness. He is now at least willing to ponder the question, but he is unable to situate the question among positive associations. Thetis's mixed ancestry is indelibly linked for him to her potential for sexual promiscuity.

At the end of the same poem, Achilles's anxiety has overtaken him. He now blames his weak heel on her "unspeakableness":

> she had promised him immortality
> but she had forgotten to dip the heel
> of the infant Achilles
>
> into the bitter water,
> Styx, was it?
> careless, unspeakable mother
>   (*Helen in Egypt*, "Eidolon" 53)

He blames her "unspeakableness" on her supposed desire "to encounter another / whose eyes slant in the old way." Achilles repeats his obsession: "is she Greek or Egyptian?" (*Helen in Egypt*, "Eidolon" 254). Clearly, part of the synthesis that Helen must accomplish on her quest includes coming to terms with Achilles's racial preoccupations.

As Helen works toward a meaningful clarity, an image occurs to her that enables her to perform the synthesis. She sees a pattern of old Egyptian pictures, but superimposed on these pictures, she views "the 'marble and silver' of her Greek thought and fantasy" (*Helen in Egypt*, "Eidolon" 264). Helen's idea of synthesis reveals itself as an image of whiteness accommodating blackness, her Greekness as an overlay atop her Egyptian ancestry. H.D. obviously correlates the idea of incorporation with synthesis; however, she does not recognize the superiority of the incorporating body. Likewise, in her analysis of H.D.'s synthesis of patriarchal / feminist dualities, Friedman mistakenly correlates incorporation with synthesis: "Helen's revelation in 'Eidolon' is her final recognition that this dynamic process of opposition can become synthesis. The wholeness that incorporates all conflicting forces ultimately transcends the duality of a sexually polarized world" ("Creating" 396). I argue, instead, that any incorporating "wholeness" exerts a power and control over its incorporated "conflicting forces" as evidenced in Helen's celebration of a synthesis that permits her to superimpose her Greek thoughts over her Egyptian hieroglyphs. Greece still embodies Egypt; Egypt does not embody Greece. H.D. supports racial synthesis as long as white mastery, in some form, is maintained.

The final words of *Helen in Egypt* do not revel in an exaggerated white liberal sense of having solved the racial ancestry problems of Western civilization through a simplistic version of ancestral synthesis. H.D., rather, like her Helen, suspects that someone greater must provide the answers and that we would most likely not comprehend the answers should we hear them (*Helen in Egypt*, "Eidolon" 303). H.D.'s *Helen in Egypt* breaks new ground in its exploration of the origins of white mastery as it simultaneously reveals the magnitude of the threat that such excavation exposes. As Bernal makes clear, if the Afroasiatic origins of Western civilization become unearthed,

> *it will be necessary not only to rethink the fundamental bases of "Western Civilization" but also to recognize the penetration of racism and "continental chauvinism" into all our historiography, or philosophy of writing history.* (2)

H.D. furthers the fundament of Bernal's proposition by alleging that white people might be so psychologically, socially, and culturally inveigled of white purity, goodness, superiority, and primacy that we could not apprehend, never mind rethink, an Afroasiatic source to Western civilization.

HERMETIC DEFINITION

Hermetic Definition, written in the late 1950s and early 1960s and published posthumously in 1972, is H.D.'s last work and another complex trilogy. Deborah Kelly Kloepfer insightfully notes that H.D. uses tripartite structures as controlling devices (187). *Hermetic Definition* contains three parts: "Red Rose and a Beggar," "Grove of Academe," and "Star of Day." Chisholm describes *Hermetic Definition* as "an unconventional love story, which begins with an enigmatic encounter between an aging, seventy-year-old H.D. poet-persona and an ordinary stranger, a certain Lionel Durand, a forty-year-old newspaper reporter" ("Autoheterography" 102). Rather than a "description" of the situation, Burton Hatlen views this text as an exploration of love rhetoric: "What happens to the rhetoric of love when the lover becomes a 70 year old white woman, and the beloved becomes a 40 year old black man?" (148). DuPlessis reads *Hermetic Definition* as H.D.'s bold suggestion of negotiations that may finally unify Others (*H.D.: The Career* 124–125). Edmunds recounts the race shame that *Hermetic Definition* inspires, a shame that originates from Edmunds's suspicion that H.D. exploits Durand's black body in the poem (14). Edmunds contends that H.D.'s erotic fantasies may "draw on the racist modernist tradition of primitivist myth-making" (15). Although most critics and scholars agree that *Hermetic Definition* obviously proclaims racial relations as its subject, no one to date discusses the problematic of H.D.'s white body, her white authorship, her white positionality, her white privilege, nor her white power as it relates to the contents of or the construction of the poem. I argue that the "problem" in *Hermetic Definition* is not only the exploitation of Durand's body, but also the unspeakable wielding of white authorship, especially female white authorship.

In a journal entry, H.D. records her gaze on Durand:

> He looked so dark in the shuttered hall-room downstairs, when he turned to greet me that I thought he might be *Creole*, but he is not, he has possibly a touch of Spanish, there seems Africa, the Moor in him. Is this poor Lawrence's Dark God? (Quoted in Edmunds 156).

H.D. first notices Durand's skin color. The skin color signifies multiple ethnic possibilities, the first of which speaks to a mixture of European and Latin American or Spanish ancestry. As her gaze continues, she sees more possibilities in his darkness. She continues to see the Spanish possibility, then her eye captures an African possibility, and finally she sees a particular type of Northwest Muslim Berber-Arab African in him. The longer H.D. scrutinizes Durand, the more specific and refined her sense of his blackness becomes. Yet, the final sentence circles back to the beginning of her journal entry; Durand becomes a "Dark God," just as in the beginning he "looked dark." H.D. has developed a sensitivity to degrees of blackness, but ultimately, she encases the particulars in the realm of the general. The man begins in darkness and ends as a subject of a white man's, D. H. Lawrence's, Dark God signifier. H.D. met Durand twice in her life. Each time, he merely interviewed her regarding her poetry and recent awards. As far as we know, the sexual fantasies stimulated by his black body were hers alone, and they were never consummated.

In lyric 1, the very first poem of "Red Rose and a Beggar," the H.D. persona immediately offers an apology for the attraction and its seeming inappropriateness. She understands the inappropriateness as having to do with her age:

> I am old (I was old till you came);
>
> the reddest rose unfolds,
> (which is ridiculous
> in this time, this place,
>
> unseemly, impossible,
> even slightly scandalous),
> the reddest rose unfolds
>   (*Hermetic Definition*, "Red Rose" 3)

She displays no sense of herself as exploiting a racially marked body, a body encompassing a human who has simply interviewed her twice. H.D. wants to shed responsibility for the attraction by claiming that her sexuality, "the reddest rose," simply became enlivened upon glimpsing Durand. Although thirty years have passed since H.D. cast Robeson's body into bronze, and although H.D. has become more educated and more fully aware of difficulties in racial relations, her desire to write yet another black man into poetry reveals an uncanny inability to resist the white mastery that compels her imagination. She self-consciously realizes the similarities between the two situations and makes reference to them in "Red Rose and a Beggar":

> So my *Red Roses for Bronze* (1930)
> bring me to-day, a prophecy,
> so these lyrics that would only embarrass you,
>
> perhaps reach further into the future;
> if it took 30 years for my *Red Roses for Bronze*
> to find the exact image,
>
> perhaps in 30 years,
> life's whole complexity will be annulled,
> when this *reddest rose unfolds*
>   (*Hermetic Definition*, "Red Rose" 16)

Neither Robeson nor Durand actually enter the poems as full human beings. They enter as significant inspirations for H.D.'s possessions—"my" *Red Roses for Bronze*. They enter as bronze or dark bodies, and they leave as bronze or dark bodies. They never become anything more than figurative sites of white female desire.

In lyric 3, H.D. wrenches another figure out of the darkness; she calls to her muse, Isis: "come out, come out of the darkness" (*Hermetic Definition*, "Red Rose"). Isis, like the Durand of H.D.'s journals, emerges from the darkness because H.D. wants specifically to situate Isis among her northeast African, Ethiopian, and Egyptian ancestors (Snowden 97). As in previous poems, H.D. recuperates Isis in her Afroasiatic skin. This conjuration affords H.D. an important display of hermetic knowledge,[4] particularly that regarding the "transmigration of souls from one body to the next" (Bernal 133). Not only has H.D. called to Isis in the poem, she has also suggested a dangerous alchemical transmigration of her self into Isis: "I would enter your sense / through burnt resin and pine-cones" (*Hermetic Definition*, "Red Rose"), and she ends the poem in fear of the change: "will I be burnt to cinders in this heat?" Interestingly, H.D.'s concern with being burned has a literal and direct connection to Isis's blackness. Snowden informs us that

Aithiops (Aeithiops), the most common generic term in the Greek and Roman world applied to blacks from the south of Egypt and from the southern fringes of northwest Africa, highlighted the color of the skin. The word meant literally a "burnt-faced person," ... a reflection of the environment theory that attributed the Ethiopians' color as well as their tightly coiled hair to the intense heat of the southern sun. (7)

H.D.'s fear of being burned reflects hermetic transmigration of souls as well as the environmental theory of skin color. H.D.'s persona fears that her white skin might not be able to make the changeover from "I" to Isis without being burned to death. Figuratively then, she understands the difference between occupying a white body and occupying a black one as a matter of life and death.

By lyric 9, H.D. has entered the mystical state of transmigration and ventured on a quest to understand how she will be judged for her scandalous desires. L. S. Dembo claims that H.D. embarks on these "quests for an ultimate knowledge or experience that is eternally approached, never acquired or known" (222). I argue that H.D. never acquires the knowledge because she fears the loss of white power and privilege as evidenced in her concern with security in lyric 9: "there is time yet to crawl back / to security? no—there is not time left" (*Hermetic Definition*, "Red Rose"). Although the transmigration will presumably allow her mystically to enter Isis and explore a relationship with the Durand figure, as she proceeds, she experiences fear. H.D. chronicles a scattering of new foods, sands, winds, flowers, and spices and compares their newness and difference to Durand's newness and difference. All of the newness becomes "nothing," however, when a desert wind kicks up a "white / gumblossom eucalyptus' fragrance" (*Hermetic Definition*, "Red Rose"). H.D. reaffirms the power and the potential of whiteness by having its perfume lay a coating over "all." Her immediate reaction to an excess of newness is to assert the dominance of whiteness, but this reaction only lasts for a moment. H.D. calls out "no, no." She wants to avoid escaping into whiteness and to test her capacity to endure the change and the potential judgments.

Lyric 16 situates H.D. asking whether the sesame seeds she strings on a white thread will split when pierced by her needle:

> Sesame
> seed,
> string
> minute granules
> on a white thread
> or red,
> will they split
> on my needle?
>   (*Hermetic Definition*, "Red Rose" 18)

Metaphorically, this poem interrogates whether the white thread, with the seeming power to hold all the seeds together—those from South Asia, those from India—serves as vital connector of Others or as immolator of Otherness. The thread poses either the power to pierce each seed or to damage the seed altogether.

Ironically, H.D.'s concern lies with whether she needs a thimble for her own white finger. Pushing the needle through the seeds portends a bloody indentation on the finger, thus accounting for the possibility of a "red" thread. This lyric aligns the power of the white thread with that of white assimilation of Others. The assimilator understands that the "seeds" might be destroyed, but the major concern is of the potential bloody white finger and thread. In this poem, H.D. artfully demonstrates the self-concern involved in assimilation, and she decides that she needs "no rosary of sesame." "Rosary" aligns assimilative practices with alleged unifying institutions such as religion. H.D. renders the horrifying power and narcissism of whiteness in this poem, and for a moment, she chooses not to participate in it.

The first four lyrics of "Grove of Academe," the second part of *Hermetic Definition*, flaunt a flourish of white images: "a *dahlia blanc*," "snow-owl," "strung snow-flakes," "white rosary," "virgin flower-clusters," "cloudy ghost-convoy," and "snow." These white images interweave throughout revelations of weariness with being at "the top of the hill," weariness with homages paid to "masters and imperators," weariness with acclamation and recognition. H.D. speaks of her long road to literary acclaim and asserts that many times she thought of leaving that road for "a red rose and a beggar." The first four poems turn on H.D.'s declaration that Durand changed all of that:

> when you greeted me,
> I was paid fully
>
> for the long search
> and the meagre lamp
> (*Hermetic Definition*, "Grove of Academe" 26)

Her epiphany is that there is "an end to the whole adventure, / it stops here." She claims that no one taught her about various unities such as the botanical unbels until he came along, but interestingly, a cluster of white imagery gathers just as H.D. makes this claim:

> no one strung snow-flakes
> for a white rosary,
> nor invoked unbels,
>
> virgin flower-clusters for her
> (*Hermetic Definition*, "Grove of Academe" 27)

The snowflakes, the white rosary, and the virgin flower-clusters gather to ensure the representation of whiteness even as the poet speaks of a botanical center from which many equal-length stems would grow. The poet seemingly blankets the umbel in natural, religious, and social whiteness in spite of her own spoken desire to seek a different nature.

By the end of the poem, the poet / persona, daunted because she must be satisfied with mere recognition of how separate peoples are, starts as if from a trance. At first she finds herself on the "other side" with no whiteness, "no cloudy ghost-convoy" to accompany her, but she soon realizes that not all of her white accoutrements have disappeared. The snow and the white rosary remain with her. H.D. struggles in this poem with the hierarchical relationships among peoples of different races and rhetorically sets out to dismantle them. However, she discovers the incongruence that exists between rhetoric and actual racial unity. Should one white person step over to the "other side," without the convoy of the entire white world, she would still carry with her a few, but significant, remnants of the white world.

H.D. wrote "Star of Day," the last part of *Hermetic Definition*, after she learned of Durand's untimely death. The racial markings of these lyrics occur in contrasts of darkness and light. This part of the poem depicts stars emerging from midnight shadows (lyric 1), long desperate nights (lyric 1), depths of night (lyric 2), candles burning out (lyric 2), dark winter (lyric 2), desire to light candles (lyric 4), visits by angels (lyric 4), and drizzly snow (lyric 6). H.D. suffers through the pain of Durand's death until she figures out a way to revive him from this darkness and, figuratively, from the darkness of his skin. She experiences an epiphany based on the sensation that through her pen, he had walked into her. H.D. describes the event as "unprecedented" and "fiery" and one that brought him nearer to her than ever. Then, she italicizes an incredibly commodifying statement: *"you are my whole estate"* (*Hermetic Definition*, "Star of Day" 50). Because he had entered her, she possesses him as one would possess any personal property. Hollenberg claims that H.D. "revives" both Durand and herself so that they could "exist together inside the text she has created" (241–242), and Hollenberg associates this revival with the "peaceful homecoming of the imagination that H.D. wished for" (242). H.D. arrives at her imaginative peace by turning the deceased black man into her belongings, into her "Star of Day," thus reinstating the "unalterable law" that whiteness will always emerge from and control darkness. In H.D.'s terms, "Night brings the Day" (*Hermetic Definition*, "Star of Day" 55). She does not permit the poem to end with an image of the familiar sun cycle (night brings day and day brings night), which would suggest a daily exchange of power between darkness and lightness. H.D. determinedly concludes the poem with the movement of bringing day to suggest the cinematic fade into light which leaves the viewer with a frame of nothing but impenetrable whiteness.

In a fundamental way, this image takes us full circle back to *Sea Garden*. The early poems also evidenced H.D.'s desire for an ultimately white world. In *Sea Garden*, colors other than white constitute H.D.'s imaginative palette, but they exist only to highlight the importance of whiteness as an aesthetic imperative in the imaginary landscape. Likewise, darkness is a profound element of "Star of Day," but darkness's most significant purpose is to usher the final day, with its white light, to the finale of the poem.

CONCLUSION

H.D. presumes a whiteness equivalent to and inseparable from a positively masterful existence. The poet recognizes, interrogates, and struggles with this presumption only to succumb to its invincible allure each time she confronts it. H.D.'s "white" often signifies perfection, in particular, the perfection, power, and dominance of white people. Paradoxically, the poetry also intimates the unspeakable Afroasiatic heritage, including the black bodiliness, fixed in white Western civilization.

NOTES

1. Friedman argues "The Moravians were able to live with the Indians in peace because they were themselves persecuted exiles, 'political and religious refugees' whose history went back at least to a Greek church in 9th-century Constantinople. . . . The Moravians who founded Bethlehem [Pennsylvania] came from all over Europe, brought a love for learning and music with them, and looked even to the cultures of Asia, Africa, and Arabia, as well as the Native Americans" ("Exile" 46).

2. A palimpsest is a paper which has been written upon more than once, both the surface writing and fragments of the erasure(s) are visible.

3. The "writing-on-the-wall" experience, also referred to as the Corfu vision, occurred to H.D. in April 1920 while she was with Bryher on the island of Corfu. The images that H.D. saw took shape on the wall between the foot of her bed and her wash stand. They were outlined in light. They formed sequentially a profile of a head, a chalice, a ladder, and an angel named Victory or Nike. These images seemed to her to have been projected cinematically onto the wall.

4. *Hermetic Books* is a written collection dating from the first century A.D. to the fourth century A.D. of Thoth's (the Egyptian god of wisdom) revelations.

Chapter 3

"A Sort of Inheritance; White": Elizabeth Bishop and Selective Self-Reflection on Whiteness

Poet Elizabeth Bishop was born in 1911 in Massachusetts to parents of white Canadian descent. Her father died during her first year, and her mother subsequently suffered illnesses causing her to be institutionalized. Relatives from both families raised Bishop in Massachusetts and in Nova Scotia. Educated at Vassar, she became friendly with young white writers Mary McCarthy and Muriel Rukeyser. These early friendships anticipated the close literary friendships she would maintain throughout her life with white poets Robert Lowell and Marianne Moore. Bishop wrote poetry throughout her life. She won the Pulitzer Prize in 1955 and the National Book Award in 1969. She spent almost two decades of her adult life in Brazil living with her Brazilian lesbian lover, Lota de Macedo Soares. Bishop died in Massachusetts in 1979 of a cerebral aneurysm.

Bishop writes a diverse whiteness, one that differs in each discourse she undertakes. In *The Body and the Song: Elizabeth Bishop's Poetics*, Marilyn May Lombardi argues that each of Bishop's works contains "levels of manifest and latent meaning" and that the diary entries and early drafts are "often far more forthright than the final, enigmatic version "(4). Similarly, Bishop employs a racial discourse in her letters far different, far more overtly racist, than that used in her poetry.

Lombardi suggests that Bishop continuously directs "attention to the differences among people and the otherness of nature" (*Geography of Gender* 6). However, I argue that what proves most intriguing about Bishop and her white positionality are the ways in which she directs attention to the issues of alterity in the letters and those in the poetry often without attention to her own racial markings as a white person. Lombardi asserts that the impact of Bishop's body on her art has been ignored (*Geography of Gender* 5), while Lombardi, herself, overlooks the fact that Bishop's body is white. Granted, Lombardi's main concern is Bishop's bodily illnesses such as excema, asthma, and alcoholism; but nonetheless, Bishop's body was also white, and this fact has been unduly overlooked. Anne Colwell, too, writes a wonderfully informative book about Bishop's bodily existence, and she also never mentions the fact that Bishop's body is white:

> Many of the poems explore what it means to inhabit a body. . . . [T]hey depict the body as both the imperfect vehicle, the reason for distortion, the limit of the otherwise boundless imagination, and yet the only means of connecting with other people and the external world. (3)

Neither Lombardi nor Colwell question the ease or the ramifications of pursuing connection with others when one is housed in white skin. The whiteness of Bishop's body has been invisible in scholarly discourse because white scholars deem it the bodily standard.

In letters to friends, lovers, family members, and colleagues, Bishop demonstrates that whiteness is the standard of being in multiple ways. She discusses musical "Negro voices" as disembodied attributes for the entertainment of whites. She expresses her disregard and disrespect for ethnic minorities as servants. She romanticizes and infantilizes blackness. She denigrates a "too-muchness" about "Latinity." She discusses certain peoples of color as "primitives" and "savages." She refers possessively to "our blacks." Bishop does not express her attitudes regarding her own whiteness overtly, but rather the superior attitude of the language she uses to discuss racial Others in her letters mirrors her sense of privilege and authority.

In contrast, the poetry provides a much more thought-out and self-reflective language, a language that rids poetry of any discussion of savages or primitives, but that simultaneously leaves readers suspicious of a language too well crafted and too different from that of the more colloquial letters to be regarded as purveyor of a singular truth about Bishop's racism and/or her awareness of white privilege. Bonnie Costello suggests that we do not yet understand Bishop's complex and contradictory nature when it comes to situations regarding mastery in the poetry (4–5). She argues specifically that Bishop vacillates between celebrating hierarchy and resisting it (5). Lorrie Goldensohn, upon visiting Bishop's house at Samambaia in Brazil, denies the overwhelming evidence of wealth and elitism that she sees in Bishop's home:

> This house, this lavish spread of buildings and grounds, was only another rich person's country place. The traces of the occupancy I was interested in had long been eliminated. (*Biography of a Poetry* 25)

Goldensohn did not wish to see the privileged, white, masterful Elizabeth Bishop standing before her. Bishop enacted many white personae in life, in letters, and in poetry. Her poetry presents a hierarchical view of the world with whiteness firmly situated in power. However, when we compare the poetry to the language of the letters, or to the "lavish" texts of her living arrangements, poetry clearly inspires Bishop to construct a persona capable of rising to occasions of discourse most "apt" and "bright," a reflection of poetry's responsibility to express the best thinking of its time. Jay Martin calls such persona construction in Sylvia Plath's *The Bell Jar* her "fictive personality" (quoted in Axelrod 11). Similarly, Bishop constructs a "poetic personality" who attempts to write with an eye to the authority enacted by her whiteness; however, I argue that she cannot always see the authoritative burden that whiteness manifests in the poems.

Lombardi claims that Bishop eradicated the more sensitive aspects of language related to race to rid poetry of "the excessive morbidity" apparent in the world (*Body and the Song* 30). Bishop believed that she better served the link between reader and writer by squelching the urge toward morbidity, thereby promoting poetic language as equivocal, as "always hiding something in the process of revealing everything" (Lombardi, *Body and the Song* 31). Thus, Bishop toned down the "savage" attributes of the letter discourse in order to write a more polite whiteness into the poetry. However, as thoroughly as Bishop tried to tidy up the poetic discourse, she recognized the power of language to betray any attempts at sheltering attitudes, politics, or emotions. Bishop not only knew that "the unconscious spots" would be left in the work, she argued that it is impossible to erase or negate them. Lombardi describes Bishop's argument about the unconscious spots as specifically surrealist in their reflection of Bishop's interest in "the biblical parable of the whited sepulcher (a shining surface belying the corruption beneath)" as an imaginative foundation for her work (*Body and the Song* 177). The insidious white surface plays an important role in Bishop's poetry, a role that she does not always control. In particular, Bishop does not always recognize that the whiteness of her poetry reveals her own ingrained and privileged expectations about life. Nor does she realize her own body as a shining whited sepulcher.

Colwell suggests that Bishop was sensitive to the body as bearer of cultural weights and meanings. Bishop tells us that "what we have in this world is bodiliness" (quoted in Colwell 4), but neither Colwell nor Bishop articulate the poet's bodily whiteness. What Bishop has in this world is white bodiliness—a body that is racially marked.

Bishop was probably not sensitive to the cultural weight that her whiteness would bring to bear on the reading of her letters. Her letters unselfconsciously reflect classic Romantic racism and the white writer's consistent ability to overlook political and social realities in order to reify an aesthetic moment associated with people of color. On one occasion in 1934, Bishop correlates the beauty of a Negro singer whom she heard in a Gertrude Stein opera with the beauty delivered by the inanimate setting pieces on a stage (*One Art* 19). Bishop clearly coordinates Negro voices with theater set pieces as though the two had synonymous value. These voices provide romantic, exotic sounds that emanate from an indefinable source. Bishop fails to discuss the rare success achieved by African-American artists during this period of time. Bishop hears only the beautiful sound of the voices; she does not think to address the political, economic, nor social situation of the African-American musician of this time. She is not sensitive to the cultural cost of hearing such voices. Yet, Lombardi reminds us that the terrifying screams of Bishop's mentally unstable mother haunted the poet's life and her work, which should have made her more sensitive to the power of disembodied voices:

Long into adulthood Bishop is haunted by nightmare images of dark, shrouded, caterwauling women whose grating voices threaten to invade and animate her own body, and whose intrusive presence she attempts to expel. (*Body and the Song* 3)

The dark women with grating voices haunt Bishop's unconscious while the Negro voices of her conscious existence seem beautiful to her. Clearly an ambivalence between the conscious and the unconscious exists in Bishop and becomes centered on the African-American women's voices. The attraction for her is at once compelling and threatening.

Further evidence of her appreciation for the African-American voice as separate from its body and its politics appears in a 1938 letter to Frani Blough in which Bishop describes a Negro cook's potential to be an entertaining singer for Blough. Bishop suggests that her Negro servant might perform a concert for Blough (*One Art* 72). Bishop does not offer to introduce Blough to the "Negro cook, etc." so that she may engage with this woman's interesting humanity, rather Bishop views the Negro cook's talent to entertain, her value as aesthetic "etc."—separate from her bodily humanity and her personality—as the enticement to Blough.

Years later, in 1959, Bishop maintains her interest in these voices but has at least developed more interest in the individual names of the singers. She mentions Odetta, Bessie Smith, and Billie Holiday, and she strangely groups them with a succeeding "etc." (*One Art* 378). The use of "etc." proves most intriguing in this letter as well as in other associations with race and Otherness. The "etc." used after naming Billie Holiday makes clear that Bishop has grouped all Negro voices together in a Bessie Smith, Billie Holiday aesthetic category. It seems that the reason Bishop likes Odetta is simply because Odetta's voice is black and because Bishop is prone to like them. The second "etc.," used in a clause that grammatically clarifies what Bishop wants to know about "this girl," Odetta, only states an interest in whether May Swenson, the letter recipient, has "heard" the voice. The "etc." adds a vagueness to an already vaguely expressed interest in Odetta, the woman.

In another remarkable connection between "etc." and racial Otherness, Bishop writes to Frani Muser (née Blough) in 1970 of her living conditions at Harvard. She describes her Graduate Center as housing Chinese, Hindus, " . . . etc." (*One Art* 533). The ellipses as well as the "etc." are Bishop's. With these markers Bishop presumably expects that the reader of the letter will fill in the spaces marked as infinitely blank. These ellipses signify Bishop's disregard for Otherness and ethnicity. Clearly, what makes her temporary living situation "awful" includes having to share the space with people of color—any people of color.

In many of her letters, Bishop uses anecdotes about people of color—especially Negro servants—not as examples of her complaints about her living conditions, but rather as narrative flourishes aimed at entertaining the letter recipient. Bishop offers these anecdotes as items of interest, part of the daily goings-on in her life; however, reading these anecdotes with an eye to white privilege, one confronts Bishop's feelings and attitudes of mastery and superiority. In one such letter, Bishop infantalizes Flossie, a Negro servant to Marjorie Carr, as a person incapable of making a mundane decision about eyeglasses (*One Art* 116). Bishop's all-knowing and patronizing tone expresses her ideological sense that whiteness, especially upper-middle class whiteness, endows one with the capability to comment upon, "hang on to," make decisions for, offer money to, assume the happiness of, and design narratives to describe a Negro woman servant's life.

The Bishop letters also blatantly portray people of color in romanticized and childlike ways. In an early letter to poet Marianne Moore, Bishop remarks upon the Portuguese Negroes' abilities to choose cars that accent their black skin (*One Art* 44). Bishop remains painfully unaware of the white privilege required to note only the color coordinated symmetry of this scene. No mention of these people as persons or laborers makes it into the letter nor into her imagination.

These letters also portray adults of color as childlike by virtue of associating infantile antics or diminutive adjectives with them: "We have a *little* [my italics] black man who sleeps outside our door to protect us from burglars—clutching a knife two feet long in one hand & a large rock in the other" (*One Art* 183). In order to diminish the power of the black man positioned to secure her, Bishop describes him as "little," thereby infantilizing him and his power. This discourse speaks quite clearly to the white woman's privileged position, steeped in desire to situate black men as her protectors but also wanting to maintain an imperious distance and superiority.

A particularly paradoxical part of this discourse involves Bishop's relationship to and repulsion from "Latinity." In the early letters, a decade before Bishop ever knew that she would spend almost twenty years of her life living in Brazil with a Brazilian lover, Lota de Macedo Soares, she writes with disdain for Latin peoples. In a 1940 letter to Muser, she describes a visit from Louise Crane and three Spainards. Bishop comments on the excess of Latinity and on the noisiness of the Spanish language (*One Art* 86). Not only the people, but also the "noise," the (lack of) aesthetic quality of the language, irritates Bishop. Once again, Bishop constructs an ideology of race and ethnicity not solely on the basis of flesh color, but also on voice.

In "The Body's Roses: Race, Sex, and Gender in Elizabeth Bishop's Representations of the Self," an essay remarkable for its breakthroughs in understanding some of Bishop's ideological framework regarding race, sex, and gender, Goldensohn presents the complicated way in which Bishop made sense of her relationship with de Macedo Soares:

Bishop's pictures of Lota, held close to her in alternating terms as both a privileged aristocrat and a tropical other, reflect how within metaphors of race that engage our sharpest sense of self and other, we draw the portrait of our conflict ridden allegiances to love and community.... For Bishop, on the mythic map of her southern descent, her Latin American lover, however aristocratic or however correctly *engaged* in upbringing, could still represent in the chain of color her own embrace of a darker, more primitive self and a less disrupted definition of the feminine. For Bishop, Lota could be seen both as a dark and subordinate other *and* as an aristocrat. ("Body's Roses" 86–87)

What Goldensohn does not say specifically is that Bishop's whiteness demands for de Macedo Soares to be viewed both as dark and subordinate.

Arthur Gold, speaking of Bishop in Gary Fountain and Peter Brazeau's *Remembering Elizabeth Bishop: An Oral Biography*, also feels comfortable describing de Macedo Soares as Bishop's "Latin side," without naming the poet's whiteness as the element in need of a darker side. Bishop's whiteness proves unmentionable, but de Macedo Soares's darkness constitutes an important utterance when discussing the lovers' relationship:

One has to understand Lota to understand Elizabeth because Lota was the most volatile, outgoing, almost exhibitionist Latin type. She was very small, not particularly good looking, but immensely vivacious, and in a sense, everything Elizabeth wasn't. She was Elizabeth's south, the Latin side of her character. (136)

What Gold expresses here, by way of saying without saying, is that in order to understand privileged whiteness (Bishop), one has to understand the darker subordinates (de Macedo Soares) that surround this whiteness. What author Toni Morrison in *Playing in the Dark* has specifically asked scholars to begin to think about is the accompanying study of the mind of the privileged white master. Why does one have to understand de Macedo Soares in terms of her Latinity in order to understand Bishop? Why has it been that, until recently, it would be odd at best to think about labeling whiteness and searching whiteness for understanding of the white mind?

If de Macedo Soares does represent a dark side of Bishop, then it is a side for which Bishop expresses no respect:

We are now planning to go to Amsterdam . . . and I think that possibly a few weeks of Dutch stolidity (if they really are that way) and English stoicism will be good for Lota after all this Latin hysteria. WHY do they carry on so? I am so sick of it, and I think it exhausts L. without her realizing it, she is so accustomed to it. (*One Art* 453)

Bishop, the white woman, assumes "stoicism" to be both desirable and English, whereas she denotes "hysteria" as negative and Latin. She divides attributes into ethnic origins making sure that the "white" group has something better to offer.

Often when discussing people of color in her letters, Bishop resorts to assumptions of primitiveness and savagery. Goldensohn asserts that in many of the texts, Bishop's "fascination with the primitive, becomes in part an assumption of a childhood perspective with a liberating and adaptive force" (*Biography of a Poetry* 7). Goldensohn's instincts in this instance seem to be overly protective and redemptive of overtly racist writing. In describing a Haitian painter, Bishop writes about savagery (*One Art* 192). When discussing a cook hired by de Macedo Soares, Bishop writes about her dirtiness and, again, her savagery (*One Art* 243). After four years of living in Brazil, Bishop confesses to her friends Ilse and Kit Barker that she has tired of the primitive people (*One Art* 290). Bishop set herself apart from people of color both by virtue of her whiteness and her sense of herself as cultured and civilized.

In order to maintain the relationships with people of color that most suited her ideological position of separateness and superiority, Bishop related to people of color in terms of possession. In describing the cook's child, a child the cook named after the poet, Bishop elevates her position as possessor of the child and only parenthetically mentions the mother: "I also have a Negro namesake, 'Maria Elizabeth,' aged 19 months now (the cook's)" (*One Art* 326). She refers to this same child in a later letter: "Day before yesterday, Easter, I gave an egg-hunt party for them up here, the three older ones and our little black one" (*One Art* 358). Fountain notes,

Since Bishop was not Roman Catholic, she could not be a godparent with Lota, but she began a parody of Yeats's "A Prayer for My Daughter" (uncompleted), which began, "My negro namesake in my crib." (In Fountain and Brazeau 140)

Fountain's excerpt makes it clear that Bishop, although said to be honored and proud, could not bring herself to write a more serious occasional poem. The idea that she saw something in the situation worthy of parody signifies that Bishop viewed the event as an imitation event, as a travesty, as a poor and feeble rendition of something usually exquisite.

Bishop's own discourse in her letters regarding the event demonstrates a constant awareness both of the child's blackness as well as a type of possessiveness toward the child. This discourse clarifies the relationship for Bishop as well as for the reader. Bishop proves in the letters to be quite aware of racial inequities, and she views the distinctions as the clarity needed in order to maintain her masterful position as white woman.

Although I do not wish to overstate the case, artistically, in her poetry, Bishop treats her white positionality with a bit more awareness and self-reflection than in her letters. Bishop does understand that when confronted with art and art forms, one has the opportunity to unveil (albeit politely and artistically) the darker parts of the self and the culture. Colwell refers to this realization, this centering on the double nature of the self, "as simultaneously a living organism connected to the contingent world of other organisms and objects, and also the mediator through which the invisible self comprehends the visible world" (43). This type of realization was not frightening at all to Bishop (Colwell 48). She would have been well aware that she, as poet, was responsible for "writing down the times" in which she lived (Dickie 5). Margaret Dickie argues that although Bishop rebelled against writing doctrinaire political poetry,

> she published frequently in *Partisan Review* ... where her work was surrounded by political writing, and her poetry, if not partisan, was at least concerned with the public issues of poverty, of race, and, in her Key West poems, of class. As the country moved toward war, so too did she turn to war as a subject. Later, in her Brazilian years, she lived in the middle of a revolution in a household immersed in politics, and she wrote again of poverty, race, and class, as well as social injustice.... In traditional verse form, Bishop could express political sympathies with marginal elements in society from maids to drunkards to impoverished children. (15–16)

Dickie's research is concerned with the role of Bishop's "secret" lesbianism and this lesbianism's association with the marginal, but the same awareness of Bishop's political nature holds true for Bishop's role in assuming the cultural work of her age (5). Bishop writes to Muser, "I am utterly disgusted with 'social-conscious' conversation—by people who always seem to be completely unconscious of their surroundings, other people's personalities, etc. etc." (quoted in Dickie 111). Bishop obviously presumed herself to be one of the socially conscious people aware of her surroundings. I argue that Bishop's sense of her own awareness is valid to a point but that her lack of awareness regarding the privileges of her own centered whiteness might "utterly disgust" her had she recognized it.

Dickie makes a case for Bishop not as part of a center, but rather as an outsider. However, "outsider" does not reflect the totality of Bishop's position. Bishop's whiteness, the element of her bodily being that "shows," is not the coloring of an outsider. In racial terms, Bishop fits in with the dominant culture. She may have had an "interest in other classes and races, as if she could study in their conflicts something of her own conflicted identity" (Dickie 116), but that interest is not the same as having flesh encoded Latina or encoded black. Bishop was not a racial outsider; she was, in fact, implicated in the continuance of racial outsiderness, a situation that she does come to suspect and fear.

NORTH & SOUTH

Bishop writes whiteness into one of her earliest poems, in her earliest book, *North & South*. The whiteness in "The Imaginary Iceberg" intrigues especially because it has been repeatedly overlooked. Strictly speaking, I want to discuss the meaning of the line in the second stanza that reads "The wits of these white peaks / spar with the sun"; but a fuller discussion of the entire poem as well as its critical reception is necessary. Many scholars have discussed this poem; some have discussed this exact line; and some have discussed the "wit" in the line, but no one has discussed the whiteness of the "peak" itself.

Jeredith Merrin discusses the relationship of the entire poem to religiosity and moralism (59, 114). James McCorkle sees in the poem attempts at "provisional moments" of communion with others (12). C. K. Doreski explores this poem's suggestion that imagination is more powerful than eyesight (6). Anne Stevenson cannot see "how to read this poem in any light other than Transcendentalist" ("Iceberg" 708), and Dickie reads the iceberg as an allegory of lesbian love's secret attraction. Each of these readings displays an incredible knowledge and integrity, but the scholarship of Betsy Erkkila, Marilyn May Lombardi, Anne Colwell, and Susan McCabe paves a more direct path toward an understanding of white authorship. The readings by these four scholars address the relationship of the "Imaginary Iceberg" to female subjectivity and the authorial body, readings that enable us to discern what it means for a woman poet in a white body to write white, and therefore, to write about an indisputable, yet invisible, dominance. These readings, which are nonetheless political and culturally embedded, also encourage us to consider meanings not necessarily related to literary influences nor steeped in literary traditions. The works by Erkkila, Lombardi, Colwell, and McCabe permit me to suggest meanings in Bishop's poetry that tend to "gurgle up" rather than stem only from consciously determined and poetically manipulated language.

Erkkila writes an expansive and meticulous article about Bishop's political affiliations during the time that the poet wrote "The Imaginary Iceberg." Bishop was a New York radical who dutifully read her Russian Marxist criticism daily; however, Bishop balked at doctrinaire pronouncements, idealism, and utopianism. "In the mid '30s, however, she herself began to move toward an increasingly self-conscious attempt to give her work more social weight and significance" ("Modernism" 290). More important during this time, Bishop was moving away from the art world's Eurocentric focus on high modernism and making moves toward the geography bordering North and South America (291). Bishop was not apolitical (a critical notion that Thomas Travisano blames on Alicia Ostriker in "The Elizabeth Bishop Phenomenon"), she was simply not doctrinaire. Because Bishop's politics are only subtly portrayed or invisibly foundational in the poetry, her work provides an important template through which to read the subtleties of racial whiteness. Erkkila's work supports the presumption that at the time of "The Imaginary Iceberg," Bishop was politically aware and was already reflecting upon Key West and South America as geographical and imaginative places of difference. In fact, Erkkila's work makes it clear that Bishop's texts invite readings of racial markings (although relatively few have been done), especially as they connote difference and Otherness in relationship to a white standard of being.

As Dickie points out, until feminist poet and critic Adrienne Rich told us differently, it was quite typical to discuss Bishop as apolitical. Rich and Dickie, however, make sturdy claims for Bishop as a poet who often writes "about multiracial Brazil, about the poor and the tenant ... lives marginal in ways that hers is not" (Dickie 7). Dickie and Rich praise Bishop's "acknowledgment" of "other outsiders" (7) without questioning the value of mere acknowledgment, especially when the acknowledgment of Others in art equates with cultural gain for the acknowledging artist. What do the acknowledged Others gain?

Dickie recognizes that Bishop had the "leisure for the 'perfectly useless concentration' that such art requires" and that Bishop chose her art and "devoted herself to the discipline of 'heroic observations'" (14), but Dickie does not name this particular leisure as white, privileged, woman's leisure. Colwell sees more than mere acknowledgment in Bishop's writings about Otherness, but she suggests that Bishop may only be able to "connect" with Otherness by "taking it into herself" (122). Further on in her book, Colwell writes that for Bishop, "connection occurs not because the body moves beyond its boundaries into another body but because the body expands its boundaries to take something into itself" (146). This movement of accommodation is indeed more than acknowledgment; it is a possessive attempt at co-optation or erasure. Colwell proposes Bishop as a poet fully aware that acknowledgment and accommodation fall short as gestures toward connection with Otherness; Bishop understands "we cannot know what we experience because of our subjective walls, because of our flawed human senses, our tendency to imagine our own bodies everywhere" (122). However, even the "our" in Colwell's proposal suggests a privileged, white position in the tendency to imagine "our own bodies everywhere." In Morrison's *The Bluest Eye*, for instance, the African-American child cannot imagine her body anywhere. She wants to imagine her body as another body, a white one, and to see with other eyes, blue ones. She would not be included in the "our" of Colwell's proposal.

I want to shift this aspect of Bishop studies. Rather than looking at Bishop's images and representations as those that express her acknowledgment and concern for others, I want to look at such poems as "The Imaginary Iceberg," which opens with the bold declaration, "We'd rather have the iceberg," as racially marked texts that connote what it means to "have" and to prefer whiteness.

Lombardi's research on the origins of "The Imaginary Iceberg" describes R. H. Dana's *Two Years Before the Mast* as the "scaffolding on which Bishop builds her vision of the iceberg" (*Body and the Song* 88–89). In this mariner's tale, Dana describes an iceberg sighting. Lombardi notes that the "enmity between the ice mountain and the heavens" particularly appealed to Bishop (*Body and the Song* 90). This animosity becomes a type of hostility that can be handled by "wit" in Bishop's poem, especially the wit of whiteness as it faces off with its only comparable warrior, the heavens. Bishop's addition of whiteness to the peaks adds an element of purity, strength, and excellence to their already named wit. Whiteness dominates the peak in this poem, and not with grace, but with flailing limbs raised in attack. Bishop's pure and intelligent whiteness quickly fades to gracelessness as the ridiculous sparring occurs—the white peaks cannot win against the heavens. The racial markings of this poem suggest that whiteness, although glorious in its attainment of the peak, might have gone too far in its increasing enmity toward the heavens and in its insistent hierarchical journey.

McCabe concentrates a portion of her analysis on the exact lines regarding the white peaks. In discussing them, she notes the "allegorical genius and courage" of the line (51). McCabe does not discuss the whiteness of the peaks, but I add to her analysis that the allegorical genius and courage of the line stem matter-of-factly from the established whiteness of the peaks. The word "white" in English is emblematic of excellence. At the sound level of the line, Bishop plays with the way in which deleting the silent letters in the word "white" would give us "wit." Wit exists in white. White does not exist without wit. Better yet, wit is white (with a few minor, humble additions). Although a white writer might write "white," she is always already assuming and including an embedded wit. McCabe reminds us, "Everything of this poem reveals as it conceals" (52). In looking at white as a racial marker of an automatically assumed wit—an intelligence, sagacity, perception, cleverness, or shrewdness—McCabe's claim about "The Imaginary Iceberg" could not be more accurate.

Colwell's argument about "The Imaginary Iceberg" provides the most illuminating reading of Bishop's white-peaked iceberg: "It remains both ineffable and the mirror of human understanding" (39). Bishop's iceberg, as Colwell sees it, "does not search out its own reflection, cannot move, change, or be changed by the adornment of the perceiver's gaze" (42). The iceberg, remember, is witty. Due to its size, its hierarchical imperative, it stares down at others. It is white. It is all-powerful. Like all-powerful white people, the iceberg has no cause to change.

Bishop prepares her readers for the power of the white peaks throughout the first stanza of the poem. In this stanza, she has already whitened the terrain by way of multiple similes and metaphors: "like cloudy rock," the sea like "moving marble," and the "breathing plane of snow." This terrain prepares us for the dazzling display of the "white peaks" themselves: "The wits of these white peaks / spar with the sun." In this poem, to be covered in whiteness (as is the iceberg) is a peak experience, only to be topped by witnessing whiteness (as do the sailors/people on the witnessing boat). Although Bishop will not always present whiteness as related to mountaintops, dominance, and power, such displays do occur repeatedly. Their repetition suggests an imaginative, if not an ideological, pattern. Interestingly, Colwell asserts that Bishop developed a pattern of living atop mountains and that she was fond of observing landscapes from these positions: "Everywhere she worked—her apartment in Rio de Janeiro overlooking the beach, her study above the waterfall in Petropolis, her mountain house in Ouro Preto, her Lewis Wharf condo above Boston Harbor—had a magnificent view" (1).

In a discussion of H. G. Wells's use of whiteness, David J. Lake also notes the importance of mountaintop whiteness:

[W]hiteness seems to be shifting its meaning, or at least its emotional tone, from negative to positive, as it becomes associated with high mountains and, in general, elevation, both literal and metaphorical. The link between whiteness and height is provided by *ice* or *snow*, which are found on mountains. (16)

An ideological link may also be drawn between the literal elevation of a white mountain peak and the hierarchical nature that we associate with whiteness and the power of white people. Richard Dyer argues that both the Aryan and the Caucasian models of white supremacy share "a notion of origins in mountains" and that these mountainous origins endow the white race with a particular power:

Such places [mountains] had a number of virtues: the clarity and cleanliness of the air, the vigour demanded by the cold, the enterprise required by the harshness of the terrain and climate, the sublime, soul-elevating beauty of mountain vistas, even the greater nearness to God above and the presence of the whitest things on earth, snow. All these virtues could be seen to have formed the white character, its energy, enterprise, discipline and spiritual elevation, and even the white body, its hardness and tautness (born of the battle with the elements, and often unfavorably compared with the slack bodies of non-whites), its uprightness (aspiring to the heights), its affinity with (snowy) whiteness. (21)

White mountains in poetry signify for the white woman poet what they signify for the white male writer. White women writers participate in the ideological regard for the hierarchical nature of that which is white. But intriguingly, white women only stand for and support such power: They do not "exercise it effectively or . . . change its abuses" (Dyer 30). In "The Imaginary Iceberg," Bishop concludes the poem by waving good-bye to the iceberg, thereby recognizing its power and letting it stand.

Other authors have written a patterned whiteness into their texts. Writing about whiteness in poet Edgar Allan Poe, Mary F. Sisney notes that whiteness does not always pose a fixed meaning for the white writer (88). Arnold G. Bartini finds that whiteness can correlate with particular authorial fears such as poet Robert Frost's "inner fear" of an indifferent, "morally neutral" nature (353). Bishop's use of whiteness as descriptor in her poetic work is not fixed, nor particular to an inner concern of the poet, but rather, it is a crucial signifier of culturally embedded, and unquestioned, beliefs about the inherent strength, courage, power, and goodness of that which is white, and those who are white.

Bishop often reveals power and goodness through the size and dimension associated with whiteness and blackness. In "Large Bad Picture," she notes "small black ships" (*Complete Poems* 11). In "Cape Breton," she describes "little white churches" (*Complete Poems* 67). In "View of the Capitol from the Library of Congress," she forms a simile with "a big white old wall-eyed horse" (*Complete Poems* 69). In "Letter to N.Y.," she writes of "big black caves" (*Complete Poems* 80). In "In the Waiting Room," she notes "a big black wave" (*Complete Poems* 161). "Five Flights Up" houses a "little black dog" (*Complete Poems* 181). "Bigs," "littles," and "smalls" as descriptors of blackness and whiteness seem interchangeable in the poetry; however, the effort initiated is always toward mastery, toward controlling not only the color of an object or life form, but also the size of it. Bishop molds blackness and whiteness with descriptors to suit the authoritative need apparent in the poem. She understands that the words "white" and "black" are already fraught with dimensions; her adjectives of size serve as her attempt to manage, as well as she can, the effects of whiteness and blackness on her poetry.

At this point, it seems fair to ask: When is a white mountain peak simply a description of an actual peak with snow on it? How can we make the leap from snow-capped mountains to white racial representation? Lombardi astutely turns to Frank Kermode's *The Genesis of Secrecy* for revelations that relate to Bishop's poetics. Kermode and Lombardi encourage readings that enable our "divinatory powers" to grow, readings that compel us beyond the most obvious images and toward deeper understandings (Lombardi, *Body and the Song* 45–46). In other words, a white mountain peak in poetry is never simply a literal snow-capped mountain. It is a prophetic image that asks for our openness to its foresight. I divine this image as a blatant display of white racial dominance. By blatant, however, I do not mean that Bishop controls the mountain's revelations about whiteness in "The Imaginary Iceberg."

Many Bishop scholars argue that the poet deliberately incorporates multiple layers and uncertainties of meaning for well-designed and well-controlled interrogative purposes. Although these arguments for control do persuade to a certain point, and although I have the highest regard for Bishop's intellectual capabilities and am convinced that she eventually developed a deep concern for racial and social injustice, the whiteness that manifests in her poetry is not the result of her own managed incorporations. Bishop knows that the language of her poetry must be more well mannered than that of her letters, and she does exert control enough to make the poetry acceptable, even impeccable at times. However, the content of her letters, combined with the pervasive racial unrest in the world and the connotative burden that the word "white" bares, often seeps through the decorum of Bishop's poetry to manifest a white positionality undetermined by her.

I believe that the repetition of words as well as modes of imaginative display in her poetry provide keys to the poet's ideological makeup. Merrin similarly claims that Bishop's poetry works through "figures and tropes" that "are actually ingrained habits of mind, powerful psychological gestalts" (in Lombardi, *Body and the Song* 48). Lombardi claims that Bishop's habits of reiteration reveal her determination to "see a thing clearly" (*Body and the Song* 97). Bishop's reiteration of whiteness is an attempt to reach further and further toward an understanding of it, but I argue that this particular attempt is not determined on Bishop's part. Colwell stresses that Bishop does understand the struggles that being embodied generates and that Bishop, therefore, "translates her ambivalence about embodiment in flesh into ambivalence about embodiment in poetic form, and her evasions, her richly ambiguous phrases, words, and structures, all preserve that ambivalence and, by saying two things in one utterance, express her uncertainty, her struggle, and her openness to multiplicity" (202). Colwell does not mention that the authorial body under discussion is white; thus her argument succeeds up to the point of naming the color of the flesh. She does not name the flesh, as Bishop does not, because whiteness is invisible. To say flesh is to assume white flesh. I suggest that some of the multiple layers and meanings in Bishop's poems are as invisible to her as is her own whiteness. For Bishop, knowledge about whiteness is in a sense like knowledge about writing in that, as McCabe points out, "Bishop is, almost above all, an epistemological poet who reminds us at every turn that we cannot know anything fully or absolutely, and that the activity of writing cannot save us with its 'magical powers,' but reveals our 'grave difficulties'" (xiv). Recognition of whiteness has been a grave difficulty, not only for Bishop, but for many who are white. Bishop's poetic language reveals the magnitude of this lack.

In "Love Lies Sleeping," also from *North & South*, Bishop again confronts us with a whiteness looming overhead, but this time, the whiteness is "weak," and it is embedded in a poem that Erkkila reads as a protest against the overbearing attributes of large cities ("Modernism" 288). The "I" of the poem describes what she sees from the window:

> An immense city, carefully revealed,
> made delicate by over-workmanship,
>   detail upon detail,
>   cornice upon facade,
>
> reaching so languidly up into
> a weak white sky, it seems to waver there.
> (*Complete Poems* 16)

At first glance, the whiteness in this poem seems to lack the wit endowed to the white peaks of "The Imaginary Iceberg." In bringing together the usually unrelated adjectives "weak" and "white," Bishop appears to suggest that not all whiteness is dominating; however, her grammar informs us that "white" by itself does connote strength and an additional adjective must be used to weaken it. This grammatical issue proves important to reading the racial markings of this poem because it demonstrates Bishop's assumption that "white," by itself, connotes excellence, strength, and the ideal. The adjective "weak" literally modifies what she assumes "white" to mean on its own. This poem is about modified whiteness and its relationship to industrialization, the city, and the disheartened (white) worker.

Victoria Harrison claims that "Love Lies Sleeping" addresses Bishop's interest with inverted figures as well as with inversion as a possible way for gaining insight into order (60). Lombardi argues that Havelock Ellis's[1] "inversion" as a term to refer to homosexuals provides another subtle foundation for Bishop's interest in inverted images in this poem (*Body and the Song* 48). I am persuaded that sexual inversion signifies, but I also think Bishop bemoans the inversion of a powerful whiteness in this poem.

The racial markings of the poem are tricky, and Dyer reminds us, "The point is to see the specificity of whiteness, even when the text itself is not trying to show it to you, doesn't even know that it is there to be shown" (14). At first reading of the whiteness in "Love Lies Sleeping," it seems that Bishop's imagination houses a malleable connotation of whiteness: In "The Imaginary Iceberg," she delivers white peaks arrogant enough to spar with the sun, but in "Love Lies Sleeping," whiteness is not enough to make the sky strong. With a cursory reading, I surmise that, to Bishop, whiteness has been misperceived and too rigidly defined as representing dominance; therefore, she wants us to look at it as potentially weak and malleable in connotation. McCabe sees reason to believe that this poem signifies a Bishop "swerving and turning between possibilities" (91), but actually the hierarchical assumptions about whiteness in the poem are similar to those witnessed in "The Imaginary Iceberg." The political dimensions of these hierarchies are far more subversive in "Love Lies Sleeping."

In the line "Hang-over moons, wane, wane!" Bishop protests by grammatical exclamation that fuzzy and out-of-balance moons, ones not as bright or white as moons might be, are waning. She not only bewails the loss of the moon's light, and thereby its power, but also exclaims that the whiteness had already been dimmed by intoxication. For Bishop, the experience of a hangover is a shameful thing. Thus, the dimmed light of these moons signifies a looming, shameful image. Its further waning could be read as a demand for the moons to recede because they have caused so much shame already, but the punctuation demands we read the line as exclamatory. The line "Hang-over moons, wane, wane!" expresses outrage that bright white moons have become intoxicated by the polluting elements rising from the industrial city below. Metaphorically, Bishop's exclamation about the waning moon exudes a nostalgia for the former power of whiteness.

In addition to an exclamation regarding waning whiteness, Bishop writes a "Boom!" into "Love Lies Sleeping" that immediately initiates a cloudy whiteness: "Then in the West, 'Boom!' and a cloud of smoke." This particular exclamation, "Boom!" has an important literary history as regards the construction of whiteness. In "'HOO, HOO, HOO': Some Episodes in the Construction of Modern Whiteness," Rachel Blau DuPlessis discusses the "BOOM" in Vachel Lindsay's poem "The Congo: A Study of the Negro Race" as precursor to the booms in the poetry of Bishop's generation. The "BOOM" in "The Congo" occurs as a representation of percussive sound that emanates from black Africans who pound their hymn books against a surface as repentance for having resisted Christianity. The "BOOM" also occurs in the Lindsay poem in lines referring to killing Arabs and white men. DuPlessis notes the popular appeal of "The Congo: A Study of the Negro Race" as well as Moore's displeasure with Lindsay's "Aryan doggerel" ("Some Episodes" 675). Lindsay toured with the poem and invited audience members to chant the percussive sections. DuPlessis suggests that poets using such words as boom and hoo after 1914 "are probably responding to the enormous provocation of 'The Congo'" ("Some Episodes" 668). What "The Congo" provokes is a denial of African ethics and values and an assertion of Euro-American ethics and values.

Bishop's "Boom!" in "Love Lies Sleeping" directly recalls Lindsay's provocation, but with an added twist. Her poem addresses this boom's effect on sleeping workers and notes that the sound now says "Danger" to them, when once upon a time, it said "Death." Bishop's "Boom!" emits a weak whiteness, "a cloud of smoke" into the sky as a contradictory signal of the waning, yet polluting, effects of whiteness. This poet suggests that although whiteness will not die and may not cause death, it certainly has become endangered. Steamy emissions from the street-cleaning vehicle also throw a "hissing, snowy fan" across the street. The polluting white smoke and the polluting white steam from the streets are the causes of the dimming of the white sky. Oddly, Bishop's poetic argument is that whiteness from below pollutes the whiteness above. The white working classes pollute the privileged white classes.

Erkkila's reading of "Love Lies Sleeping" as an understated, but nonetheless ardently, political poem that Bishop had published in the *Partisan Review* in 1938 informs my reading of whiteness. Erkkila finds that Bishop breaks down any possibility for sense of upward mobility in this poem ("Modernism" 289). I argue that Bishop not only breaks down this opportunity, but more specifically, she metaphorically lays blame on the white working class for the loss of an ideal whiteness. Bishop claims that what was once white has been weakened and, figuratively, that upward mobility and the ideal, which would have been represented by the white sky (unweakened), is on the wane. Dyer reminds us "White cultivation brings partition, geometry, boundedness to the land, it displays on the land the fact of human intervention, of enterprise" (33). Bishop sees a blight in this cultivation. What once loomed as white ceiling and backdrop before the slow growth of the "cloudy," "snowy," "smoky" city was the ultimate, was white, and now it stands weakened.

Ironically, as Bishop tries to argue for us to recognize the plight of "all the employees who work in plants," she bemoans their inability to strive toward the ultimate in whiteness, and in fact, she argues that their work emits the cloudy and snowy fumes that dirty the whiteness above. In "White Savagery and Humiliation, or A New Racial Consciousness in the Media," Annalee Newitz argues that such set-ups of an ultimate whiteness against a lower form of whiteness are emblematic of the great shame and the great loss unconsciously exhibited by many whites. The real great shame is white failure in a system created by whites and in which whites are purportedly favored (145). Bishop's "Love Lies Sleeping" dramatizes the felt shame and loss of white people. Dyer claims that because whiteness purportedly "carries such rewards and privileges, the sense of a border that might be crossed and a hierarchy that might be climbed has produced a dynamic that has enthralled people who have had any chance of participating in it" (20). The people in Bishop's poem, however, begin to suspect this enterprise. The only benefits offered to the worker in the current world of the poem are a gradual decrease in the whiteness of the moon, a weak white sky, a cloud of smoke, and a hissing, snowy fan of spray. For the privileged whites, the seers at the window of the poem, the only benefits are knowledge of the white world lost or nostalgia for an always already waning one.

In "Cirque d'Hiver" from *North & South*, Bishop further reflects upon a nostalgic whiteness when she describes a special toy "fit for a king of several centuries back." This toy turns out to be "A little circus horse with real white hair" (*Complete Poems* 31). Even though Bishop occasionally demonstrates malleable connotations for "white" and for "black," she often situates whiteness in a slippery polar opposition to blackness. As polar opposites, they are infrequently actual equivalents in value. Most often, white is deemed standard, and black is Other. For instance, in "Cirque d'Hiver," the circus horse has "real white hair," and "glossy black eyes" (*Complete Poems* 31). In this poem, white is real and black is merely glossy. Colwell argues that the central point of this poem is the meaning that derives from endowing a toy with humanity (27). More importantly, Colwell claims that the poem suggests levels of difficulty in "embodying the invisible in the visible" (28). I further her argument by adding that Bishop's poem also expresses the difficulty of rendering the visible in the invisible, of rendering real in the glossy.

As Hazel Carby points out in Dyer's book *White*, making a determined effort to look at whiteness as a racial marker enables us to "make visible what is rendered invisible when viewed as the normative state of existence" (3). To make the white racial markings of this poem visible, I point immediately to the line in which Bishop identifies the source of the horse's white hair, a line in which she figuratively produces a genetic origin for the horse's hair coloring: "His mane and tail are straight from Chirico." Giorgio de Chirico, an Italian painter (1888–1978) whom we typically herald as having founded the metaphysical school of painting, greatly influenced the surrealist painters. Exemplifying Chirico's works, whether metaphysical or surrealist, are contrasts between darkness and light and particular sculptural images such as faceless, white mannequins.

In a painting aptly entitled "The Uncertainty of the Poet," Chirico positions the white, headless, limbless torso of a female facing a cluster of phallic bananas or plantains. In the background of the painting, a horizontal streak of white steam emits from a moving train. The whiteness of the torso and the steam ostensibly provide sources for the "real" whiteness that constitutes the horse's mane and tail in Bishop's "Cirque d'Hiver." McCabe, too, analyzes the Chirico connection, but she opts for a more generalized association with Bishop's poem, one that tints the poem "with the extravagancies and strangeness of the surreal, with the eeriness and heavily symbolistic quality of a Chirico landscape" (71). More to the point is that Bishop makes a specific claim in the poem regarding what she has borrowed from Chirico; she writes, "His mane and tail are straight from Chirico." I suggest that the authentic, the "real" whiteness that Bishop needs for this poem, whiteness special enough to be "fit for a king," is really surreal like Chirico's work, really truncated like Chirico's torsos, and really pollutant like Chirico's engine steam.

Although McCabe notices a "split" in the poem that results from the speaker identifying with the horse both in its playfulness and in its wintry "hibernation and isolation" (71), I suggest that Bishop's reference to Chirico signifies far more than a binary split between darkness and light. The uncertainty that Bishop exhibits in her recognition of the multiple dark sides or the absent truncated pieces of the white body and its connotations of perfection will haunt her poems and her sensibilities as a white person from this moment on.

Interestingly, Lombardi notes a fascinating diary entry of Bishop's from 1950 (later than this poem was written, but pertinent to discussion of Bishop's imagination regarding whiteness and statuary) that directly points toward Bishop's awareness of whiteness as corrupt: "A perfectly ghastly brief nightmare—I was looking at a head, showing it to someone—no one I recognized, white and neat like a statue and very perfect. Then I said 'See' and opened the mouth to show that the inside was corrupt and running with ants" (*Body and the Song* 183). The whiteness of the early poem "Cirque d'Hiver" does not yet refer to the corrupted mask of whiteness, but it certainly, in its figuration of absence and lack and in its reference to the horse as having a "formal melancholy soul," alludes to something more suspicious and worrisome than the playful surface first exuded by the white-haired, cantering toy.

The canter of this horse, oddly enough, also permits analysis of whiteness. Dyer asserts that the significance of the power of whiteness has to do with its enterprising and active leadership. As a primary example of such enterprising whiteness, he refers to the Western in cinema. "It is in the visceral qualities of the Western—surging through the land, galloping about on horseback, chases, the intensity and skill of fighting, exciting and jubilant music, stunning landscapes—that enterprise and imperialism have had their most undeliberated, powerful appeal" (33). Ironically, Bishop's toy horse is the most enterprising, "the more intelligent," being in the poem: "He canters three steps, then he makes a bow, / canters again, bows on one knee, / canters, then clicks and stops, and looks at me." This horse moves with a purpose, a familiarity, a rhythm, and a routine, but this horse is not the rough-riding, intense horse of Westerns.

In fact, Bishop's "Cirque d'Hiver," like "Love Lies Sleeping," bemoans a whiteness (and a canter) that is not now what it used to be or what it has been mythologized to be. The whiteness flowing from the toy horse in "Cirque d'Hiver" is one that "flits," one that is "little," and one that is only "fit for a king of several centuries back." This horse with its "real" whiteness is merely a circus horse, an entertainment, a representative of the humiliation (Newitz 140) of having been brought low, of having been reduced to a toy. Upon coming to terms with this humiliation, the toy horse and the "I" of the poem face each other "desperately." They reinstate and reiterate the idea that they have been enterprising even if they have not achieved extraordinary heights, when they say in unison "Well, we have come this far." The whiteness that originates from Chirico is special in what it fails to embody, in what it lacks. It has no head, and it has no limbs. The horse and the speaker of the poem unite in their recognition that given their heredity, that having been sprung from Chirico's whiteness, they must be satisfied with, or they must settle for, the current limits of their whiteness. At least they have their heads and their limbs. At least their bodies are not pierced through the soul liked that of the dancer's. At least they have not turned their backs on each other nor on the future unlike the dancer, who, "by this time, has turned her back." The poem also ends on a note of opportunity for whiteness to regain its power when it suggests that having come this far, the speaker and the horse, descendants straight from Chirico, might be capable of going farther.

However, opportunities for blacks to further themselves in Bishop's poetry are limited. In "Cootchie," Bishop designs a grammatical parallelism that actually undermines any parallelism between black life and white life. In this poem about the death of a woman of color, Cootchie, who served a white woman, Miss Lula, Bishop opens with two lines suggestive of a parallel structure:

> Cootchie, Miss Lula's servant, lies in marl,
> black into white she went
>   below the surface of the coral reef.
>   (*Complete Poems* 46)

If we read these lines with both a grammatical eye and an eye to Bishop's sense of whiteness, we read in the first line that Cootchie is renamed as and subsumed into "Miss Lula's servant" in an appositive, just as in the second line black folds into white. Bishop thwarts our tendency to read black as opposed to white, as polar opposite to white. Harrison argues that "the position of each figure in this poem is fixed" (97), but I disagree. In this poem, black drifts into white both in the sense that Cootchie becomes a white woman's servant and in the sense that Cootchie's blackness becomes invisible to Miss Lula's needs and her whiteness. White is the ever-accommodating and more powerful factor in this polarization.

The stanza ends with another attempt at coordination of black and white: "The skies were egg-white for the funeral / and the faces sable" (*Complete Poems* 46). Bishop again defies any equivalency between the two by situating that which is white above, and that which is human and "sable" below. Her ideological sense of equivalency falls into a hierarchical or subsuming pattern. Apparently, Moore chastised Bishop for exploiting peoples of color in her poetry, but Bishop only heard the criticism as a reproach against the inaccuracy of her portrayals (Harrison 97), which resulted in further and further attempts to get the Otherness right.

In "Songs for a Colored Singer," Bishop's attempt to get the Otherness right only results in trite stereotyping. She writes from the perspective of a colored woman upset with her partner, LeRoy. An obvious cliché, right down to the use of the name LeRoy for the man, "Songs for a Colored Singer" simply reflects upon Bishop's sense of white privilege as that which enables a white woman to narrate a fictionalized black woman's story.

The last poem of *North & South*, "Anaphora," a poem put to music by Elliott Carter, flaunts a white sky, more specifically a "white-gold sky." Once again, Bishop does not leave whiteness unadorned; it must have an added wit, an added weakness, or an added color to enhance its whiteness or to draw attention to its significance. Although white connotes excellence, to further associate white with gold elevates the connotation to one of richness, luxuriance, and regality. The sky that Bishop employs to open "Anaphora" is a noble and spiritual sky, and the poem, from this point on, chronicles the fall of an "ineffable creature" from a glorious sky.

As with the poetics of hierarchy and humiliation that play a role in "Cirque d'Hiver," here, too, Bishop delivers a parable that Newitz associates with the transgression of hierarchy (140). Erkkila also reads this poem as having politically transgressive implications especially as regards the failure of class revolution: The poem "records a fall into time and history as the dream of earthly plenitude, perhaps associated with the promise of the Left and the hopes of the '30s" ("Modernism" 296). Doreski discusses "Anaphora" as one of Bishop's deliberate attempts to subvert the power of "author function." Doreski explains that Bishop was intent on neither naming nor engendering the authority of her poems (63–64). I push Doreski's argument further and claim that in Bishop's attempt to unname those elements of a self that she assumes wield too much power, Bishop fails to withhold the power of whiteness from the poem. Lombardi furthers the argument by recognizing that by not "naming the body in either graphic or conventionally erotic terms, she conveys her sensual experience through her tender reiteration of certain talismanic words—words and phrases that gain their power through insistence, through playful echoing and reversal" (*Body and the Song* 96–97). One of these talismanic words so incredibly important to understanding the racial markings of Bishop's work is the word "white." Lombardi claims that Bishop's reiterations were emblematic of a process by which Bishop pursued "seeing a thing clearly" (*Body and the Song* 97). The "thing" that Bishop's reiterations reveal are not always those upon which she determinedly focused. I believe that while her famous eye tracks certain things, certain other ineffable things, such as the naming of a "white-gold" sky, emerge as powerful repetitions on the periphery of her vision.

In "Anaphora, " the "white-gold" sky emits an ineffable creature who falls and takes on an "earthly nature." As he falls, Bishop describes him as "darkening" and "condensing all his light." Dyer speaks of the light in artworks that comes from above as representing the virtuous and celestial (118). He argues that a "culture of light" exists that makes "seeing by means and in terms of light central to the construction of the human image" (121).

Those associated with the light should inherit and rule the earth; those not touched are lesser beings. Bishop's creature emerges from the celestial place only to lose his grace as he falls toward earth and mingles with the lowliest of people and classes. The creature

> sinks through the drift of bodies,
> sinks through the drift of classes
> to evening to the beggar in the park
>   (*Complete Poems* 52)

The beggar in the park has no lamp, no light, however artificial, by which to shine. The ineffable creature, by virtue of association, becomes a lowly creature who must hereafter struggle upward. Bishop sees this struggle of falling from a white hierarchical place into the poverty of drifting bodies, darkness, and beggar-filled parks as a daily and endlessly occurring ordeal. Clearly, whiteness is up and darkness is down.

The voyeuristic aspect of her authority positions Bishop at a safe distance from either up or down. She is somewhat outside, a position that many scholars have assigned her. Travisano reminds us, however,

> if one looks at Bishop's life from an alternate perspective, it is clear that she also enjoyed many privileges of an "insider." She attended fine schools; she was supported for most of her life by a modest inheritance; she shared a beautiful house and estate in Brazil with Lota de Macedo Soares, a member of the intellectual and cultural elite; she won prestigious fellowships and awards; and she closed her career by teaching at Harvard. Indeed, Charles Tomlinson once dismissed Bishop's portraits of the disadvantaged with the remark, "The better-off have always preferred their poor processed by style." ("Phenomenon" 911)

Bishop's poor, her working classes, and her embodied people (as opposed to the brilliant, white, ineffable creatures) occupy the bottom of a hierarchy. Her poetry describes the position as one with constant upwardly mobile potential: "the fiery event / of every day in endless / endless ascent." As apocalyptic and beautiful as the attempt toward ascent might seem, Tomlinson's point is well taken, for those who live at the bottom, away from the "white-gold" sky, the artistry of daily thwarted ascendance goes unnoticed.

A COLD SPRING

Bishop's next book of poems, *A Cold Spring*, included in *The Complete Poems*, continues reiterating various forms of "white." In the poem "A Cold Spring," Bishop uses variations of "white" four times in a relatively short two-stanza poem. Her aim in this poem is to debate with Gerard Manley Hopkins's line: "Nothing is so beautiful as spring." As McCabe reminds us, however, the poets discuss two different springs: Hopkins's is Edenic and innocent; Bishop's is not so warm and untainted (115). McCabe reads Bishop's connection to spring as having less to do with nature and a signifying earth than it does with Bishop's own body (117). I concur with McCabe about the bodily signifiers, but I also read this poem as culturally and politically significant due to the whiteness of Bishop's body.

In order to create a particular spring with a particular type of beauty, Bishop decides that whiteness is aesthetically helpful. In the first usage, she orchestrates a virtual spotlight of whiteness that provides a birth site for a calf on the side of a hill: "One day, in a chill white blast of sunshine, / on the side of one a calf was born" (*Complete Poems* 55). This spotlighting by sunshine, a technique used in painting, theater, and cinema, directly recalls Dyer's work on the use of lighting to target subjects. White people are not only associated with light, but they also control the amount of light cast in art and where that light is cast (84). Dyer claims that occasionally subjects other than white ones are lit in art, "but this is only to indicate the triumph of white culture and its readiness to allow some people in, some non-white people to be in this sense white" (103). Bishop performs a similar type of triumph with the calf in "A Cold Spring." She isolates the calf and designates its importance by casting a white light on it. This white light changes things in the poem by virtue of its brilliant endowment; the next day, which begins the next stanza of the poem, is a "much warmer day." Interestingly, Bishop employs the word "white" differently in "A Cold Spring" than she has in previous poems. Rather than modifying white, she uses white as a modifier of "blast of sunshine," an element that already connotes whiteness. The first stanza thus flaunts a spectacular white explosion signifying that when brilliant change occurs, even if it occurs under the guise of an ordinary occurrence such as the changing of the seasons, then the catalyst will have the power of whiteness.

In the second usage, Bishop changes the hue of whiteness into the particular "greenish-white" needed to describe a dogwood. The aesthetic complexion of whiteness in this poem proves malleable. McCabe says of this stanza "Colors meddle with one another" (118) in a "blurred" "infiltration." The significance of this line and these words when associated with the vagueness of the adverbs "apparently" and "almost" is that the colors do indeed meddle, but we are not quite sure why or in what form. The scene is a blur, but not enough of a blur for the verb "infiltrated," a verb connoting force, to go unnoticed. This beat-up, greenish-white dogwood, with its burned petals and its red blurry buds, has the force of infiltration on its side. The dogwood is "motionless," but significantly, it is "more like movement than any placeable color." For Bishop, even when whiteness stands still, against any of the other discernible colors, races, peoples, it will appear to be moving quite forcefully.

Colwell rightly interprets the verb "infiltrates" as signifying the militaristic aspects of the poem:

> In "A Cold Spring," the landscape and the speaker, as well as the elements of the landscape themselves, are at war.... Certainly, the battle to get born and grow is in the forefront, but also important is the conflict between the speaker's expectations and demands for permanence and beauty and absolute truth and knowledge, and the landscape's transience, its changing violently from moment to moment. (96)

The whiteness of the poem signifies further the power and forcefulness of the changing aspects of the poem. In each stanza, the element that most consistently motivates change is that of whiteness. In the first instance, white makes change through explosive brilliance and, in the second instance, through force.

Bishop uses white the third time in "A Cold Spring" as a verb that again illustrates a process of change: "the lilacs whitened" and "fell like snow." This usage connotes a natural, fading type of change that does not remind us of death or aging, but rather remains (unnaturally) brilliant and pure in its transformation. These lilacs do not yellow nor grow brittle as they fall from their branches. It seems natural to Bishop, as natural as the seasons changing, that whiteness would both be the catalyst for the change as well as that element into which nature transforms. When the lilacs change, they change back into the whiteness that Bishop uses to describe the blast of sunlight that begins the whole process. No matter what natural changes occur, all begins and ends in whiteness.

Then, finally, Bishop shifts from descriptions of whiteness in nature to the humanmade whiteness of a painted door:

> Beneath the light, against your white front door
> the smallest moths, like Chinese fans,
> flatten themselves, silver and silver-gilt
> over pale yellow, orange, or gray.
> (*Complete Poems* 56)

This closed, white entryway serves as the white backdrop to a group of colorful moths. Elizabeth Dodd writes that the moths are "clearly drawn, through that fascinating attraction to light, to the home of the 'you.' For the 'you' is the center of the poem—owner of the land, the home, the very occasion of spring" (131). The white door signifies universal possessiveness. Ideologically, this poem offers as its last instance of whiteness, a thorough backdrop to the entire imaginative landscape of change. As in the beginning of the poem, a spotlight designates that the white door is the signifier *extraordinaire*; in this instance, it signifies that all change begins and ends in whiteness. The spring calf is born beneath whiteness in the beginning of the poem, and the white door is closed beneath whiteness at the end of the poem. Bishop knows that words carry with them the burdens of their time: "Words, time-laden, themselves embody displacement, so that when adults speak of 'mourning,' the child hears them say 'morning'" (McCabe

6). When racially conscious readers read "white," they not only read color, but they are beginning to read race. Bishop's use of white resounds with its late twentieth-century racial burden. McCabe argues further, brilliantly I think, "What permits art and forging ahead is not erasure or transcendence but an acceptance of the 'unexpected gurgle,' of the permeating scream and the insistent frailty of all objects" (12). Bishop's poetry forges ahead into the twenty-first century because it unexpectantly screams the power of whiteness and the presumption of this power in the white imagination.

Colwell sees as the ruling power of "A Cold Spring," an emperor of peace who deigns to balance the conflicts on the landscape: "[T]he personified spring appears as a kind of emperor, a force capable of balancing, if only momentarily, the opposing factions of the landscape" (99). Whiteness that blasts explosively, that infiltrates, that enhances, that stands firmly as backdrop, and that thrives on obliged glory bestows this emperor's power. The poem ends with a feudal suggestion:

> And your shadowy pastures will be able to offer
> these particular glowing tributes
> every evening now throughout the summer.
> (*Complete Poems* 56)

The peace offered by this emperor comes at a great cost, the cost of mandatory adulation by subjects to their white ruler.

Throughout the poetry, Elizabeth Bishop also employs language associated with racial, religious, national, and ethnic categories; as well, she attempts to represent dialects marked as differing from standard white language. By incorporating such words as "Chinese," "Indian," "Muslim," "Arab," and "American" in her poetry, she invites political, cultural, and ideological readings of her poems. Bishop is known to have a penchant for accuracy of word choice and a particularity of observational skills, but this precision is not in place when she chooses to categorize peoples.

Bishop stereotypes Arabs in her poem "Over 2,000 Illustrations and a Complete Concordance." She opens the poem with a tone of ennui regarding having seen pictures of the Seven Wonders of the World and having found them "familiar." She continues to observe and report on "other scenes" that are more "foreign" when she happens onto an Arab:

> The Seven Wonders of the World are tired
> and a touch familiar, but the other scenes,
> innumerable, though equally sad and still,
> are foreign. Often the squatting Arab,
> or group of Arabs, plotting, probably,
> against our Christian Empire,
> while one apart, with outstretched arm and hand
> points to the Tomb, the Pit, the Sepulcher.
> (*Complete Poems* 57)

Bishop immediately associates Arabs with terrorists plotting against "our" Christian Empire. She assumes a readership who is predominantly part of the "our"; who will harbor the same concern when spotting an Arab and who will have the same reaction to a plot against one's "Empire." She aligns herself as other than the Arab. This Arab is not a wonder of the world because he or she is not "familiar"; however, Bishop familiarizes the figure by stereotyping probable activities for him or her.

Another way in which Bishop expresses her whiteness and its whispering ideology is by using whiteness as the veil through which the rest of "nature" struggles to exist. Often a fog or mist, a blanket of whiteness, covers the people in a poem or emerges to cloud the visibility of something in a poem. This particular type of whiteness expresses the whiteness of Bishop's imagination. It is interesting to note when such misty scenes occur.

In "Cape Breton," the mist that Bishop attempts to see through veils poverty and distinctions in class. Looking out over the water at the islands of Ciboux and Hertford, just off Cape Breton, the narrator of the poem describes a mist that occasionally lifts, but mostly "incorporates" scenes and sounds:

> The silken water is weaving and weaving,
> disappearing under the mist equally in all directions,
> lifted and penetrated now and then
> by one shag's dripping serpent-neck,
> and somewhere the mist incorporates the pulse,
> rapid but unurgent, of a motorboat.
>   (*Complete Poems* 67)

This "same mist" becomes much more sinister even though the veil is described as "thin":

> The same mist hangs in thin layers
> among the valleys and gorges of the mainland
> like rotting snow-ice sucked away
> almost to spirit; the ghosts of glaciers drift
> among those folds and folds of fir:
> spruce and hatchmatack—
>   (*Complete Poems*, 67)

These "rotting" layers of mist leave a ghostly, haunted aura of dullness and "death" hanging over the valley. In this description, Bishop writes layers of whiteness that cover the earth with complex veils of ghosts from the past. Heavy with death, this mist lingers over the rotting aura of winter. The whiteness that masks this terrain is burdened with the past.

Only a slight action occurs on this veiled landscape. A bus enters and "a man carrying a baby" disembarks. This man heads off into a meadow, "which establishes its poverty in a snowfall of daisies." This mundane epiphany becomes swallowed up by the mist:

> The thin mist follows
> the white mutations of its dream;
> an ancient chill is rippling the dark brooks.
> (*Complete Poems* 68)

The action and reaction between mist and darkness in this poem is choreographed as an ancient dance by Bishop. As the emblem of poverty, the man and his child walk off into the meadow. The whiteness of the mist blankets them. This dance, this activity of whiteness chasing itself and of making poverty and certain peoples invisible in order to chase its own mutations and permutation, is an ancient one, one upsetting to the dark brooks. The ancient dance sends a too familiar chill rippling through the brooks. The mist in this poem represents the white imagination that blankets and makes invisible all that it does not want to have seen.

In "Faustina, or Rock Roses," Bishop does not use mist to signify the ubiquity of whiteness; instead, she appears to dismantle the power of the white/black polarity only to recoup the power of whiteness in the end. In the poem, an interesting slipperiness regarding the reading of the servant and the "white woman" lying in bed occurs. The situation involves three people, presumably three women: Faustina, the servant; the visitor; and the ill white woman lying in the bed. Bishop describes the ill woman deliberately as "a white woman" making issue of the difference in skin color. Intriguingly, Bishop uses description to dismantle typical polarizations. Usually only people of color are described in terms of the skin they occupy. However, in this poem, the white woman is the one whom Bishop designates. We then assume that Faustina, from her exotic name and her position, is at least Other in class, but presumably also Other by race. Bishop designs this polarization in an unusual way, and she proceeds to use "white" as an operative word throughout this poem.

After we are introduced to the "white woman" in the second stanza, we read in a later stanza of the white woman's "fine white hair" and her "white disordered sheets." Lombardi astutely notes, "Whiteness appears as if it might eliminate difference; the very weakness and powerlessness of the unnamed mistress 'with her pallid palm-leaf fan' wilts and bleaches away into her sick room" (*Body and the Song* 126). In stanza 6, an interesting interrogation of the attributes of whiteness occurs when Bishop describes the garments strung about the sick room:

> —Rags or ragged garments
> hung on the chairs and hooks
> each contributing its
> shade of white, confusing
>   as undazzling.
> (*Complete Poems* 73)

Bishop destroys any sense of direct polarization with blackness by drawing attention to the degrees and variations within whiteness. She also associates whiteness in this poem with rags, with confusion, and with an undazzling effect. These atypical associations might lead us to believe that Bishop can imagine a whiteness that is vulnerable and imperfect, but Newitz reminds us that race is only marked as white when it represents deteriorating or "white trash" whiteness: "Whites who are not 'trash' . . . seem innocent of racially marked whiteness" (138). Whiteness can only stand in polar opposition to blackness when the whiteness is ragged and undazzling.

In stanzas 7 and 8, Bishop has Faustina enter the bedroom in response to a call from the white woman. Faustina not only serves the white woman but also makes requests of her and complains and explains some problems in the terms of her employment. Interestingly, Bishop literally labels the white woman "other" in this poem when she has Faustina bend over her patient. Clearly Bishop creates a reversal of the typical polarizations, but the reversal is not a complete and easy switching of roles and places:

> On bare scraping feet
> Faustina nears the bed.
> She exhibits the talcum powder,
> the pills, the cans of "cream,"
> the white bowl of farina,
> requesting for herself a little *conac*;
>
> complaining of, explaining,
> the terms of her employment.
> She bends above the other.
> Her sinister kind face
> presents a cruel black
> coincident conundrum.
>   (*Complete Poems* 73)

The servant's face, situated above the Other white face, and described from the point of view of the visitor, seems alternately a "sinister kind" face and a "cruel black" face. Of the three adjectives, two of them—sinister and cruel—have negative connotations often associated with blackness, but the combination of one-third kindness throws the formula off a bit. Again, Bishop is not suggesting any ideological ease with change; rather, she is suggesting that the change will occur in an unbalanced way, a complicated and complicating way, rather than in any strict polarized way. Black will not become equivalent to purity and innocence and neither will whiteness become associated only with rags, but rather, an undazzling "conundrum" will be the most likely outcome of changing race relations and changing racial discourse.

In "Invitation to Miss Marianne Moore," Bishop again appears to dismantle a white/black polarity only to reinstitute the power of whiteness at the culminating moment of the poem. Although Bishop designs a witchlike persona for the flying Moore, fully equipped with a "black shoe," a "black capeful of butterfly wings," and a hat with a "broad black brim," she makes it clear that in poetry certain types of blackness, especially a blackness that has been donned for purposes of disguise and safety, can be aesthetically whitewashed. To whiten the figure of Moore, Bishop does not use the typical paint, rather she surrounds her representation of Moore with light. Light causes transformation (Dyer 109). Light contributes to plant growth, to fire starting, and to the relief of depression in humans. In "Invitation to Miss Marianne Moore," light washes away blackness, and as it does so, Bishop's poem becomes racially marked. The poem that Bishop writes as a tribute to her friend and mentor becomes something more. It becomes an artifact that represents the ways in which any contemporary vocabulary speaks in multiple ways to what the writer plans, what the culture embeds, and what the words signify to future readers. Bishop's essay on English poet W. H. Auden evidences her knowledge of just such disjunctures inherent in language:

One of the causes of poetry must be, we suppose, the feeling that the contemporary language is not equivalent to the contemporary fact; there is something out of proportion between them, and what is being said in words is not at all what is being said in "things." (Quoted in McCabe 54)

In words, Bishop writes that Moore's black garb is an accurate depiction of the living poet's dress habits, and the description defines her as eccentric. In "things," Moore's black garb signifies an earthboundedness that needs to be shed, that will be shed, should Moore decide to fly triumphantly, and whitely, through the sky. Black equates with heaviness and fear; white equates with lightness and freedom. The "things" happening among those who wear black skin and those who wear white skin will become progressively more articulated throughout the century, but the tensions whisper in this poem. The poem's language about blackness and whiteness is not equivalent to the contemporary racial facts, but from the future perspective, we can read a language that is highly suggestive.

What is out of proportion in "Invitation to Miss Marianne Moore" is the blackness of Moore's garb and the whiteness of her power, presence, and impact on Bishop's imagination. Dickie claims that although Bishop comments on the fear that underlies Moore's structured dress and her likewise structured poems, Bishop, too, "encased her body, if not in the peculiarity of costume that Moore chose, at least in the uniform of the middle-class matron that protected her from full disclosure of any departure from such a lifestyle" (135). Moore adorns herself in black in order to feel safe in the world, and Bishop adorns herself in the body of an asexual, matronly white woman for the same purpose. The ideological current in each case is that white women are inherently desirable and, therefore, in need of disguise;

that white women are free to choose a disguise for their bodies should they want them; that blackness shrouds and weighs down the otherwise soaring white spirit; that aging, like blackness, shrouds the incredibly desirable white woman. White people accord whiteness an "aspirational structure," an "ecstasy," and a "luminescence" (Dyer 80). In "Invitation to Miss Marianne Moore," Bishop reveals her imagination's aspirational, ecstatic, and luminescent hold on the figure of Moore.

In the last stanza of the poem, Bishop turns the Moore figure into a blaze of whiteness regardless of the black garb so meticulously provided in stanza 3:

> Come like a light in the white-mackerel sky,
> come like a daytime comet
>   (*Complete Poems* 83)

A mackerel sky is one already spotted with white, fleecy clouds. By specifically naming just such a sky, Bishop negotiates a white figure against a white speckled backdrop. In a study of classic literatures, proverbs, and sayings, P. J. Heather argues that "ideas of purity and innocence are ... intimately present in the minds of our people and in the imagery of poets when white is introduced" (quoted in Dyer 73). Bishop invites her poetic muse and mentor, Moore, to fly whitely through a white-speckled sky, thereby figuratively allowing us to read Bishop's imagination as masterful white space. McCabe finds in this poem that Bishop takes an important step toward "seeing others in unfixed relationships as equal and not subordinate" (135). As indebted as I am to McCabe's close reading of the poem, I must disagree in this instance because while Bishop does not subordinate Moore in her Otherness, she elevates Moore and herself to beings associated with the heights of the sky. Dyer aptly analyzes the white woman in the sky as angelic, extreme, and idealized. These idealized beings are prominent in times of "perceived threat to the hegemony of whiteness," and they symbolize a racial specialness predicated on "their non-physical, spiritual, indeed ethereal qualities" (Dyer 27). Bishop's angel, Moore, flies as an idealized symbol of the white woman poet. Furthermore, Bishop claims a "we"-ness with this symbol. Although in the poem Bishop makes it clear that the two poets may write in different grammatical structures and may employ different details when writing, ultimately the poets are joined in their aspirations and are joined by their whiteness.

Bishop asks Moore to fly "like a light in the white-mackerel sky" and to journey "like a daytime comet" as provisions for the safety that Moore needs. Bishop's method is to supply a white sky as backdrop for a daytime comet. A white figure against a white backdrop could journey in safety. In this way, Bishop not only glorifies Moore's likeness to the white sky but also claims for her a moral and aesthetic superiority worthy of angelic travel and visible only to those with special sight (Dyer 70). Therefore, what reads to Dodd as a shallow emotional poem, "an indulgent exercise in cataloguing detail" (107), reads to me as white women poets claiming the superior space and the superior connections that their whiteness affords them.

QUESTIONS OF TRAVEL

In "Brazil, January 1, 1502," from *Questions of Travel*, Bishop weaves a tapestry of nature, which will ultimately serve to hide the Indians when the good Christians in the poem hunt. In this poem, the Indians appear as female animals in a hunt, calling to each other from behind the quilted squares of nature. From the perspective of the good Christian men, the Indians seem "maddening." Here Bishop employs Indians with irony in order to comment on the Sunday activities of the Christian men:

> Directly after Mass, humming perhaps
> *L'Homme arme* or some such tune,
> they ripped away into the hanging fabric,
> each out to catch an Indian for himself—
>   (*Complete Poems* 92)

But she ends the poem with an image of "maddening little women who kept calling, / calling to each other" and who were "always retreating" behind nature. This scenario romanticizes the situation of the Indians for the purpose of art. These women did not simply always retreat. They died. They died of "civilized" diseases brought to the Americas by European explorers, good Christian European explorers. What first appears to be an ironic treatment of the Indians in order to interrogate the actions of the white people only serves to placate the reader with gorgeous images that make invisible the reality of the retreats that did occur. Bishop uses a racial category, an Indian, for her own purposes to craft an aesthetic moment in poetry separate from the tragedy that occurred in reality.

By the time of the poems written while living in Brazil, Bishop had become much more self-reflective about her position as a privileged woman, although it is unclear whether she thought of herself as white. McCabe writes, "While Bishop is not among the rich of Rio, she certainly regards herself as privileged, cannot but see herself in the position of those protected from the poverty of those on the hill of Babylon" (179). In " Arrival at Santos," the first poem of *Questions of Travel*, Bishop lets us know that she has been thinking about what it means just to travel, to live in a different country, or just to visit another country. She becomes particularly self-reflective when thinking about the assumptions, both the overt ones and the latent ones, a traveler makes. Upon arriving at Santos, the "I" of the poem comments in an internal monologue: "So that's the flag. I never saw it before. / I somehow never thought of there *being* a flag, / but of course there was, all along" (*Complete Poems* 89). The pause after "but of course there was," and then the inclusion of the phrase "all along" adds a dimension to the reflection that occurs for Bishop. The present observation not only allows her to comment on the actuality of the flag, but the added phrase "all along" makes it clear that Bishop understands the importance of there having been a flag regardless of whether her imagination took the time to imagine it. For a white woman to reflect upon that which exists and has existed outside of her imaginative domain is extremely important. Lombardi reminds us that

> by the beginning of the twentieth century, the *flaneur*, or artist-pedestrian, had gained unprecedented access to the colonized cultures once the exclusive purview of the explorer, the settler, the missionary or the trader. There is something of this "holiday fool" in Bishop's traveling persona. When she lived in Lota's luxury apartment in Rio, Bishop viewed the miserable hillside slums of the city from the *flaneur*'s perspective. From that height the poet could survey the vast fairground of Rio. (*Body and the Song* 152–153)

In the poem "Questions of Travel," Bishop takes herself to task for surveying "the vast fairground":

> Should we have stayed at home and thought of here?
> Where should we be today?
> Is it right to be watching strangers in a play
> in this strangest of theatres?
>   (*Complete Poems* 93)

Bishop questions whether it is right for the traveling persona to be "watching strangers" as if they were playacting a life. The answer suggests that the choice to travel is "never wide and never free"—apparently as long as one recognizes one's lack of innocence, one's intrusion, and one's own compulsion, then one can travel and observe because one will. At least in writing, at least in the notebook that the traveler keeps, this is the way she can justify her actions to herself.

In *Questions of Travel*, Bishop also refigures traditional aesthetic associations that align whiteness with goodness and blackness with evil in literature. An intriguing aesthetic connection for Bishop is that between fear, death, and whiteness. In "Electrical Storm," Bishop calls attention to the cat's fear of lightening by describing his eyes as "bleached white." When depicting the color of the hail that emerges from the sky in this same electrical storm, she uses the phrases, "Dead-white," and "wax-white." She takes this refiguring further in "First Death in Nova Scotia" in which she writes of a young white boy's, Arthur's, death. The "I" of the poem, when taken into the viewing room where Arthur rests, first focuses on a series of chronographs depicting white rulers: "Edward, Prince of Wales, / with Princess

Alexandra, / and King George with Queen Mary." All of these figures are dead, but their white representations boldly and powerfully remain.

The narrator's eye then shifts to a stuffed owl whose breast "was deep and white" and who sits on a "white, frozen lake." The "I" in the poem then delivers a white flower, a "lily of the valley," to the hand of her dead cousin who is being eyed by yet another stuffed bird, perched on yet another "white, frozen lake." The associations between whiteness and death continue into the third stanza of this poem in which the narrator describes Arthur as "all white, like a doll / that hadn't been painted yet." This lack of color ultimately leaves Arthur "white, forever" (*Complete Poems* 125–126), and within Western art, the dead white body is to be venerated in Christlike fashion (Dyer 208). To be white forever is to be simultaneously powerful and nonexistent, a situation analogous to the one in which all white people arguably exist; whiteness is virtually invisible and yet it exudes tremendous power, like that of God. Dyer explains the paradox: "The slippage between white as a colour and white as colourlessness forms part of a system of thought and affect whereby white people are both particular and nothing in particular, are both something and non-existent" (47). Thus, whiteness wields power even (or especially) in its absence. Not only does Bishop refigure whiteness in terms of its typical association with life, she also rewrites white as a state of lack—a state of lacking color and a state of lacking life.

Representations of the white body as lacking in life are not altogether threatening to whites because, as Dyer points out, it is the "spirit" inherent within whiteness that makes whites special. However, Dyer does think we need to interrogate this site of denial because "[i]f it is spirit not body that makes a person white, then where does this leave the white body which is the vehicle for the reproduction of whiteness, of white power and possession, here on earth?" (207). In the case of cousin Arthur's body in "First Death," the white body becomes forever lodged in the imaginations of white gazing children who are to become poets. These white poets will then embed and venerate white images forever into the landscape of art.

In *White*, Dyer devotes an entire chapter to the relationship between whiteness and death. He writes that "within much of the white tradition it [death] is a blank that may be immateriality (pure spirit) or else just nothing at all" (207). Whether immaterial or nothing, the imagistic power of the whiteness of death, as Bishop demonstrates it, is everlasting.

White writers typically associate whiteness with beauty, purity, innocence, clarity, mastery, and perfection. In *Questions of Travel*, Bishop's representation of whiteness is atypical. The poetic value she associates with whiteness shifts; as well, the value she associates with blackness also shifts. Typically white writers associate blackness with savagery, death, fear, and threat; however, Bishop describes many beautiful situations in terms of blackness. For instance, in an early poem, "Large Bad Picture," Bishop writes of "hundreds of fine black birds" (*Complete Poems* 11), although one could argue that the addition of "fine" only points out the connotative power of "black" to presume evil.

Bishop is not the first white writer to employ a transformative aesthetic for the words "white" and "black" in her texts. In his work on H. G. Wells, Lake also notes a transformative whiteness:

> In general [in Wells's work] cold blank whiteness can symbolize death through the absence of expected color: corpses are pallid, bones bleached, the Moon and snow are white, unlike the living green Earth; and so on. (13)

What remains peculiar about Bishop's associations with whiteness and blackness is that both may refer to death. As previously mentioned, Arthur's white body connotes an everlastingness beyond death, but to Bishop, blackness is also deathlike.

Robert Giroux, Bishop's publisher and friend, tells of the time he assigned Harry Knopf to design the dust jacket for Bishop's translation of *Helena Morley*:

> He used yellow, blue, and green colors against a black background to make a most elegant design, but Elizabeth protested against *the use of black*.... Harry and I thought that the bright colors were heightened and made more festive by the black, but I learned that black to Elizabeth was *always* funereal. (In Fountain and Brazeau 154)

By "unfixing" the connotations of the words in her poetry, Bishop hints at the possibility for imaginative change regarding the connotations and ideological underpinnings associated with these words. However, she employs whiteness in relationship to death as having an eternally positive effect, and her associations with funereal blackness are ones she tries to avoid. We cannot, therefore, confuse the evidence of associative transformation in Bishop's poetry with an ability to disengage from fixed cultural meanings. In words similar to the opening line of "The Imaginary Iceberg," Bishop might write "we'd rather have the white-forever-death than the black-funereal-cover." Whiteness provides for a preferable and more long-lasting representation.

Although whiteness is preferred, throughout *Questions of Travel*, Bishop represents whiteness as that which shrouds, veils, and blankets often to the point of invisibility. In "Manuelzinho," Bishop describes the Brazilian "half-squatter half-tenant's" children as seen through a veil of fog:

> along with Formoso, the donkey,
> who brays like a pump gone dry,
> then suddenly stops.
> —All just standing, staring
> off into fog and space.
>   (*Complete Poems* 98–99)

The "I" of the poem "sees" but does not really see. A blanket of fog rests over the children, reflective of the white imagination's incapability of getting a clear take on the subject. By making this fog visible, Bishop figuratively admits to the presence of just such an imaginative veil in her perspective.

Likewise, in "Song for the Rainy Season," Bishop shrouds her home in whiteness:

> Hidden, oh hidden
> in the high fog
> the house we live in,
> beneath the magnetic rock,
> rain-, rainbow-ridden,
> where blood-black
> bromelias, lichens,
> owls, and the lint
> of the waterfalls cling,
> familiar, unbidden.
>   (*Complete Poems* 101)

It is hidden from sight, from the public, by a naturally created barrier of privacy—a white fog. In this poem, nature works with white people to grant them a luxurious and aesthetically appealing privacy by shrouding them in whiteness:

> vapor
> climbs up the thick growth
> effortlessly, turns back,
> holding them both,
> house and rock,
> in a private cloud.
>   (*Complete Poems* 101)

Whiteness works effortlessly to protect its own. Further on in the poem, Bishop admits that it is only natural for whiteness to linger over those who have attained "membership":

> House, open house
> to the white dew
> and the milk-white sunrise
> kind to the eyes,
> to membership
> of silver fish, mouse,
> bookworms,
> big moths; with a wall
> for the mildew's
> ignorant map
>   (*Complete Poems* 102)

This white dew is "kind to the eyes" of those in membership, and it walls out those undesirables—those mildewed others. But the poem prophesies a different era: an era that will kill the small "shadowy," private life:

> For a later
> era will differ.
> (O difference that kills,
> or intimidates, much
> of all our small shadowy
> life!) Without water
> the great rock will stare
> unmagnetized, bare,
> no longer wearing
> rainbows or rain,
> the forgiving air
> and the high fog gone;
> the owls will move on
> and the several
> waterfalls shrivel
> in the steady sun.
> (*Complete Poems* 102)

She seems nostalgic for the fog-covered private world, even while she exists in it. She knows that a time will come when a different light will be cast on the top of the mountain, when a different light will penetrate the blanket of fog to reveal something perhaps unforgivable in the small shadowy life sheltered by elevation and whiteness. When a "steady light" is held to this "high fog," then a different era will ensue.

Perhaps in this new era, a blending of whiteness and blackness will occur as evidenced in "The Armadillo." In this poem, Bishop entwines the colors black and white by creating a natural swirl brought on by the flying of owls:

> We saw the pair
> of owls who nest there flying up
> and up, their whirling black-and-white
> stained bright pink underneath, until
> they shrieked up out of sight.
> (*Complete Poems* 103)

Bishop forms one hyphenated word out of the usually polarized white/black usage. She distinctly designs a poetic language that allows the dismantling of polarizations between black and white. She imaginatively creates connectors between the two and a blur, a combination, rising together.

But such romanticized moments do not last in Bishop's poetry. Further evidence of a white life as a preferable life, occurs in "The Riverman." This poem opens with a magical Dolphin speaking to a *cabolclo* (a mixed Indian and European man) from within a "mist." This enterprising man leaps from his bed naked to follow the Dolphin. From the beginning of the poem, Bishop orchestrates a white place from which the leader—the Dolphin—speaks, and into which the dark man follows. The man continues down the river where "the moon was burning bright / as the gasoline-lamp mantle / with the flame turned up too high." There is something not quite right about this moon. Bishop's simile brings a technological excess to the light. Too much whiteness glows here.

In a moment of doubt, the *cabolclo* looks back: "I looked back at my house, / white as a piece of washing / forgotten on the bank." Harrison reads the whitewashed house as a "stabilizing force" in the poem that permits the riverman's voyage (156). I read the whiteness at which he glances back as an image dingy in comparison to the gasoline-lamp moon that guides him. Given a choice between white house and white moon, the man chooses the brighter one. As he continues on his journey, smoky mist rises through the water clouding his sight. From this smoke emerges an atypical serpent. White writers typically present serpents as dark, shadowy, barbaric, and Satanic forces. In "The Riverman" Bishop offers a different version:

> a tall, beautiful serpent
> in elegant white satin,
> with her big eyes green and gold
> like the lights on the river steamers—
> (*Complete Poems* 106)

This beautiful serpent, dressed in white, with well-lit eyes, positions Bishop as a poet who refigures beauty in language by undermining typical connotations of blackness and whiteness, but only for a moment. In the context of the poem, one transformed serpent does not amount to an imaginative refiguration of the ways white people imagine a racialized world. The man in the poem continues his journey by returning upon three occasions to the misty river.

Significantly, the riverman's wife begins to notice a color change in her husband: She says that he now looks "yellow." The man is changing races. In his move to follow the brighter white moon on a more enterprising journey than that signified by existing behind the dingy white door, he is trading in the darker Indian side of himself for the white European part of himself. "Yellow" signifies this transition.

The riverman becomes more and more connected to the life associated with the bright moon. He now receives invitations to important parties at the river in rooms that "shine like silver / with the light from overhead, / a steady stream of light / like at the cinema." Dyer argues that light technology such as that used in movie theaters "produced new expectations of everyday life" (108). In particular, cinematic lighting flooded space with meaning and movement. In "The Riverman," the *cobolclo* understands that he is pursuing something more meaningful because the cinema lights are glowing above him. He is near the source (albeit false) of meaning.

As he continues on his path toward whiteness, the man asks, "Why shouldn't I be ambitious?" The enterprising man justifies his journey by naming people he wants to be like. He claims that the path he follows is lined with great people. McCabe writes, "By the poem's close, the riverman has become as one with the river, surpassed his landed relatives, though still linked to them as medicine men; he is powerful and elusive, not commensurate with the physical" (176). In other words he has become whiter, and now, he must move away from the darker peoples.

Goldensohn tells us that Bishop felt uncomfortable with "The Riverman":

In 1960 she wrote to Lowell: "You don't have to like the 'riverman' poem—Lota hates it, and I don't approve of it myself but once it was written I couldn't seem to get rid of it." As Bishop explained in letters, Lota's distrust of the poem stemmed from her dislike of Bishop's or anyone's interest in the primitive; an activist in advance of her country's backwardness, she was impatient with what seemed to be her American friend's regressive fascination with Indians, or in this case, the cabolclo, or mixture of Indian and European. (*Biography of a Poetry* 209)

Bishop's passivity regarding the production and then publication of the poem suggests an irresponsibility and disregard for her own racist tendencies even when she does notice them.

Travisano sees it differently. He finds an authenticity in Bishop's depictions of Brazilian peoples:

Fifty, forty, or thirty years ago, when Bishop was writing all of those poems and stories and long letters studying and appreciating the individuality and integrity of indigenous peoples—or examining the "history" (to use her word) embodied in postcolonial artifacts—in ways that dramatize and hold up for contemplation the gaps between Western and non-Western modes of conditioning, perception and social behavior, she was simply following her own proclivities in a way that placed her characteristically ahead of the curve. ("Phenomenon" 912)

Although it is true that Bishop lived two decades in Brazil before it became popular to theorize Otherness, her first sight of Otherness is no less racially marked with whiteness than that of her successors. McCabe disagrees. She finds in this poem a genuine attempt on Bishop's part to get near to Others, to adopt the voice of the riverman, and to initiate a political sensibility and an empathetic encounter between two worlds (171–173). I find it difficult to read such attempts at understanding as remarkable or politically astute. It is white privilege that permits anyone to think they can get near to Others, that they can mimic the voices of Others, and that they can initiate worldly encounters. Shira Wolosky finds that Bishop's poetic desire is to imagine other worlds and experiences without appropriating, penetrating, possessing or absorbing the experience (9). In poems such as "The Riverman," try as she might not to, Bishop does enact a self-projection onto the poem. Only a sense of oneself as active, powerful, and correct could even compel a poet to make the assumptions that nearness, mimicry, and encounters are desirable on the part of Others.

The facts of Bishop's living arrangements at the time she wrote this poem portray her as a naïve romantic desirous of an impossible political tidiness and an upward mobility for those people she deemed less fortunate than herself:

Bishop's residence in Brazil in the '50s and '60s coincided with a period of rapid industrialization and modernization, runaway inflation, and an increasingly violent struggle between the landless, impoverished, and mostly illiterate urban and rural masses and an essentially feudal system of land ownership by a few powerful aristocrats. As a white middle-class North American woman living with an aristocratic Brazilian woman who owned an apartment on Copacaban Beach in Rio de Janiero and a country estate in Petropolis with several servants, Bishop was a benefactor of the system. She was simultaneously drawn to the communal rhythms and seemingly harmonious race and class relations of precapitalist Brazil and repelled by the massive poverty, illiteracy, and governmental corruption that were the marks of the old patrimonial system. (Erkkila, "Modernism" 299)

Bishop's urge toward mastery enables her poetry to find a resolution for such people as the riverman, and the resolution is to have him journey away from poverty and toward a "brighter" existence, an existence that will allow him to "go to work," and to attain "health and money."

Bishop, however, questioned her own motives in writing such poems as "The Riverman." In a letter to Robert Lowell, she ponders whether she might exoticize the people of South America (*One Art* 140). Dyer discusses this tendency toward worry, anxiety, and ultimate passivity in the face of decisions regarding race and empire as a particularly white female trait. He argues that although white women voice a "liberal critique of empire," in reality they do nothing to eradicate the enterprise (205–206). White women write the "spectacle of moral suffering" and demonstrate an "exquisite agony" over the problem, but ultimately, they enact no change. Although Bishop worries about poems such as "The Riverman," she has it published anyway.

Bishop may occasionally question her motives, and she may break some minor ideological constraints in order to imagine "fine black birds" and a white serpent, but she does not consistently struggle toward such breakthroughs. In the same book of poetry that includes "The Riverman," Bishop includes "The Burglar of Babylon," which opens with a metaphoric construction that likens Rio de Janeiro's Brazilian poor with a "stain" on the landscape:

> On the fair green hills of Rio
>   There grows a fearful stain:
> The poor who come to Rio
>   And can't go home again.
> (*Complete Poems* 112)

In this stanza, Bishop permits the reader insight into the stains upon her own imaginative landscape: stains typically named race and class. For every move Bishop makes to aesthetically refigure the connotations associated with race-related words and images, she also makes it clear that the refiguring occurs inconsistently at best. At any moment, the darkness or blackness that stains may make its mark on a poem, and the whiteness with wit may wield its mountaintop mastery. David Weimer, a visiting Fulbright scholar to Brazil, claims to have been a little startled to come face to face with Bishop's "elitist attitudes." He evidences the elitism in an anecdote about her treatment of the servants:

Elizabeth was a genuinely humane and decent person, and also she was a poet, so that the funny things that these servants did were exactly the kind of things she liked to write about with that wonderful sharp wit of hers.... Elizabeth told us one story about the man and the woman who were the servants up in Petropolis. She said there would be coffee available in Petropolis, which either the man servant or the maid would make, but she said we had better get it early in the morning because they would just keep it on the stove all day letting it boil. Elizabeth said it was sludge by the end of the day. She said this in a way to suggest that it was funny of these people to do that, and at the same time she was a trifle scornful that these people really didn't know how to treat good coffee. That's the edge. (In Fountain and Brazeau 179)

Yet, in certain poems such as "Filling Station," Bishop seems incredibly aware of the relationship between her privileged white position and her aesthetic creations. In these poems, she actually interrogates the negative attitudes toward Others that her whiteness imposes upon her and affords her.

"Filling Station" situates a "disturbing" blackness in the beginning stanza of the poem:

> Oh, but it is dirty!
> —this little filling station,
> oil-soaked, oil-permeated
> to a disturbing, over-all
> black translucency.
> Be careful with that match!
> (*Complete Poems* 127)

At first, the omniscient narrator's attitude seems harshly judgmental, but the following stanzas highlight the determinedness with which this narrator looks into the translucency in order to see the humanity existing at the filling station. Five stanzas later, the narrator comes to an understanding about love and potentially about God. Clearly, we can surmise, via Bishop's aesthetic design in this poem, that her imagination proves capable of transcending certain white racist and classist attitudes.

Importantly, however, if we read this poem as a replica of the ideological structure of at least one transformable white racist, the first stanza makes it clear that the foremost thought expressed will be that of disturbance and that of a negative attitude toward blackness. As well, the first stanza's last line implies fear of the explosiveness of too much blackness. It then takes five times as much processing, equivalent to the five succeeding stanzas, for the white imagination to come to a transformed place. The process of change, at least according to this poem, requires no intervention or action on the part of the Other, but rather, the white person must observe, question, and transcend. What she will observe includes one human being, a family associated with that human being, the work situation of the family members, a pet who looks "comfy," some domesticating accoutrements, and the recognition that "someone" chose to decorate this place to make it livable and comfortable. This recognition is stimulated by a string of questions beginning with "why ": "Why the extraneous plant? / Why the taboret? / Why, oh why, the doily?" (*Complete Poems* 127). Upon having recognized the particular someones and their particular choices, the observer reaches a place of transcendence, a position that accepts love as one of the ultimate levelers of humanity.

Regarding white discourse, white ideology, and the white imagination, "Filling Station" looms as an epiphanic and, ultimately, unsustainable moment in the Bishop oeuvre. McCabe states that many of the poems like "Filling Station" in *Questions of Travel*

> attempt to give voice to the Brazilian culture she appropriately feels outside of. While many of the poems "feel" calm, they unsettle us with open questions—a tension emerges in her voice, a struggle with a historical guilt for oppression, social inequality, poverty. She never forgets her potential for being a "tourist" and the dangers involved in such a position. (147)

Bishop was always a tourist in Brazil. Although she expressed enthusiasm for the culture, she withdrew from the people. She preferred the places—Ouro Preto, the Amazon, Petropolis—to de Macedo Soares's friends. She loved language but would not speak Portuguese for fear of making mistakes (Besner 2). Bishop never really connected with Brazil or Brazilians.

Further evidence of her defiant tourism comes in "The Sandpiper." This poem describes the situation of a bird obsessed with searching for something along the sand. He runs and runs looking for this indefinable something. The poem ends with an image of multiplicity in grains of sand: "poor bird, he is obsessed! / The millions of grains are black, white, tan, and gray, / mixed with quartz grains, rose and amethyst" (*Complete Poems* 131). Bishop blends the black and the white in an inclusive scheme when viewed from the point of view of a sandpiper. However, the blending was not a comfortable one for her; Lombardi claims that "The Sandpiper" is a self-portrait that depicts Bishop as losing perspective within a "controlled panic" (*Body and the Song* 219). Harrison suggests that the multitudes of colors at the end of the poem do not "answer fully to the vital search for 'something.' . . . The grains of sand can ever only partially meet the terms of 'the world'" (41). Bishop understands that multiplicity should be the answer, but she also declares straightforwardly, "The world is a mist." Try as she might want to dismantle polarities by imagining pluralities, she also firmly believes that a misty whiteness constitutes the world.

No where is the belief in the glory of the white body more firmly stated than in the prose poem "Giant Snail." Bishop opens with the giant snail narrating in the first person. The snail takes a "walk" after a rain and begins to describe its body: "It is white, the size of a dinner plate." This white figure moves invisibly like a ghost; however, it imagines itself as "heavy, heavy, heavy." Interestingly, the snail claims, "I give the impression of mysterious ease, but it is only with the greatest effort of my will that I can rise above the smallest stones and sticks." This white figure is aware of the names it is called, and although it looks as if it is doing fine, it really takes a lot of effort for this snail to creep along. The most intriguing part of the text is the commentary that the snail makes regarding awareness of its own perfection:

> Ah, but I know my shell is beautiful, and high, and
> glazed, and shining. I know it well, although I
> have not seen it. Its curled white lip is of the
> finest enamel. Inside, it is as smooth as silk, and I,
> fill it to perfection.
> (*Complete Poems* 141)

This amazing bit of self-reflection reeks of a self-satisfaction based on vanity and gloating in one's whiteness, and it undermines the end of the poem as the snail calls out for pity: "But O! I am too big. I feel it. Pity me." Bishop appears to argue that whiteness needs to be pitied because, like the snail, it cannot see its own body. It can feel the body, the bigness, and the heritage, but it cannot see it as anything other than perfect. It cannot get a handle on the shell of itself; it can only vaguely register a heaviness, a burden. Bishop writes a white persona in this poem who acknowledges the largeness and excess of its whiteness, but equally the white figure is seduced by its sense of its own perfection.

GEOGRAPHY III

In Bishop's final book, *Geography III*, her famous identity poem, "In the Waiting Room," not only addresses the discovery of one's gender, but it also includes Bishop among women of color. The persona of the poem is young and not quite certain that she wants to belong to this world of "breasts." The girl understands little about women, but she does discern that the world of women, with whom she is suddenly identified, includes many women of many colors, including white.

While waiting for her Aunt Consuela in the dentist's office, the young Elizabeth scans through a *National Geographic*. She surveys among the pictures some black, naked women with interesting necks:

> wound round and round with wire
> like the necks of light bulbs.
> Their breasts were horrifying.
>   (*Complete Poems* 159)

While she is reading, her Aunt Consuela lets out an "*Oh!*" of pain, and the young Elizabeth of the poem experiences a moment of sheer empathy with the aunt. She empathizes in multiple confusing ways: with the pain, the fact of Aunt Consuela's femaleness, with the family sound of the voice. The sensation is overwhelming and causes a feeling of vertigo for Elizabeth.

By talking to herself about her upcoming birthday, the child stops the swirling sensation of discovering her connectedness to women, to a particular family, and to pain. She contemplates the situation and questions:

> But I felt: you are an *I*,
> you are an *Elizabeth*,
> you are one of *Them*.
> *Why* should you be one, too?
>   (*Complete Poems* 160)

Her question, "why," occurs again, with a greater sense of the similarities:

> Why should I be my aunt,
> or me, or anyone?
> What similarities—
> boots, hands, the family voice
> I felt in my throat, or even
> the *National Geographic*
> and those awful hanging breasts—
> held us all together
> or made us all just one?
>   (*Complete Poems* 161)

She cannot quite put her finger on the similarities, but Bishop makes clear in the poem that the persona recognizes the similarities regardless of the awfulness she ascribes to the breasts themselves. This coming of age poem is an important signifier in terms of understanding Bishop's ideological framework regarding whiteness and connections among women.

Clearly, at least for the moment of this poem, and at least beyond the initial awful surprise at the observation of the black breast, this white female child does recognize herself as connected to women of color. The frightening part of this recognition comes when the child then feels herself sliding beneath a series of black waves. To feel remotely connected to women of color, to black women, especially by virtue of femaleness, brings on a feeling of being drowned in blackness:

> The waiting room was bright
> and too hot. It was sliding
> beneath a big black, wave,
> another, and another.
>   (*Complete Poems* 161)

Sadly, Bishop recognizes the connection but also expresses the workings of her imagination, which claim that any connection to blacks feels like suffocating, like being smothered in blackness. Recalling "The Imaginary Iceberg" and Dyer's claim that whites associate themselves with mountaintops and purer forms of oxygen, "In the Waiting Room" reaffirms that connections with blackness cause difficulty in breathing and threaten death.

Bishop cannot locate a consistent ideological base from which to derive comfort regarding this issue of race. She understands the need for change and connection, but the attempts at connection are not long lasting or they threaten to overwhelm.

One indirect way to address the whiteness that must, for Bishop—mask, coat, shield, and blanket the world is to use whiteness as the veil through which "nature" appears. In "The Moose," white mists and fogs are emblematic of the white imagination. In this poem, the rhythmic bus ride and the scenes passing by the windows together form a pulse of reverie, a situation in which the mind can contemplate. To write the contemplative mind, Bishop again turns to whiteness:

> The bus starts. The light
> grows richer, the fog,
> shifting, salty, thin,
> comes closing in.
>
> Its cold, round crystals
> form and slide and settle
> in the white hens' feathers,

> in gray glazed cabbages,
> on the cabbage roses
> and the lupins like apostles;
>
> the sweet peas cling
> to their wet white string
> on the whitewashed fences
>   (*Complete Poems* 170)

Reverie equates with a settling in of whiteness—the fog, the crystals, the white hens' feathers, the wet white string, the whitewashed fences—in Bishop's imagination. The whiteness settles in on every thing in the poem with the effect of "whitewashing."

Further on in the poem, the moonlight accompanies the mist to form a thicker whiteness:

> Moonlight as we enter
> the New Brunswick woods,
> hairy, scratchy, splintery;
> moonlight and mist
> caught in them like lamb's wool
> on bushes in a pasture.
>   (*Complete Poems* 171)

The whiteness becomes threatening in its ability to scratch or splinter and in its ability to abandon its natural position (on the lamb's body) and leave its mark on the rest of the world.

From out of this deep white reverie, a she-moose emerges, an otherworldly moose that gives "all" a "sweet sensation of joy." That female otherworldliness should emerge from this white-shrouded contemplation evokes an interesting attempt on Bishop's part to have something Other emerge from the thick mind of whiteness. This Other is not a human; it is a moose, and its Otherness cannot even be accurately articulated. It can only be sensed by smell, the smell of something acrid mixed with gasoline. Although Bishop can imagine something Other emerging from whiteness, she is not yet able to liken that Other to the white self.

The poem entitled "Poem" takes the reader through the process of reading whiteness in an unknown work of art. In this process, Bishop suggests that certain recognitions come from an aesthetic appreciation of reading whiteness. "Poem" begins with the "I" describing a small, unknown painting (*Complete Poems* 176). The first and second stanzas surmise what landscape the painting depicts. One of the ways that the landscape can be identified is through its colors, particularly in this case, white, gray, green, brown, blue, and yellow. Bishop uses both "gray" and "white" five times each in the first thirty-one lines of the poem. The white aesthetic markers include white houses, white geese, a wild white iris, and a particular "titanium white" barn. The sudden recognition of this titanium white barn causes the narrator to exclaim, "Heavens, I recognize the place, I know it!" From this moment on, in a poem that extends for another thirty-three lines, Bishop does not mention another color.

Reading this poem with an eye to the aesthetic importance of whiteness to the imagination of a white woman writer allows us to note with emphasis that recognition of a place coincides in this poem both with the moment at which the narrator claims her "I" and the final dab, just "one dab" of titanium whiteness. Titanium, used as an adjective to distinguish a type of whiteness, serves in its definition to mark a sturdy, resilient whiteness. Titanium is a lustrous, hard, light, corrosion-resistant element. It is long-lasting and makes the whiteness that Bishop associates with it in this poem equally long-lasting. Whiteness permits the recognition of this particular artwork; whiteness permits an accurate rendering of its meaning and its location. Whiteness serves to locate the reader vis-à-vis the artwork. Ideologically speaking, Bishop looks for whiteness as an indicator of who she is and where she is in relation to art, and in particular, in relation to poetry.

Whiteness associated with the power of nature is further evident in "The End of March," in which Bishop correlates a full-sized man with a white snarl. In the midst of a storm taking place on a beach, Bishop situates a set of people walking on the beach, a "we." As nature storms onto the shore, it offers up with "every wave," a particularly malleable whiteness: a whiteness in the form of a ghost, a ghost in the form of a man, a man in the form of a white snarl, a white snarl made out of white kite string:

> Then we came on
> lengths and lengths, endless, of wet white string,
> looping up to the tide-line, down to the water,
> over and over. Finally, they did end:
> a thick white snarl, man-size, awash,
> rising on every wave, a sodden ghost
>   (*Complete Poems* 179)

This image of a white snarl the size of a man aesthetically refigures once again the typical associations between whiteness and a natural innocence. Bishop poses instead a haunting whiteness in nature that snarls and that rides every wave in man-sized form. By doing so, she suggests a white aesthetic as equal in its threatening capabilities as it is in its innocence. Bishop does have moments of refiguring and inversion of word connotations that reflect her imagination as one that resists fixed aesthetic representations. However, I emphasize that these are imaginative moments that occasionally surface from within a poetry heavily burdened with masterful white racial markings. It is not the case that a "real" racist looms beneath Bishop's impeccable aesthetic facade, nor is it the case that a good-hearted nonracist emerges now and then from beneath a language that enforces racism. As

Dyer argues, racism is "part of the cultural non-consciousness that we all inhabit" (7). Bishop is responsible for her language, and simultaneously, she is not to blame for its burden. She would most likely be shocked to understand fully that the whiteness she writes reflects a construction that she deems normal and standard, and yet, it is a world constructed in her own white image.

CONCLUSION

In a poem written during the last year of her life, "Santarém," Bishop actually discusses the literary compulsion toward designing polar oppositions and suggests that time helps to dissolve such limited dimensions. Lombardi discusses the power of Bishop's late poems as the ability to "hold contrary notions or aspects of existence simultaneously, without letting one submerge the other, and without hoping for a seamless suturing between them" (247). I agree with Lombardi insofar as we are discussing polarizing moments in the poetry; however, I do not believe that Bishop thought this balancing act sustainable.

The situation of "Santarém" is a memory of having arrived at Santarém, at the "conflux of two great rivers, Tapajos, Amazon." The "I" in the poem writes of "liking" the place and being tempted to literary interpretations that support binary readings:

> Even if one were tempted
> to literary interpretations
> such as: life/death, right/wrong, male/female
> —such notions would have resolved,
> dissolved straight off
>   (*Complete Poems* 185)

If we read "Santarém" as a signifier of her own imagination, Bishop is saying outright that in certain places polarizations will dissolve, and these are places she likes. It is important to note, however, that Bishop does know that she cannot maintain this ideology all the time in all places; but she clearly wishes she could: "I really wanted to go no farther: / more than anything else I wanted to stay awhile / in that conflux of two great rivers" (*Complete Poems* 185). She desires to stay, interestingly, not forever, but for a while. The truth is that she did not and could not stay forever in the literal Brazil, nor in the imaginative place where balance seems a bit more achievable.

Bishop frequently preserves the domain of whiteness and expresses a nostalgia for the mastery that whiteness seems to have had in the past. Simultaneously, Bishop does also want to see her way through the mist of whiteness, even though she is not always able to do so with a brave heart and open mind. As she writes in "The Imaginary Iceberg," her whiteness "saves itself perpetually and adorns / only itself" (*Complete Poems* 4).

NOTE

1. Havelock Ellis (1859–1939) was an English psychologist who supported sexual liberation. He wrote *Sexual Inversion* (1897) and the six-volume text *Studies in the Psychology of Sex*, published between 1897 and 1910.

Chapter 4

"White: It Is a Complexion of the Mind": The Enactment of Whiteness in Sylvia Plath's Poetry

Poet Sylvia Plath was born in 1932 in Massachusetts to a first generation Polish-American father and a second-generation Austrian-American mother. Educated at Smith College, she wrote and published numerous early works. The summer after college graduation, she met the English poet, Ted Hughes, and soon married. During the next six years—the last of her young life—Plath settled in England; continued to write poetry, fiction, and children's literature; gave birth to two children; and also supported her husband's writing career. In the early 1960s, although her poetry was becoming more frequently published and well-reviewed, Plath's marriage slipped into turmoil, and the burdens of a writing life along with the ensuing threat of single-parenthood added to a number of factors that caused Plath to take her own life in England in 1963.

To a certain degree, Plath understood herself as a privileged person. Her poetry, much of which focuses on discovering, recognizing, and dramatizing the self, sometimes acknowledges and sometimes evades a mindfulness about the privileges associated with a self embodied in whiteness. During her years at Smith College, Plath wrote in her journal of the "terrifying" realization of her multiple privileges (*Journals* 61). Ostensibly, these privileges terrify her because, regardless of her advantages, she still occasionally succumbs to insatiable desires for more: more achievements, more comforts, more recognition, and more understanding of herself. However, Plath only affirms the terror of recognizing one's privilege; she rarely quarrels with or repudiates its endowments.

In another journal entry, Plath understands enough about her whiteness as a privilege to market it as a sexual commodity. She markets herself as white, and yet interestingly, she modifies her whiteness into a "colorful" one (*Journals* 77). Such modification signifies an understanding of whiteness—and its associated purity, cleanliness, and virtuousness—as lacking, particularly lacking in regard to love and sexuality. This scenario, which depicts whiteness as sexually lacking and colorfulness or darkness as sexually fulfilling or excessive, occurs repeatedly throughout her poetry.

Ted Hughes, the man who figuratively responded to Plath's personal advertisement by literally becoming her husband, affirms her attractiveness in exactly the same terms as she delineates. In his recent book of belated love poetry to Plath, *Birthday Letters* (1998), Hughes describes in "Fulbright Scholars" the signifiers of her spellbinding whiteness: her long blond hair and her likeness of Veronica Lake (3). However, Hughes, too, understands that mere whiteness is not as attractive as a "colorful" whiteness. In "18 Rugby Street," he describes the "colorfulness" of her face as related to her "aboriginal" and thick lips, and to her broad Native American nose (23).

In yet another poem, "You Hated Spain," Hughes again refers to Plath's lips in terms of Otherness: "The juju land behind your African lips" (*Birthday Letters* 39). Hughes directly associates her features with her Americanness, the America he marvels over (*Birthday Letters* 24). Plath's (and Hughes's) investment in depicting a whiteness that lacks unless marked by features of racial Otherness, along with the sheer accumulation of color, whiteness and blackness in her poetry, evinces Plath as a poet both produced by the racial politics of the 1950s United States and superficially aware of a need to focus particular attention on racial politics.

Although Plath might claim her own whiteness and its lack for particular purposes, the only real subject matter she scrutinizes in her poetry is that of the self spiraling in on the self. She considers her relationship to Otherness and "colorfulness" only insofar as it affects her own sense of attractiveness. She considers her whiteness only insofar as it affects herself and her personal goals. Author Toni Morrison argues that in the case of another white American writer, Herman Melville, realizations about white privilege are radical:

> [T]o question the very notion of white progress, the very idea of racial superiority, of whiteness as privileged place in the evolutionary ladder of humankind, and to meditate on the fraudulent, self-destroying philosophy of that superiority . . . that was dangerous, solitary, radical work. ("Unspeakable Things" 18)

Plath's realizations do not signify radical work; they do not challenge her, as Melville's realizations do for him, to analyze the "philosophy" of her privilege and superiority. Instead they serve as a catalyst for her to study the value of her embodied self to herself. Plath is a gifted delineator of whiteness, but she does not comprehend, nor pretend to comprehend, the complex relationships among her whiteness, the dominant culture's perception of her whiteness, and the terror she experiences when chronicling her privileges.

Margaret Dickie Uroff claims that both Plath and her poet husband thought the purpose of poetry to be the "enterprise of recovering a genuine self" (12). In this recovery process, Plath reveals the white embodiment of herself although she does not always recognize the significance of a racially marked white self. Other critics have also noticed Plath's insistence on her whiteness and have used such language to describe her, but no one remarks on this whiteness as a significant racial marking. Janet Malcolm refers to Plath as a "plump and golden" American child who "became the woman, thin and white in Europe" (66). Such images have been employed to symbolize the biographical lore of Plath and to trace her maturation from youthful American to stark European, but I argue that the whiteness embedded in discussion of this transformation bears racial implications. Plath's body, when in America, and when youthful, signifies as a vessel better than white—a corpulent repository of light. When in Europe, her body becomes pure, lean, and bare. In racial terms, European whiteness indulges no excess, needs no modifying color, nor any added weight. Plath's transformation from American to European is analogous to a recovery of a genuine and original white self.

Susan R. Van Dyne assures us that such readings of Plath's representation of herself and her body may enable us to understand her embodiment "in ways the subject inhabiting it could not read or represent herself" ("More Terrible" 79). Likewise, Wai Chee Dimock notes that as "unwelcome" readers, readers with sensibilities unfamiliar to the author, we may hear "nuances the author did not" (1067). From an early twenty-first-century perspective on whiteness as racial marking, Plath's poetry unwittingly reveals complex and contradictory notions regarding the privileges of occupying a white body.

Of the 224 poems printed in Plath's *The Collected Poems*, a remarkable fifty percent of them (117 poems) use the words "white" and/or "black" as intricate signifiers of power, (im)purity, fear, and thought. Eleven poems address skin color, twelve poems discuss the significance of whiteness, and fourteen poems refer to peoples other than whites such as Africans, Indians, Latinos, Chinese, and Negroes. Such an accounting coincides with what author Joyce Carol Oates calls a diagnostic approach to cultural studies. In her essay "The Death Throes of Romanticism: The Poetry of Sylvia Plath," Oates claims that Plath's work enables us "to diagnose...the pathological aspects of our era" (26). In the case of Plath, Oates suggests, "What needs desperately to be seen is how she performed for us, and perhaps in place of some of us, the concluding scenes in the fifth act of a tragedy, the first act of which began centuries ago" (27). Oates refers particularly to the death of Romanticism as performed by Plath; I argue that Plath also enacts the tragedy of persistent white dominance over Others.

Plath invites us to read her poems as figurations of whiteness via her plentiful renderings of "black" and "white." To best analyze this production, we must understand the expectations Plath had of words. She believes that every word could be thoroughly and pervasively analyzed (*Journals* 31–32). Furthermore, Plath claims that writing makes her feel like a small god (*Journals* 131). This poet conjures the flux and smash of racial ideology without realizing the cultural embeddedness and meaning of such language. Oates maintains that Plath's poems disturb us because of her "passive, paralyzed, continually surfacing and fading" capabilities as cultural mediator. Against her own will, Plath summons "with deadly accuracy the regressive fantasies we have rejected—and want to forget" (Oates 33–34). In terms of whiteness as racial marker, Plath's poetry convenes an exhibition of the power and dominance inherently assumed, yet overtly denied, by white peoples.

Many critics have discussed the use of colors, particularly white, black, and red, in Plath's poetry. Anne Stevenson claims that sometime during 1958–1959 "symbolic colors entered Sylvia's poems, to disturbing effect: white suggesting the purity of annihilation, red signifying the blood and pain of continuing life" (*Bitter Fame* 137). Steven Gould Axelrod rightly notes the polarity that Plath designs with her insistent use of black and white. He says that while she understands the "inadequacy of thinking and feeling in opposites" her poetry "implies that such a mode can locate truths denied more complex cognitive and affective systems" (58). Racism, one of this century's significant truths denied an articulated complex system, becomes repeatedly enlivened through Plath's insistence on the black/white binary. Although Plath persistently reiterates this binary throughout the poetry, Axelrod reminds us that her linguistic world is "inchoate, uncontrollable, and ultimately foreign to her purposes" (74). Plath writes an unfamiliar whiteness into her texts. She articulates the existence of the black/white power binary without posing a consistent argument regarding its essence.

Plath's poetry renders racial markings by way of sheer accumulation. She amasses references to blackness and whiteness with a brash innocence of aggregate effect. Her poetry gathers and flaunts blackness:

black look	black fingers
black pond	black statements
black marauder	black yew
black rooks	black tree
black November	black lake
black luck	black boat
black pilgrimage	black, cut-paper people

black seeds
black busybody
black alacrity
black deus
black-gowned examiners
black feathers
black stone
black winter
black compost
black frost
black Stone-built town
black goats
black fathoms
black sheep
black bull
black ducks
black sea
black coat
black shoes
black hair
black cypress
black-sharded lady
black armorplate
black rocks
black shadow
black apples
black pillbox
black slots
black keys
black agonies
black twigs

black spikes
black gap
black wall
black boot
black pocketbook
black edges
black eye-pits
black discs
black head
black eyes
black veil
black roses
black pine tree
black ball
black intractable mind
black asininity
black detector
black shoe
black man
black telephone
black heart
black sack
black horsehair
black sweet blood mouthfuls
black bat airs
black Alps
black muzzles
black car
black amnesias
black Circle
black air

Likewise, Plath accrues references to whiteness throughout her work:

white reflection
white noon
white air
white cloud
white hulks
white frost
white heat
white-jacketed assassins
white hands
white fire
whitehot noon
white leg
white edge

white days
white-haired jeweler
white china
white hiatus
white lines
white mice
white Mummy-cloths
white Nike
white person
white walls
white lids
white caps
bonewhite light

corpse-white Giant
white fizz
white, triumphant spray
white saint
whitewashed walls
white pillars
white-bellied
white horse
white hair
white beard
Grub-white mulberries
white catalpa flowers
white shadow
white petals
white fan-tails
white fingers
white palms
White bruises
white Niagaras
white stars
white flesh
white bone
white stomach
white down
white horse
white-smocked boys
white stones
white gull
white mist
Zinc-white snow
white heather
white maggots
white daisy wheels
white tumuli
white lady

white disease
white light
white coat
white, handsome houses
white, awful, inaccessible slant
white sky
white, cold wing
white clean chamber
white pickets
white mute faces
white ship
white sheets
white eyes
white cuffs
white crib
white soul
white sea-crockery
white fists
white shop smock
white straw Italian hat
white hive
white box
white smiles
white linen
white busts
white sticks
white, high berg
white gape
White Godiva
white spit
white cigarette
white towers
white, tight drum
white skull
white serpent

Linguists Ronald Carter and Deirdre Burton argue that studies of such grammatical litanies yield insight into the stylistic "norms" of the writer (32) and into attributes "permanently ingrained" in the text (32). The words "black" and "white," used as adjectival descriptors in Plath's poetry, point toward a habitual perception of the world as definitively sorted. Oates suggests that literary criticism regarding any twentieth-century American poets should serve to "illustrate how the work of a significant artist helps to explain his era and our own" (27). Plath's poetry helps to ascertain, although it does not always explain, the white urge to classify, modify and qualify its artistic subjects in terms of the twentieth century's most difficult debate: power relations among black and white peoples.

EARLY POEMS

In the poems written from 1956 to 1959, some of which Plath published but chose not to collect, extensive evidence exists to help discern how Plath's imagination constructs whiteness. In these poems, Plath interrogates the power transformations that might occur should we view the world through a black gaze rather than a white one. However radical such a repositioning might seem, it remains the case that a white imagination constructs this black gaze, and therefore, the black gaze signifies a threat to whiteness. The early poems also demonstrate an obsessive repetition of the black/white binary. This repetition signifies the penetrative will of the culture's racial issues to pervade the white imagination and its art. Morrison details this will as evidenced through lurking shadows in white American literature; Plath's early work is replete with such shadows. In these poems, Plath begins to focus on the body, not only as a vessel culturally constructed by patriarchy to entrap woman, as many Plath critics have discerned, but also as an organ significantly marked by color. These poems also house Plath's first attempts at creating the white, godlike, masterful "I" and at referencing the white woman's role in upholding the Western "culture of light" (Dyer 103), which asserts an association in art among white people, light, power, action, enterprise, and knowledge. Plath's early poems provide maps of her imagination's relationship to her own whiteness as well as to her sense of power as a white woman.

In "Conversation Among the Ruins" (1956), Plath associates the word "black" with the power of initiating change in language:

> While you stand heroic in coat and tie, I sit
> Composed in Grecian tunic and psyche-knot,
> Rooted to your black look, the play turned tragic:
> With such blight wrought on our bankrupt estate,
> What ceremony of words can patch the havoc?
> (*Collected Poems* 21)

The controlling gaze of this poem belongs to the black look(er). Read with an eye toward racial markings and implications, Plath suggests that a black gaze has the power to reinterpret (life or literary) performance. She proposes that all was fine; all was "elegant" in the house before this black looker cast his/her eye and its "wild furies" upon the place. The "look" casts a tragic pall upon a previously decorous performance. The conversation among the ruins implied by Plath can be read as the discussion of racial relationships in the United States during the 1950s. Plath suggests that it might be poetry's job to "patch" things up; however, she does not know the words and ends this particular poem in a state of interrogation, perhaps the major cultural interrogation of her life.

The second poem in *The Collected Poems*, "Winter Landscape, With Rooks" (1956), addresses blackness as a bleakness that threatens whiteness:

> Water in the millrace, through a sluice of stone,
> plunges headlong into that black pond
> where, absurd and out-of-season, a single swan
> floats chaste as snow, taunting the clouded mind
> which hungers to haul the white reflection down.
> (*Collected Poems* 21)

In this poem, a white swan "chaste as snow" floats atop a black pond. The black pond, also referred to as a cloudy mind, hungers to destroy the white reflection. This poem establishes blackness as a particular cloudiness of mind that threatens to demote whiteness, threatens to drown its uniqueness. In her first two poems, Plath establishes the word "black" as reference to threat of bleakness and to administrator of havoc.

"Pursuit" (1956), the third poem in *The Collected Poems*, flaunts a black panther who stalks the "me" of the poem. Critics typically read this poem solely as an occasional one chronicling Plath's first meeting with Hughes. However, when reading the poem in relationship to the two that precede it, it becomes clear that Plath also continues to write a complex and cultural blackness into the poetry. In these earliest poems, Plath positions the threatening gaze, the threatening elements, and the threatening stalker as colored black. In "Pursuit" the "I" must travel through the "hot white noon" while the black panther stalks her. Thus, the "I" walks through a whiteness shadowed by blackness. The second stanza, when read with an eye to racial politics, refers to the white "ancestral fault" that caused the black panther to want to seek revenge:

> Insatiate, he ransacks the land
> Condemned by our ancestral fault,
> Crying: blood, let blood be spilt;
> Meat must glut his mouth's raw wound.
> Keen the rending teeth and sweet
> The singeing fury of his fur;
> His kisses parch, each paw's a briar,
> Doom consummates that appetite.
> In the wake of this fierce cat,
> Kindled like torches for his joy,
> Charred and ravined women lie,
> Become his starving body's bait.
> (*Collected Poems* 22)

In this poem, Plath devises the panther as victim of a heritage that causes him to stalk for revenge. In particular, he stalks women. Plath does not say *white* women, but part of the heritage of racism has been the white assumption that black men want to rape white women in order to make the white world feel insecure and unsafe. Plath's poetry clearly declares that black creatures stalk and that white women, although they share the heritage that produces the need to stalk, are innocent prey. Plath dedicated "Pursuit," a poem she associates with the dark forces of lust (Hayman 96; Stevenson, *Bitter Fame* 78), to Hughes, the man who became her husband. Even though she never articulates an association between her poetic dark forces and the role of dark peoples in the world, the poem likens sexual predatory prowess with blackness, thereby suggesting the overdone and stereotypical relationship between blackness, violence, and bestiality.

With these three poems, Plath sets the stage for an enactment of blackness and whiteness throughout her *oeuvre*. Neil Fraistat reminds us to read a body of work as an ongoing text, rather than as separate units and to attend to repetition:

As readers, we gather data about the cohesiveness of a volume not only from explicit prefatory material or cues such as titles and epigraphs but from our growing awareness of the formal and thematic repetitions, contrast, and progressions among the poems. (8)

Plath's vocabulary provides us a thematically repetitive scheme that speaks to the character of racial politics in the 1950s. Brita Lindberg-Seyersted also discusses the role of repetition in Plath's poetry:

It is certainly easy to see that through almost obsessive repetition some elements put their unforgettable mark on the poetry: themes such as the contradictory desires for life and death and the quests for selfhood and truth; images like those of color, with red, black and white dominating the palette. (509)

I argue that one of the most unforgettable marks on these poems is the obsessive repetition of vocabulary that signifies Plath's relationship to the American, and later the English, culture's racial politics. Whether Plath determinedly designed her vocabulary with racial connotations in mind is an insignificant point in Dyer's mind and also in my mind. He argues that "white people create the dominant images of the world and don't quite see that they thus construct the world in their own image" (9). In terms of repetition, "White power ... reproduces itself regardless of intention, power differences and goodwill, and overwhelmingly because it is not seen as whiteness, but as normal" (Dyer 10). Plath absorbs and reflects, more than we can prove she understands, the collective conversation and shadows of conversation about the mid-twentieth century's racial divisions.

In "Tale of a Tub" (1956), Plath alludes to an "ambiguous shadow," something that lurks darkly and cannot gain admission through the window "blind with steam." In his work on Plath's shadows, Axelrod argues that Plath's shadows represent her "imaginative identity" that transforms throughout the work from something quite unformed and malleable toward a mighty woman artist. Throughout his persuasive discussion (212–218), Axelrod follows Plath's poetic shadows through phases when authorities possess her identity, through phases of insubstantiality and victimhood, through phases of alignment with marginal figures, and through phases when literary precursors burden the shadow with influence. Axelrod poignantly proclaims that Plath's shadows in poetry signify the interaction between two of her provocatively contradictory goals: "to represent accurately and to free words from any referential aspect whatever" (218). I add a social reading to Axelrod's psychoanalytical analyses of Plath's shadows, a reading espoused by Morrison: that the shadow in American literature also signifies the lurking specter of racial issues.

In "Tale of a Tub," Plath vaguely detects the shadow and admits that it has been there for a while. Her "we" bravely "takes the plunge" under the water in the tub and agrees to shudder away "the genuine color of skin":

> We take the plunge; under water our limbs
> waver, faintly green, shuddering away
> from the genuine color of skin; can our dreams
> ever blur the intransigent lines which draw
> the shape that shuts us in?
> (*Collected Poems* 25)

Read in terms of racial markings, this poem poses a question regarding the black/white lines, the racial boundaries drawn around our bodies. Plath asks if we can shun the lines in our dreams, but she quickly realizes that no matter how much we might desire a blurring of the lines, "absolute fact / intrudes even when the revolted eye / Is closed; the tub exists behind our back: / its glittering surfaces are blank and true." The tub represents an absolute vessel that holds the secrets and the heritage of racial difference, and in these last lines, Plath argues that this tub exists regardless of our human desire to change things. Its surfaces are alight with blank truth. Plath constructs many such bodies, limbs, and skins in her poems. Van Dyne argues, "In thinking about her body Plath displays an unremitting self-consciousness; her self-perception always includes an awareness of herself as spectacle, and her self-representation contains an element of performance" ("More Terrible" 72–73). However, as in "Conversation Among the Ruins," whoever does the gazing at the spectacle proves of utmost importance in terms of being a threat to white dominance.

Besides actualizing a racial terrain by repetition of blackness and whiteness throughout the poetry, Plath also displays white mastery through employment of a godlike "I." "Soliloquy of the Solipsist" (1956) begins with such an "I" and a question mark. Each succeeding stanza begins with this "I" (without the question mark), an "I" that claims ultimate power for herself:

> I?
> When in good humor,
> Give grass its green
> Blazon sky blue, and endow the sun
> With gold;
> Yet, in my wintriest moods, I hold
> Absolute power
> To boycott color and forbid any flower
> To be.
> (*Collected Poems* 37–38)

To Plath, solipsism signifies not only that the self alone exists, but also that the self is masterful. Significantly, in this particular display of solipsistic mastery, Plath exerts power over color. In the final stanza, when the solipsist attempts to recognize an Other, the "I" only discerns the Other by virtue of the power she herself endowed upon this Other: "it's quite clear / All your beauty, all your wit, is a gift, my dear, / From me." The mastery of this "I" is marked by clarity and an all-encompassing bestowal.

In "Electra on Azalea Path" (1959), a poem said to mimic the name of Plath's mother, Aurelia Plath, as well as to designate the exact path in her father's graveyard, Plath embodies a different "I," a female child recalling the death of her father: "The day you died I went into the dirt, / Into the lightless hibernaculum." Linda Wagner-Martin notes the "striking imagery," "terse language, and "direct[ness]" of Plath's "early history" in this poem (167). Stevenson recognizes this poem as a turning point in Plath's writing, one that taught her to "capitalize on her gift for mocking pathos" (*Bitter Fame* 153). This poem discusses what Plath saw as "the central situation of her life" (Pollitt 70), her father's death and her subsequent first suicide attempt. Although all of these readings do certain justice to the poem, none addresses the "lightless[ness]," the "dress of innocence," nor the "durable whiteness" of the poem's first two stanzas. I argue that these images, again reflective of a black/white binary, strongly suggest a direct relationship between personal and cultural pain in Plath's imagination.

According to Dyer, light in white Western culture represents the emphasis that the modern world places on "seeing as the epistemic sense *par excellence*" (103). With this emphasis comes a direct association among light, knowledge, and power (Dyer 106), and, as well, a connection among light-skinned people, power, action, and enterprise (Dyer 109). Dyer asserts, and I concur, that the use of light, particularly as it reflects on peoples in works of art by white people, has long-standing associations with the cultural position of the subject: "Light is a defining term and means of the culture and how different groups relate to it profoundly affects their place in society" (121). Those subjects particularly spotlighted by light in art "are the people who should rule and inherit the earth" (Dyer 121). In "Perfect Light," Hughes projects just such a reifying light on Plath and claims that she embodies innocence (*Birthday Letters* 143).

For Plath, living under such a heavy dose of projected innocence proved devastating. In her own poetry, she often seeks lightlessness as an escape from the burning spotlight of innocence. In "Electra on Azalea Path," Plath immediately associates the death of her father with her entry into lightlessness. The absence of the powerful white father triggers an association for Plath with darkness as well as with an especial death of the self. For a young white girl, the loss of protection by the white male figure signifies a forfeiture of the white child to a black, lightless world in this poem.

Dyer analyzes the position of the white woman in imperial, colonizing, and power situations as one quick to critique the "conduct" of white males in power, but as relegated to the role of "doing nothing" to encourage change in power constructions (186–187). In "Electra on Azalea Path," Plath's climb into the "lightless hibernaculum" at the moment of her white father's death, depicts an extreme version of the white woman's "doing nothing" that Dyer describes. In the absence of the white patriarch, even the white woman's minimal role as critic becomes usurped. The twenty years that Plath's "I" hibernates in the poem correlates with the literal decades of 1950 to 1970, decades immensely important to transformations in the roles of American white women. Significantly, in the poem, as the white child grows in the hibernated state, she transfers her sense of power to the mother: "I wormed back under my mother's heart." The second stanza begins with a reemergence of the white child, now twenty years older, not innocent, but "dress[ed]" as if innocent: "Small as a doll in my dress of innocence." This doll/child/woman wears the particular mask of innocence associated with the purity of whiteness. In order to reconnect with the powerful, and still patriarchal, white world, the white woman must be adorned in purity and innocence.

The white woman, besmirched twenty years previous by disconnection with the white patriarchal father and sent into lightlessness, must rediscover her innocence in order to participate in a rebirth into a white world. By line four of the second stanza, Plath's subject has made this transformation and is, therefore, able to claim "Everything took place in a durable whiteness." It is not sufficient that "everything" take place in a mere white world; Plath makes clear that the whiteness rediscovered in this poem is durable. The whiteness Plath reclaims is stronger and more permanent than the one she left, suggesting the pervasive and ubiquitous power of whiteness.

THE COLOSSUS

Sylvia Plath published *The Colossus*, her first collection of poetry, in 1960. In his review of that work, A. Alvarez recognizes a particular, yet indescribable, sense of threat "as though she were continually menaced by something she could see only out of the corner of her eye" as the distinctive mark of her work (quoted in Stevenson, *Bitter Fame* 203). Many critics have discussed this threat as the loss of her father, anticipation of losing Hughes, or fear of insanity. The threat I read in this book is the one that Morrison describes as the "dark and abiding presence that moves the hearts and texts of American literature with fear and longing" (*Playing in the Dark* 33), the buried, but vampiristic presence of racism and its potential repercussions to white peoples.

According to Pamela J. Annas, "In *The Colossus* Sylvia Plath focuses on the boundaries between herself and her world to test the limits of action both imaginative and real" (*A Disturbance* 22). Annas also tells us that the yearnings for dark "other" worlds characterize important poems in *The Colossus* (*A Disturbance* 28). Mary Lynn Broe, too, notices a movement between the polarities of darkness and lightness in this first book of poetry: "As she attempted a 'duet of light and shade' between the forces of love and the powers of the imagination, Plath discovered that the imagination collapsed in the face of the blunt physical world" (45). Both Annas and Broe provide research that greatly aids in reading the racial markings of Plath's whiteness. When reading *The Colossus* with an eye toward revelations about white embodiment and endowed privilege, we see numerous suggestions that Plath's imagination was haunted by current racial struggles, both apparent and buried.

The fifth stanza of "Night Shift" houses "Men in white," who, in the sixth stanza, defend the "Indefatigable fact." The indefatigable fact of the poem is the poem's mystery, most commonly thought to be industrialization and its icon, the machine. Broe reads the poem as a pictorial composition revealing a "lovingly tended" machine (45). The men in "Night Shift" are "in white"; they are marked, and furthermore, they designate a targeted whiteness. Their undershirts are "circled," denoting them as condemned or fated beings. Annalee Newitz suggests that any human marked as white is typically someone more savage or more working class than a "real" white who would be denoted as "just another person" (134). Whiteness becomes most visible in conflicts or clashes within social stratifications. In other words, "Whites who are not 'trash' . . . seem innocent of racially marked whiteness and its attendant brutality" (Newitz 138). The question then becomes "what is the indefatigable fact" being tended by these working class white men during the night.

In her striking essay, " 'HOO, HOO, HOO': Some Episodes in the Construction of Modern Whiteness," Rachel Blau DuPlessis directly associates the words "hoo" and "boom" in American literature as emergent from Vachel Lindsay's "The Congo: A Study of the Negro Race," a poem whose "BOOM" resoundingly affirms Euro-American denial of equal status to Africa and its descendants (669). She argues that subsequent usage of hoo and boom in literature pays homage to Lindsay's poem and to its ideology. In light of this argument, Plath's "Night Shift" comes alive as a signifier of interracial inequality, and the indefatigable fact becomes the blunt, yet invisible, machinery of elite white dominance.

This poem opens with a "boom," not a boom from within, but a "muted boom" from outside. The men who tend this booming machine become stunned when the machinery stalls for a moment and effects a pause long enough for them to understand at the core, at the "the marrow," that they are not equal to those people who, living in the suburbs, remain unstartled. The indefatigable fact that these men tend is the fact that they are merely "in white," and as such, they are marked as different from and not equal to, the "real" whiteness that industrialization exists to support. The boom of Plath's poem vibrates with a different inequality than Lindsay's, an inequality that few whites have been willing to recognize.

In "The Thin People," Plath again describes people in service to a masterful elite, but in this poem, she explores more deeply the threat posed to a white elite. The poem opens by alluding to a "they," who are always with an "us." Although the "they," further qualified as "the thin people," are of "meager dimension," they make persevering appearances in "our bad dreams." When read with attention to the power issues important to a masterful race—an "us"—this poem emerges as Plath's suggestion that the black race constitutes a growing threat to white people. She identifies the thin people as menacing but not violent. They wield, instead, "a thin silence" from inside an "insufferable" aural cloud of victimization, and she suggests that this "race" will not "remain in dreams." In fact, she claims, they are extremely supportive of one another and, therefore, would form a bulwark against the not-thin people. "The Thin People" demonstrates an insightful understanding of collective power; but it presents this power as threat, and it also still presents Otherness as something classified from a masterful perspective. Plath proclaims vulnerability to the threat of the persevering thin people, but she does not blend or meld herself nor the "us" into the calculation of potential change. Plath situates the presence of the thin people as the deliverers of a miscegenetic grayness and singularity to the world. She claims that the presence of the thin people will make the world "grayer." Annas recognizes the racial implications of this poem. She reads the thin people as emblematic of "social guilt" ("The Self" 42–43), but she rightly warns us against presuming an activism on Plath's part: "[S]ocial history seems to stop for Plath where her own life starts" ("The Self" 135). Thus, Plath once again presents significant cultural constructions of race as she intuits them without forming an argument about them.

In her journals, Plath treats racial issues far less allegorically. In one entry she views the "colored" race as dark and ever-present (*Journals* 7). This language used to represent people of color—shadows and dark presences—is consistent with Plath's poetic language in connoting threat. She refers to "colored" children as "little," which in this instance seems appropriate; however, the word takes on a more weighted meaning when used in another journal entry in which she describes a conversation with her date, Emile. In the conversation, she and Emile had discussed "little" things which include a stereotypical view that members of the "Negro" race all resemble one another. Plath assumes, by use of the word "little," that discussion of Negroes proves nothing more than mere topical chitchat in white courtship conversation. She never recognizes such diminishment of Others as white privilege.

A similar type of diminishment occurs in journal entries that conjure a "bronze boy with dolphin." She specifically turns to this bronze boy because he does not "smite her down" (*Journals* 101). To comfort herself, Plath turns toward this pitiable figure, a boy no one else wants. She reacts to being "smited" by turning toward a figure to whom she can feel superior. Importantly, her pity for him enables her to diminish any power or threat associated with his darkness. Although she brushes a "clot" of whiteness from his face, as if to wave away even the most minute vestige of association with white masculine power, and although she describes him as weakened and fragile—"balancing on one dimpled foot"—Plath also determinedly outlines the figure in moonlight and snow. She thus marks the dark figure with just enough whiteness to legitimize her attraction to and need for him. Dyer claims that such associations between whiteness and snow have to do with Aryan conceptions of white superiority originating in the mountainous areas:

Such places had a number of virtues: the clarity and cleanliness of the air, the vigour demanded by the cold, the enterprise required by the harshness of the terrain and climate.... All these virtues could be seen to have formed the white character, its energy, enterprise, discipline and spiritual elevation, and even the white body. (21)

Plath needs the bronze boy because he signifies something less intimidating than the powerful and pure white Aryan, often epitomized by Hughes (Malcolm 38), and less threatening than the black man.

In a strange passage in her journals, Plath further makes evident her associations with whiteness and male masculine power. She feels vulnerable about attending an upcoming dinner engagement because she has not had time to study, nor to write, and she reacts by denigrating the quality of the attendees' whiteness (*Journals* 115). In this instance, Plath signifies whiteness as not necessarily having to do with embodiment. She understands whiteness as a powerful position, typically occupied by white men, but not automatically endowed upon just any white man. Dyer explains this phenomenon as particularizing whiteness in terms of "enterprise." To be really white is not only to occupy a white body, but to fulfill an enterprising spirit that is recognized by one's "energy, will, ambition, the ability to think and see things through" (Dyer 31). In this journal entry, Plath demotes the men at dinner by virtue of their lacking in the necessary demonstrable white enterprising spirit. Dismissing their whiteness enables her to feel less intimidated about her potentially lacking conversation. Plath poignantly and uniquely understands masculinity as directly related to the endowments of whiteness.

In "Mushrooms," a piece that began as a poetic exercise undertaken in 1959 at Yaddo (an artist's colony in Saratoga Springs, New York) (Stevenson, *Bitter Fame* 173), Plath substantiates the invisibility and conquering enterprise of whiteness. She quite clearly describes the mushrooms as behaving "whitely" when she depicts their stealthy undertakings. She claims that they multiplied "whitely," "discreetly," and "quietly." To behave whitely, when associated with behavior described as discreet and quiet, is to behave with an unquestionable authority that must, for the sake of decorum, remain as inconspicuous as possible. Plath furthers the association between the mushrooms and people by personifying the mushrooms: They have noses and toes. No one sees the mushrooms as they deceptively take over. In their unspeakable whiteness, they are invisible. Voicelessly, they expand through nooks and interstitial places. They eat little and ask for little, and yet there are multitudes of them. The last stanzas of the poem, when read with an eye toward whiteness as masterful, describe white people as aggressive multipliers who, in spite of themselves, will take over the earth. In a footnote, Broe aligns this poem with others that "reinforce the ominous power of diminished things" (200 n23); however, I argue that Plath's insistence on the association between whitely, discreetly, and quietly in the opening stanza suggests that Plath is not alluding to the seeming smallness of the mushrooms inasmuch as she is using them because they are flesh-white in color and somewhat fleshy in texture and, therefore, perfectly apt representatives of the inconspicuousness of white people.

Throughout *The Colossus*, Plath associates whiteness with an insidious power to multiply and expand. In "Full Fathom Five," Plath delivers a mythological old man from the sea, whom she describes as having "white hair" and a "white beard" that extends for miles over the sea. Critics read this image as reflective of the extent to which Plath figures the power of patriarchal reach and control as fixed in nature and as representative of danger (Annas, *A Disturbance* 29). However, Plath specifically describes this patriarchal power as white. In "A Whiteness I Remember," Plath does not directly allude to patriarchal power; nevertheless, she perceives the power of nature as white. This poem resulted from a 1955 horse-riding experience she had with a friend, Dick Wertz, in Cambridge. Apparently, a reputedly tame horse went bolting out of control with Plath aback of him (Stevenson, *Bitter Fame* 66n). However, she did not actually write the poem until she was on her honeymoon with Hughes. Because Plath later used the imaginative force undergirding this piece to write the poem "Ariel," critics typically do not discuss "A Whiteness I Remember" in any depth, but the poem sheds an interesting perspective on a discussion of whiteness.

Plath begins the poem by claiming that whiteness is what she remembers of the ride and of the horse, Sam. Initially, she denotes the whiteness particular to Sam by virtue of what he is not: "White, / Not of heraldic stallions." Plath understands that a royal, official whiteness exists, and she further understands what it looks like and that Sam does not have this status. Rather, Sam is:

> off-white
> Of the stable horse whose history's
> Humdrum, unexceptionable, his
> Tried sobriety hiring him out
> To novices and to the timid.
>   (*Collected Poems* 102)

The aspect that Plath remembers about Sam is the history of his alleged reliability, stability, permanence, and steadiness as reflected by his off-white color. However, Plath makes it clear that the history and humdrumness of the horse do not define the entirety of him, especially not his temper: "the dapple toning his white down / To safe gray never grayed his temper." Regardless of his mottled, disfigured whiteness, the horse has maintained a stubborn white, domineering attitude and a determination to subdue the world "to his run of it." For the rider, Plath, the experience becomes a blur of participating in a ride that turns the world into a mass of "all colors / Spinning to still in his one whiteness." Becoming caught up as a participant in the horse's stubborn and independent run, the rider finds herself simply a part of his powerful whiteness.

Although Plath will cover this material again in "Ariel," I find it significant that Plath writes the poem on her honeymoon with Hughes in Benidorm, Spain. Hughes tells us in "You Hated Spain" that Plath did not enjoy Spain as he did, particularly because the "African Black edges" to the Spanish world unnerved her (*Birthday Letters* 39).

The whiteness that emerges in Plath's poetry upon this occasion—upon marrying an Englishman and honeymooning in "colorful" Spain—is a nostalgic and safe whiteness. She does not conjure the regal whiteness associated with England, but rather a more spotted, mottled whiteness associated with America. Hughes's foreign Englishness, coupled with Spain's foreign "African Black edges" and "Arab drum[s]" causes Plath's imagination to seek comfort in a more familiar, off-white type of whiteness. Recall that Oates referred to her as a golden child in America who transforms into a white woman in Europe. The whiteness in "A Whiteness I Remember" signifies a nostalgia for the (off-)whiteness left behind as well as a loss of equilibrium signified by the spinning entrapment she feels in Hughes's new (more pure) white world.

In an analysis of whiteness, "Moonrise" proves immeasurably important. In this thirty-line poem, Plath uses derivatives of white twenty-one times. Critics have not yet justly scrutinized this singular occasion of whiteness. Stevenson describes the poem as "macabre," never noticing the flamboyant whiteness (*Bitter Fame* 137). Broe reads this whiteness as representative of a "spent" and exhausted imagination, an imagination resigned to living with void (64). Annas comes closest to recognizing the whiteness as potential racial marking although she does not directly refer to the excess of whiteness in "Moonrise." She analyzes the natural images in *The Colossus*, including the moon, as significantly contextualized in a "social and socialized world" (*A Disturbance* 96–97). I argue that the social world of this poem is decidedly white.

Plath begins the poem with the image of a particular genus of the mulberry tree, the *Morus alba*, which bears a dirty white fruit. Like the buds of the mulberry, Plath claims that she wants to immerse herself in whiteness in order to do nothing. The white world of this poem is not the superior, enterprising, Aryan world previously conjured by Plath. This white world is dingy and encourages languor. However, Dyer argues that the white world occupied by white women is significantly less venturesome than that of men. He analyzes "end-of empire fictions" for depictions of white women and discovers "Doing nothing, nothing, . . . provides the basis for the complex construction of a particular white femininity" (187). Plath directly connects lack of activity with images of grubby whiteness and thereby reflects an understanding of whiteness as racially marked. In particular, she marks the whiteness of women in this poem as a soiled position of frustration and impotence.

The second stanza resonates with associations that mark the park landscape as hopelessly and deficiently "fleshed." White, bell-shaped flowers hang from the catalpa trees, casting ominous shadows. Plath's revision of whiteness away from its Aryan associations and toward threatening ones suggests that Plath somewhat comprehends the power associated with whiteness as potentially negative. Newitz contends that white people can "generate images of a whiteness which is marked, imperfect and disempowered" (133) and that whites can occasionally see themselves as Others see them. However, when white people do represent a tainted whiteness, they often depict this whiteness as somehow discolored and as not truly white, thereby simultaneously criticizing the power of whiteness while salvaging it in its purest form. Plath's description of the park landscape as deficiently fleshed and as blooming with dingy blossoms portrays just such a defiled whiteness while making space for, by not besmirching, a "real" whiteness outside the poem.

Dyer, too, warns us against reading white writers' revisions of whiteness in association with death and threat as positive evidence of remarkable change in the white imagination. He points out "Within Western art the dead white body has often been a sight of veneration, an object of beauty" (208). Thus, in "Moonrise," when Plath writes about the whiteness shrouding death, she is not necessarily writing of the fall of whiteness. She may just as well be celebrating an image of whiteness in rapturous humility and wholeness, as signified by the "round" shadows cast upon dying. Although I am mindful of Newitz's and Dyer's warnings regarding fixed readings of whiteness, I do emphasize the significance for Plath, as artistic representative of white culture, of venturing into language that embarks on marking whiteness into visibility.

Stanza 3 of "Moonrise" links the whiteness petals of stanza 2 with white pigeon fan-tails and with white fingers in that all three share the same vocation: a version of doing nothing. Plath drolly remarks that all three have a perfunctory job she describes as "opening, shutting." However, the opening and shutting of flower petals and fan-tails is conspicuously unlike the opening and shutting of white fingers. White fingers resonate with grasping, conquering, colonizing, and enterprising action. Like the flower petals and the fan-tails, they open and close by nature, but the white fingers quiver with far more reach and power. As Plath illustrates them in the next stanza, these fingers become quite agitated when they have nothing to do.

The fourth stanza intricately contradicts the third stanza. It is not enough for the white fingers simply to open and shut. They take on an additional activity; they curl in onto their white palms and force the ten half-moons to redden in the hand that no other labor reddens. The white hands have no other purpose, no other task, save to bruise and abuse. Plath asserts that white hands, in the face of no Other, will actually turn on themselves. The poem claims that white fingers have a propensity to bruise. They will either bruise themselves or Others, or they will collapse. In terms of the white woman's proscription to do nothing, as analyzed by Dyer, Plath clearly aligns white women with white men in the tendency toward bruising Others. The tension depicted in this stanza when the white fingers curl in upon its own white hand marks the frustration that white women feel at not being permitted to participate in active racial dominance.

The fifth stanza situates another differentiation between the whiteness of nature and that of the human body. The white body, although corrupt and decaying internally, appears to all concerned as a "clean[ly]" embodied figure. Here Plath asserts that the white body is a perfect mask for ugliness within.

The "I" of stanza 6 smells the internal whiteness. She smells the rot. In stanza seven, the "I" claims that whiteness is virtually invisible because we do not name its color. Plath, then, in an effort to name whiteness and to make it visible, proclaims whiteness as a property of the mind. Plath does understand the relationship between the longevity of white dominance and the impact of its unspeakableness on the imagination. Such clarity does not bring action nor revulsion, however. Instead, the last three stanzas of the poem are fraught with exhaustion. She expresses exhaustion with depictions of declining whiteness and fatigue with the never-ending task of women to drag down the ancient white patriarchy. But the last line of the poem suggests the faint possibility of future change. Plath ends "Moonrise" with the prospect that whites may come to recognize their past and may, in fact, better "stomach," meaning better tolerate, themselves.

CROSSING THE WATER

Any attempt at discerning Plath's imagination and its relationship to racial construction as a developing process becomes difficult given the handling of her estate and her publications since the death. Although Hughes organized and published *Crossing the Water* a decade after Plath's death, I address the whiteness in Plath's poems as she wrote them, not in relationship to their publication date. Hughes took significant editorial liberties with the poems in this collection, as well as others, but I contend that whiteness continues to resonate throughout the work and continues to be under-read in Plath studies.

Annas notes that in *Crossing the Water*, Plath delivers people to these poems that are "literally colorless, objectified, and atrophied" ("The Self" 136). Annas also designates this book of poetry as housing a remarkable transformation in Plath's imagination. She claims that Plath becomes aware in this text of ways in which words resist their authors. Furthermore, in *A Disturbance in Mirrors: The Poetry of Sylvia Plath,* Annas argues that Plath's realization about words affects her sense of her relationship to the world and to her art. Plath now understands "Language structures our perceptions of self and other: In the act of labeling, it tells us what to see and what not to see" (Annas, *A Disturbance* 54). In terms of whiteness, Annas's research provides access to analyzing Plath's later work as more determinedly cognizant of its racial markings. In particular, this poetry associates whiteness with godliness, ascendance, and power. Plath marks the skin in this poetry as white, thus making the skin visibly racial. She struggles to align white women with the oppressed, while the language realigns them with white male oppressors. Finally, Plath employs "yellow" as a racial marker signifying the bottom-most level of both an articulated and secreted hierarchy.

Elizabeth Hardwick remembers Plath during the time she wrote the poems of *Crossing the Water*:

There is nothing of the social revolutionary in her, but she is whirling about in the center of an overcharged, splitting air and she especially understands everything destructive and negative. . . . She is a stranger, an alien. . . . So "crossing the water" was easy—she was an alien to nostalgia and sentiment as she was to the country itself. A basic and fundamental displacement played its part. (113)

Although Hardwick does not witness social activism in Plath, she is careful to note that Plath lives in and absorbs the social concerns of the era. Plath could not help but witness the rising racial enmity in the United States.

In *Crossing the Water*, Plath engages images of white power. When she imagines preeminent power, she repeatedly depicts a god, and she repeatedly adorns or surrounds this god in a whiteness signifying perfection or purity: the pure "pane of ice" god of "Love Letter, " and the white surgeon god of "Surgeon at 2:00 A.M." In "Love Letter," Plath situates an icy-white, godlike being ascending into the sky:

> I ascended.
> Now I resemble a sort of god
> Floating through the air in my soul-shift
> Pure as a pane of ice. It's a gift.
>   (*Collected Poems* 147)

Plath recognizes the purity and godliness of this "I" as a gift. The poem, written for Hughes, reminds us of journal entries written before she married, when she counted her whiteness as one of her many marketable commodities, as one of her many gifts and privileges.

In "Magi," Plath again denotes whiteness as related to purity and godliness; however, this poem situates whiteness more abstractly than in the previous poem:

> The abstracts hover like dull angels:
> Nothing so vulgar as a nose or an eye
> Bossing the ethereal blanks of their face-ovals.
> Their whiteness bears no relation to laundry,
> Snow, chalk or suchlike. They're
> The real thing, all right: the Good, the True—
>
> Salutary and pure as boiled water,
> Loveless as the multiplication table.
>   (*Collected Poems* 148)

In this poem, "real" whiteness equates with the whiteness of angels, not with fabricated or laundered whiteness (produced by the Chinese in "Surgeon at 2:00 A.M."). Dyer claims, "The idea of the closeness of white men to angels is especially suggestive in relation to the representation of white people in terms of light" (22). In "Magi," Plath associates whiteness with the abstract wisdom emerging from such light sources as the "lamp-headed Plato" rather than with the earthly power signified by the surgeon's role. However, the abstract powers of "Magi" do not negate the practical power of "Surgeon at 2:00 A.M." Plath views whiteness as male power, and she understands this power as having a long history of endowment granted through religion, science, and society. The power of the magi does not negate the power of the surgeon; religion and science are both white, male powers in Plath's imagination.

The magi, a priestly caste in ancient Persia and followers of Zoroaster, who practiced purification rituals involving milk, were, over time, identified with wise men and soothsayers. The biblical magi who came from the East to worship the infant Jesus were related to these wise men. However, the ancient, milk-bearing, wise visitors in Plath's poem, are not the humble admirers who visited the beloved Jesus. This magi "loveless[ly]" calls upon a girl child, and responds to her smile, not with purification rituals, nor with the standard biblical gifts of frankincense and myrrh, but with "thin air" that insinuates a "heavy notion of Evil." Stevenson reads this poem as a comparison between a baby's "bodily innocence" and the "abstracts of philosophy" (*Bitter Fame* 199). She hears in this poem a mistrust of male ideas and philosophies (*Bitter Fame* 233). I agree that Plath illustrates a mistrust of male power in this poem; however, Plath associates this undesirable power with the superior whiteness endowed upon godlike males. While Plath again marks whiteness in order to make its power and misuse of power visible, in this poem, she retains an innocent position for white females, who, she remarks, will never "flourish in such company."

Plath not only associates whiteness with godliness in *Crossing the Water*, she also directly and indirectly refers to skin as white in color. In the 1961 poem "Face Lift," Plath indirectly addresses the whiteness of skin and its fragility: "Skin doesn't have roots, it peels away easy as paper." This poem has been discussed as a vindictive and spiteful response to Dido Merwin's actual cosmetic surgery (Hayman 158; Stevenson, *Bitter Fame* 207). Merwin was the wife of poet W. S. Merwin, who was friendly with Plath and Hughes. According to Ronald Hayman, Plath was quite jealous of Dido Merwin and wrote the poem to strike a blow at Merwin's beauty (158). Stevenson states that "Face Lift" exhibits Plath "rehearsing the hatred" that would appear in later poems (*Bitter Fame* 208). Broe sidesteps the biographical references supporting the poem and analyzes the "paradoxical energy" of its passivity and the ensuing metamorphic changes that occur to Plath's sense of self (113). Axelrod, too, discusses the poetry rather than the biographical underpinnings. In "Face Lift," he also finds Plath struggling with the self. Particularly he notes "two individualities compet[ing] for possession of a single body" (200). Annas concentrates on Plath's choice of "paper" as a simile for skin, and she argues,

> Paper is symbolic of our particular socioeconomic condition and its characteristic bureaucratic labor. It stands for insubstantiality; the paper model of something is clearly less real than the thing itself, even though in "developed" economies the machines, accoutrements, and objects appear to have vitality, purpose, and emotion, while the people are literally colorless, objectified, and atrophied. ("The Self" 136)

Significantly, we assume that paper, unless described otherwise, is white in color. The rootless skin that Plath describes as paper in "Face Lift," therefore, can justifiably be read as white skin. From the first stanza of the poem, Plath prepares us for the potential disconnectness of white skin when she describes the body as "exhibiting the tight white / Mummy-cloths." "Mummy-cloth," like paper, serves a protecting purpose; thus, Plath suggests that white skin is not reflective of a self, but rather protective of a self. White coverings in this poem mask rather than reveal.

In stanza 2, Plath introduces a darkness to the poem, a darkness with power over whiteness: "Darkness wipes me out like chalk on a blackboard." Plath not only suggests in this line that darkness has the power to erase whiteness, she also implies that a foundational surface of blackness resides beneath the soft, powdery, temporary white imprint. Darkness and blackness serve as bookends supporting the deletion of whiteness. In terms of racial markings, Plath situates a whiteness threatened by an obliterating darkness and a sturdy substructure of blackness. Although the first three stanzas strongly imply that a mighty black force has finally overcome an all-powerful whiteness, within the third stanza, the "I" takes a five-day reprieve to "grow backward." During this phase, a recovery of whiteness occurs. The masked, mummified, temporary, and rootless white woman of the first three stanzas actually houses a self, who is determined by the end of the poem to rebirth herself as a white baby. Plath comes close in this poem to redefining whiteness as impotent and insecure in relationship to a sturdy blackness. However, for all her wrestling with such revisions and potential renewals, Plath cannot imagine a poem that ends in a blackness existing without a white imprint, and therefore, she cannot deliver such an image to the poem. Instead the poem culminates in a recuperation of an innocent white baby (only white babies are pink at birth) waking inside a gauze-encased mother.

In a later poem, "In Plaster," Plath struggles with the adult version of this white innocent female position. She situates two parts of one woman, "an absolutely white person" and an "old yellow one." The white one is "certainly the superior one," but this superior haughtiness agitates the other persona, and the entire poem reads as a struggle between the two factions. Stevenson understands this poem as a significant representative of "Plath's developing mythology" in which "the whited sepulcher of the cast, with its seeming security (and purity), is in reality locked in deadly battle with the living woman within it" (*Bitter Fame* 212). Stevenson claims that "In Plaster" illustrates "the fierce resentment the inner Sylvia—the real one, the poet—felt in the presence of her artificial exterior" (*Bitter Fame* 212). I argue that Plath's determination to escape from this exterior not only signifies her desire, in gendered terms, to break through the artificial female exterior designed to please patriarchy, but also expresses her intense desire to believe that white women are innocent of the connotations, represented by the white plaster exterior, of white male power.

Axelrod's psychoanalytic reading of the poem finds that it deals "less with the tortured self alone then with the self's tortured relations with the other" (223). I expand this reading by suggesting that the other may also be read as the racial Other that the white body cannot help but define. The white plaster, artificial body is treated as Other in this poem because it signifies a burden that the woman inside does not want to bear, nor share, with white men. Plath treats her white, encasing self as Other because she wants to claim a likeness with the yellow woman, a likeness in oppression. We know that likeness with yellow is associated with nationhood, ethnicity, race, and oppression because in subsequent poems Plath makes such associations clear. In "Stopped Dead," yellow scenery cannot depict England, France, or Ireland; it must represent some country more violent, like Spain. In "Wintering," Plath describes a distorting light as "Chinese yellow on appalling objects." In "Eavesdropper," Plath exclaims that yellow is "Godawful!" For the purpose of "In Plaster," however, Plath prefers alignment with the violent, distorting, godawful yellowness, rather than with the burdens of whiteness.

The poem opens with an image of a woman afraid that she will never emerge from a white cast but who also imagines the possibility of a new person emerging from this cast:

> I shall never get out of this! There are two of me now:
> This new absolutely white person and the old yellow one,
> And the white person is certainly the superior one.
> She doesn't need food, she is one of the real saints.
> (*Collected Poems* 158)

Broe associates the "saintly white cast" of this poem with the protective and containing force of the "poet's art" that keeps "disturbance at a distance" (118). I read the white cast as reflective of the white skin that also keeps the disturbing issues of oppression at bay. This whiteness is literally and figuratively impenetrable. The whiteness of the person/cast described by Plath is "absolute." Its superiority is "certain," and its saintliness is "real." Plath permits no doubt nor debate about the perfection and infallibility of this whiteness and its ability to protect the literal bones of the person as well as the figurative superior infrastructure of the white body.

But the white body does not inspire the yellow woman to admiration, rather it infuriates her:

> I blamed her for everything! But she didn't answer.
> I couldn't understand her stupid behavior!
> When I hit her she held still, like a true pacifist.
> (*Collected Poems* 159)

The yellow woman's fury stems from having no effect on the white woman. The white woman deflects blame, behaves with disregard for another's understanding, and feigns ignorance of violence. The white woman makes the yellow woman invisible, and yet in the face of such nonreaction, the yellow woman experiences the epiphany that the white woman's sole being and definition depends on the existence of the Other, the yellow woman:

> Then I realized what she wanted was for me to love her:
> She began to warm up, and I saw her advantages,
> Without me, she wouldn't exist, so of course she was grateful.
> I gave her a soul, I bloomed out of her as a rose
> Blooms out of a vase of not very valuable porcelain,
> And it was I who attracted everybody's attention,
> Not her whiteness and beauty, as I had at first supposed.
> I patronized her a little, and she lapped it up—
> You could tell almost at once she had a slave mentality.
> (*Collected Poems* 159)

The yellow woman's race is marked; she "attract[s] everybody's attention." Whiteness is not racially marked. It appears only in relationship to what yellow is not. Thus, the yellow woman realizes that the white woman needs her. The white woman's existence and power depend on the yellow woman.

For a moment, it seems that Plath designs a reversal here: yellow woman as powerful; white woman as slave. She reduces the white person to the needy one, the one pathetically grateful for another's love, but this performance is momentary and seductive. The yellow woman succumbs to the white woman/cast's need for love and deference, and the yellow woman supposes that their "relationship grew more intense." But soon enough, the white woman/cast recuperates her power: "She stopped fitting me so closely and seemed offish. / I felt her criticizing me in spite of myself." The yellow woman then realizes that the white woman is not in a relationship with the yellow woman at all. The white woman feels immortal and superior: "Then I saw what the trouble was: she thought she was immortal. / She wanted to leave me, she thought she was superior." The yellow woman suspects the white woman of murderous and annihilating impulses: "And secretly she began to hope I'd die. / Then she could cover my mouth and eyes, cover me entirely." Broe reads the yellow woman as coming to terms with a moment of "psychological realism" (119) of her dependency on the white woman when she recognizes what has occurred. I read the situation as the yellow woman's epiphany regarding the inequities that sabotage relationships between white women and Others. The yellow woman comes face to face with hierarchy and positioning among women: "I wasn't in any position to get rid of her." So, the yellow woman reluctantly surrenders: "I used to think we might make a go of it together— / After all, it was a kind of marriage, being so close. / Now I see it must be one or the other of us." The yellow woman understands far more than does the white woman about the persistence of white hierarchies. Most significantly, the yellow woman understands the incredible loss that hierarchy and power ultimately incur upon white women:

> She may be a saint, and I may be ugly and hairy,
> But she'll soon find out that doesn't matter a bit.
> I'm collecting my strength; one day I shall manage without her,
> And she'll perish with emptiness then, and begin to miss me.
> (*Collected Poems* 160)

Broe reads the yellow woman of this poem as the signifier of the real Plath, the artist determined to exist under the false white skin that patriarchal and other societal forces expect her to maintain. I argue that while Plath may actually have written this poem with just such gendered oppression in mind, her usage of the yellow woman's Otherness to represent her artistic self signifies Plath's understanding of oppression while it naïvely asserts a white woman's desire (yet inability) to disassociate from the (male) power of whiteness.

In a recently discovered and published (1996) children's book written by Plath, *The It-Doesn't-Matter-Suit,* the color "yellow" again plays an interesting role in establishing hierarchy. The story situates the youngest brother, Max Nix, in a family of seven brothers, a mother, and a father. They all live halfway up a mountain unique because of its white peaks "like three big scoops of vanilla ice-cream" (6). The story narrates a tale about a boy who wants a suit because "[e]verybody on the mountain had some sort of suit except Max" (9). Max is unique in the story because of what he lacks; he lacks a suit. Mysteriously, a yellow suit arrives at the Nixs' home. The father's first reaction to the suit is that it is "strange." Each of the family members comments on the uniqueness of the suit, and "every one of the seven brothers wished he owned just such a suit" (18). The suit is large and looks as if it will fit the father, so the father tries it on. At first he likes the suit, but then he remembers, "All the other bankers wore dark blue or dark grey suits. None of them ever wore a mustard-yellow suit" (20). The father thus decides that he is "too big" to wear the suit. Plath thereby positions a yellow suit as one not fitting to adorn high positions in the world.

The mother adjusts the suit to fit the eldest brother. The brother is happy at first, but then he realizes that his friends might think "yellow was a silly colour for a ski-suit. He would look like a meadow of sunflowers against the snow" (22). This brother does not admit his fear of being deemed silly; instead, he says he, too, is "too big" to wear a yellow suit. Thus, Plath's characters verbally articulate themselves as "too big" for the suit whereas privately the suit thus far signifies an inappropriateness and a silliness. The elder males in the family claim a superiority to that which yellow represents.

The second brother inherits the suit and publicly passes it on because he is "too big" although privately he fears the color is too attention-getting (24). The third brother is publicly "too big" for the suit, and privately he thinks the suit "too fancy" (26). The fourth brother is publicly "too big," yet privately he, who likes to fish, fears what the fish will think of him. He thinks the suit is "too frightening" (28). The fifth brother, also publicly "too big" for the suit, privately worries that if he wore the suit fox hunting, the fox would laugh at him (30). The sixth brother, publicly proclaims himself "too big" for the suit when he really thinks that the cows he milks would nibble at him and not take him seriously (32). Finally, Max inherits the suit.

Max does everything in the suit: He attends school, skis, bicycles, ice-fishes, coasts, hunts, milks cows, and walks around town. It does not matter to anyone, nor to him, that his suit is yellow. Ostensibly, Plath wants us to understand the story as one that celebrates children's disregard for community judgments about difference. However, the fact that the suit is yellow and that it passes hands downward from the patriarch to the youngest member of a family firmly establishes the encoded liability that a seemingly insignificant attribute such as color bears. Yellow in this story signifies that which is inappropriate, silly, attention-getting, fancy, frightening, laughable, and not serious. Furthermore, these signifiers are kept private. In public, all the males proclaim themselves too big, too important, too significant to adorn themselves with such a color. Plath makes clear in this story that articulated judgments regarding color do not reflect the multiple deeply encoded, privately held evaluations about color. The white speakers of this story, aligned with the never-changing white mountain peaks of their homeland, determine their own self-importance in relationship to the collectively enunciated proclamation regarding yellow. Each white "I" determines himself too substantial to inhabit yellow. Each cares immensely about suffering diminishment in others' eyes by virtue of association with yellowness. Yellowness is only acceptable when suitably aligned with the bottom-most member of a community. Furthermore, the story makes clear that, in fact, yellow may only please Max because he has no other choice. He is the only community member lacking a suit. No one, not even Max, would choose to wear (or figuratively, to be) yellow, should he be granted a choice.

The topmost community members wear white. In "The Surgeon at 2 A.M.," Plath delivers a godlike man dressed in surgeon's white to her poem. This surgeon exists in a snowy, whitely lit world likened to Chinese laundry, marble, and gauze. Stevenson experiences a "menacing yet undefined threat" in this poem (*Bitter Fame* 221). Broe rightly associates this threat with the whiteness in the poem; however, she reads the threat as that associated with "neutrality or sterility" (96). I concur that the threat of the poem emerges through the whiteness but that whiteness and its relationship to godlike mastery signify the real danger in the poem. Plath's surgeon demonstrates no ability to comprehend the bodies beneath his scalpel as similar to his. The white light that accents the bodies subject to his surgery in the first stanza is "artificial" unlike the "sun" associated with the surgeon in the final stanza. Plath aligns the surgeon with a naturally superior light.

The patient on whom the surgeon operates lies under a "snowfield" sheet laundered to this particular whiteness by the Chinese. This reference to Chinese laundries further emphasizes the hierarchical framework supporting the poem. Artificial whiteness—that which glows from electricity and that produced by Chinese labor over fabric—is not equivalent to the exceptional and uncontested whiteness associated with the surgeon. The surgeon's "natural" white hands perform the operation through the seven holes "thumbed" into sheets that have been manufactured into a whiteness contrived by the Chinese. Beneath this fabricated whiteness lies a "lumpy" human form. This human, covered with an artificial white sheet, cannot lay claim in the poem to a whiteness, a normalcy, equivalent to that of the surgeon's. Plath plainly calls attention to gradations of whiteness in the poem. Although she does situate the surgeon in a hierarchical role, it is still quite radical of Plath to make whiteness visible at all.

Broe reads this set of lines as signifying the relationship between whiteness, obscurity, and anonymity (96–97). I do not deny these relationships; however, I contend that Plath situates an omnisciently powerful white male in an all-white landscape to hew limbs from passive bodies because she wants to emphasize the unquestionable authority of whiteness to reform the bodies of Others. Broe does read the surgeon as "malignantly violent"; I read the surgeon as wielding the exact injury that the masterful white race has historically wielded over Others: assuming the white race's perfection and assuming the ability to perfect Others. The surgeon claims to have perfected another being by having amputated body parts. Plath clearly views this surgeon as more than a professional executing his job; this professional takes souvenir body parts home with him. This white-coated male simultaneously represents whiteness in its most godlike and powerful form and in its indifferent and malicious form. Typically discussed as a transitional book as related to the discovery of the voice in *Ariel* (the posthumous book of Plath poetry edited and issued by her estranged husband, Hughes), *Crossing the Water* also reveals a significant change in Plath's ability to recognize and mark the white body in poetry.

WINTER TREES

Winter Trees, published posthumously by Hughes in 1971, furthers Plath's theme of a vacillating self; however, the question Annas raises is whether movement of the self resolves anything (*A Disturbance* 96). Hardwick suggests that such irresolution disquieted Plath's well-equipped sense of mastery:

Sylvia Plath was a thorough success as a student and apparently was driven to try to master everything life offered—study, cooking, horseback riding, writing, being a mother, housekeeping. There seemed to have been in her character no empty patch or seam left for the slump, the incapacity, the refusal. (101)

In *Winter Trees*, Plath's inability to master and desire for mastery become subject matter in racial terms. I argue that the colors not only represent Plath's obsession with the ill-defined and constraining role of the mid-century female self, but the colors also enact racial furies whirling to the surface of her art in the late 1950s and early 1960s in the United States.

"The Other," when read autobiographically, addresses Plath's anger and grief regarding Hughes's adulterous affair with Assia Wevill (Hayman 176). When read more broadly, particularly in terms of Otherness, the poem offers greater complexity and speaks more relevantly to Plath's sense of whiteness as representative of mastery. In a racially tumultuous era, such representations speak volumes about Plath's socially constructed imagination. Oates peerlessly captures Plath as she faces off with Otherness:

Plath exhibits only the most remote (and rhetorical) sympathy with other people. If she tells us she may be a bit of a "Jew," it is only to define herself, her sorrows, and not to involve our sympathies for the Jews of recent European history. Of course, the answer is that Plath did not like other people; like many who are persecuted, she identified in a perverse way with her own persecutors, and not with those who, along with her, were victims. But she did not "like" other people because she did not essentially believe that they existed. (29)

According to Oates, Plath perceives herself as a master. She believes that she lives as no other can and as no other has a right to. Broe, too, argues that the poet has mastered in *Winter Trees* the pose of simultaneous "victim and victimizer" (133), but Annas claims that when faced with Otherness or when "balanced on the border between two worlds," Plath chose to write from a "privileged and precarious position, not as wondering and innocent" (*A Disturbance* 3). In "The Other," Plath is the victim of an adulterous husband; however, the attitude of the poem stems from the "precarious privilege" of this position's moral high ground. The poem opens with an accusation, "You come in late, wiping your lips." But quickly, by the end of the second line, Plath stifles the accusation with a signifying dash, and she unleashes her rage inside the extended parameters of the dash.

Inside the dash, Plath immediately poses a partial question: "White Nike, / Streaming between my walls?" In Greek mythology, Nike is the winged goddess of victory. The famous sculpture representing the goddess *Nike of Samothráki* is made of white marble. Plath deliberately describes the victorious goddess, in this case, the other woman, as white, thus further magnifying her masterfulness, but also marking her with a visibility that Plath associates with the fluids seeping from between her own vaginal walls. Plath thereby designates the victory as a sexual one, but one bound to fail because the ammunition employed by the other—"The stolen horses, the fornications"—will not suffice against a "womb of marble." In "The Other," Plath's persona positions one reputedly powerful white goddess inside her own white marble womb and vows to scratch this Other "like a cat." This poet thus aligns whiteness with female mastery, sexuality, and invulnerability.

Yet, Plath's sense of the power of whiteness could reach far beyond the power and concerns of one white woman. Marjorie Perloff claims that although "The Swarm" ostensibly addresses the particular "horrors of war" (122), Plath thought her real concerns were love, creativity, and the lives of "all people in all places" (122). In this poem, Plath takes on history, Napoleon, the power of the Western world, God, and exile, and she represents their value through images illustrated in the colors black and white. The poem flaunts "black roses," "snow," "figures of ivory," "clouds," "a black pine tree," "bone of ivory," "black ball," "white busts of marshals, admirals, generals," "an ivory palace," and "a black intractable mind." The argument that emerges through the plethora of black and white imagery in this poem is one of a whiteness determined to conquer and make a name for itself and of a blackness gullibly delusional about what white power offers it.

In "The Swarm," unnatural "black roses" created by jealousy are being preyed upon by a snow that wields "brilliant cutlery." Whiteness "marshals" a weapon of death against an unnaturalness represented by the blackness of a rose. In the third stanza, Plath issues a warning to notice the "still figures of ivory." These white, robotic, "chess people" have no feelings and no motivation of their own; they take action at the whim of a larger, more powerful, being.

Later in the poem, we discover that "the man with gray hands" controls the ivory figures. Annas argues that "the man with gray hands represents competitive capitalism and the spirit of the modern industrial West" (*A Disturbance* 153). To Plath, the end result of such manipulations of peoples and natural cycles is to live "in the furnace of greed." The repeated clouds of the fourth stanza connote a whiteness that stands firm between the mercenary greed and the rising swarm that forms a blackness so thick it creates a "black pine tree." The hovering whiteness of the clouds is both a product of Western greed as well as an enticement to black swarms. Plath does not deliver to this poem a purely binary situation that permits us to read whiteness as evil and conquering and blackness as naïve and oppressed. Rather, Plath situates whiteness as powerful and seductive to both whites and blacks.

The fifth stanza mocks the black swarm for its gullibility. When bullets are shot at the rising black horde, the swarm mistakes them for "the voice of God." The black swarm associates the whiteness of the clouds with godliness. It romanticizes all that it witnesses in nature, "the beak, the claw, the grin of the dog." Yet the grinning dog is busy gnawing on a "bone of ivory." Plath hereby associates the cloudy whiteness to which the black swarm ascends with the ivory bone reduced to a dog's prey. In "The Swarm," whiteness can be both predator and prey.

The swarming bees continue to rise above all the lands of the white peoples: "Russia, Poland and Germany!" But the bees, "in their black ball," begin to argue. Their own divisiveness initiates their fall, and the white powerful figures conquer the black swarm. History then celebrates the white figures by turning them into sculptures that will hail the power of whiteness over time: "The white busts of marshals, admirals, generals / Worming themselves into niches." However, Plath also notes that the actual bodies of these white figures, once dead, are housed in "ivory palace[s]" that are really mausoleums. Broe suggests that "the two kinds of power," the black swarm and the ivory figures, are mutually deceptive and delusional (153). The black swarm is brought down through its own gullibility and infighting, and the ivory figures die "like everybody." White sculptures do not gift the dead individual with immortality.

To the final stanza of "The Swarm," Plath delivers two unchangeable forces. The swarm of bees still maintains that their honor stems from their black intractability, and Napoleon, the representative white force, still exclaims his pleasure in terms of power and possessions: "O Europe! O ton of honey!" Plath determinedly marks these forces in black and white so that we might also reflect upon the poem in then current racial terms.

The current racial terms were not fixed in Plath's poetry, however. In "The Swarm," she illustrates the oppression and intractability of the black race as well as the dominance and seductive fallacies of the white race. In "Thalidomide," a poem that Plath wrote for the "1960 Ban the Bomb Protest in England" (Annas, *A Disturbance* 81), Plath employs the Negro as representative of the partial humans produced by this sedative. Axelrod poignantly reads the Negro shadows of this poem, similar to those that "cast a shadow" upon Melville's Benito Cereno, as representative of "the uncanny return of the repressed ... [which for Plath] means a re-encounter with feelings of marginality and bereavement" (216). Van Dyne, too, reads this poem as Plath's confrontation with "the dark interior" (*Revising Life* 152). However, the fact that Plath chooses the Negro to represent the dark and destructive force of thalidomide signifies a deeply embedded sense of the Negro's connection to horror in the white imagination.

Thalidomide is a crystalline solid chemical that was used in the 1950s and 1960s as a sedative. The drug, never approved in the United States, was widely administered in Europe. Pregnant women who took the drug gave birth to children with devastating birth defects. Plath's poem opens with a mocking reverence for the fuzzy "half" state that sedatives induce in the brain: "O half moon— / Half-brain, luminosity—." The third line of the poem initiates a metaphor that likens a Negro, "masked like a white," to the horrible birth defects masked by the sedative:

> Negro, masked like a white,
>
> Your dark
> Amputations crawl and appall—
>
> Spidery, unsafe.
>   (*Collected Poems* 252)

Dark remnants of the Negro "crawl and appall," making the world of the poem "unsafe."

The speaker of the poem claims to have been protected by some indiscernible and incomprehensible "leatheriness." Her presumably white skin has been roughened up and now serves as a protection against the ensuing "shadow." As the "dark fruits" come toward her, she emits a "White spit / Of indifference!" that causes them to "revolve and fall." Contextualized in *Winter Trees*, this poem becomes a significant representative of Plath's fear of losing mastery and of her inability to recognize or sympathize with Others. In "Thalidomide," Plath unleashes her most vehement racist images and associations; she enacts a white woman's perception of racial furies, personal and cultural, relevant to the 1950s and 1960s.

ARIEL

Ariel was the first collection of Plath's poems to be published posthumously in 1965 (England) and in 1966 (United States). As editor of her work, Hughes infamously rearranged and deleted poems from this book, which Plath had meticulously designed before she died. Although such manipulation hinders some types of scholarly analysis, in reading the whiteness encoded in Plath's imagination and illustrated in the poetry, all the poems written during this period of Plath's life render corresponding effects, regardless of their order.

Although Plath exhibited decisiveness regarding the order of the poems, she spent more time pondering the book's title and its interpretations. Wagner-Martin chronicles Plath's sense of how the poems in *Ariel* functioned together and how various possible titles emphasized different aspects of the book:

> She first called it *The Rival and Other Poems*, then *A Birthday Present*, then *The Rabbit Catcher*, then *Daddy*, and finally *Ariel*. Her first idea was that the enemy suggested by "the rival"—whether mother, sister, lover, or the self as double—was the dominant

theme. Then she focused on the issue of truth, the heart of the enigmatic "A Birthday Present." With the choice of both "The Rabbit Catcher" and "Daddy" as title poems, she was emphasizing Ted's control of her life and what she saw as his abandonment. It was only with "Ariel," God's lioness, that she chose a rich enough image to free the reader's imagination. (226–227)

The rich imagery that Plath controls in the title poem and that she hopes will pilot us through the entire book—imagery ranging from Shakespearean associations to equine associations—constitutes only some of the resonating imagery in the poems. Broe argues for *Ariel* as a book in which images bleed one into another (161); I concur and further her argument by interpreting the accumulation of images encoded with racial implications, images such as those that roar through the poem "Ariel": "Stasis in darkness," "Nigger-eye berries," "Black sweet blood mouthfuls," "Shadows," "White Godiva." Likewise, such images flow throughout the entire text.

Annas claims that by the time of *Ariel*, Plath understood, or at least suspected, language's ability to construct and maintain perceptions of self and other (*A Disturbance* 54). However, Plath only wholeheartedly experienced and noted the dilemma when it constructed her female self as Other. She did not find herself culpable in upholding language's constructions when, for instance, she fell into the trap of utilizing language such as "Nigger-eye," language that maintains slang associations that denigrate African-American people. Regardless of her suspicions about the power of language, Plath's language in *Ariel* constructs and maintains her authorial whiteness.

In *Ariel*, Plath associates whiteness with the purity of beginnings and the perfection of endings. In "Morning Song," she links a child's "clean" mouth with a "window square" lit by morning light, as it "whitens and swallows its dull stars." In "Stings," Plath renders an ordered purity in bee keeping. She delivers to this poem, a man in "white smiles" and an "I" with lily white wrists who have between them "a thousand clean cells." In "The Edge," Plath conjures a "perfected" dead woman whose children accompany her in white death: "Each dead child coiled, a white serpent."

Plath also correlates whiteness with a powerful, obliterating, and yet superficial beauty in *Ariel*. In "The Rival," Plath equates "the other woman" with the white light of the moon:

> If the moon smiled, she would resemble you.
> You leave the same impression
> Of something beautiful, but annihilating.
> Both of you are great light borrowers.
>   (*Collected Poems* 166)

Plath furthers the conjoinment between the rival and whiteness by having the woman tap her fingers on a marble table and by labeling her love letters as "white and blank." In "Little Fugue," Plath situates blackness and whiteness as dualistic controls managing the fugue-like complications of life. In this poem, "White" eyes follow-up on "black statements"; a "Black yew" shares a line with a "white cloud," nestled between lines that discuss the "horrific complications" of Beethoven. In *Ariel*, Plath unwittingly orchestrates a racially marked poetic terrain.

Plath steeps the poem "Tulips" in a whiteness depicted as powerful, peaceful, and obliterating:

> The tulips are too excitable, it is winter here.
> Look how white everything is, how quiet, how snowed-in.
> I am leering peacefulness, lying by myself quietly
> As the light lies on these white walls, this bed, these hands.
> I am nobody; I have nothing to do with explosions.
> (*Collected Poems* 160)

The wintry whiteness of the white walls presses in on the speaker, both teaching her about tranquillity and enforcing it on her. The pressure results in eradication of herself and obliteration of the volatility of life. Van Dyne links this annihilation to "the speaker's fears of carnal and contaminating flesh" (*Revising Life* 92). As well, Van Dyne suggests that the speaker enjoys the process of noting the body's drift into "anonymity and irresponsibility" (*Revising Life* 92). Hayman, too, claims that Plath luxuriates in the abdication of responsibility in this poem (155). Significantly, the body that drifts into erasure in "Tulips" is a white body in a white world, a body confronted with entrapment in or escape from its own powerful signifiers. The speaker in the poem claims to understand the tulips as signifiers of a complicated sexual world intruding on the hallowed and clean white world of the hospital. She suggests that she might elude the seductiveness of the tulips should she become a nun and regain purity.

This reading of the poem works well enough; however, when we read the poem with an eye toward racial signifiers, the poem situates the plight of many white women who ardently desire an escape from culpability in white dominance over others. Dyer argues that white women are partially responsible for white dominance, but that because of their marginal status in relationship to white men, the only way they can maintain their own honor as white women is to do nothing about their role in domination (206). Thereby, the exquisite and languorous passivity that Plath demonstrates in "Tulips" marks white women as the culpable incapables that they are in the face of white dominance. The tulips remind the woman in the poem of other worlds, of other lives, of a colorfulness outside herself, but the woman cannot acknowledge these worlds and maintain her white passivity simultaneously. She would have to sacrifice the peacefulness of whiteness.

The tulips signify, by their glorious and bold colors, glaring Otherness. The frustrated speaker of the poem prescribes an enslavement for them uncannily linked to Africa: "The tulips should be behind bars like dangerous animals; / They are opening like the mouth of some great African cat." Annas rightly notes that the speaker experiences an obligation to choose between the two worlds—the white world and the colorful world (*A Disturbance* 98)—however, I find that the speaker clearly wishes she did not have the choice. She prefers to imprison the dangerous and colorful world, so that she may remain passively white.

Perloff reads the white world of the hospital into which the colorful tulips intrude as a "dead," "dazed," and "empty" one. She reads the tulips as the entity that will force the speaker out of her whiteness (119). But I contend that in the final stanza only the image of the imprisoned tulips permits the speaker to associate the red of the flowers with the red of her heart. Figuratively speaking, Otherness may only serve as a catalyst for white introspection once it is safely ensconced behind bars.

Again, in "The Moon and the Yew Tree," images of blackness, darkness, whiteness, and mist course into one another. Plath opens the poem with images illustrating the world of the mind. "The trees of the mind are black," and "mists" also "inhabit this place." The mists are so thick that the speaker "cannot see where there is to get to." The moon in the second stanza is "white as a knuckle and terribly upset," and a despairing darkness follows the moon throughout the poem ultimately to end in "blackness and silence." Wagner-Martin claims that the "images of blackness, fear, and hopelessness" in the *Ariel* poems express Plath's "increasingly bleak sense of discomfort and foreboding" (195). Interestingly, in this poem, although blackness certainly does correlate with bleakness, Plath also makes it clear that a thick whiteness, "a mist," keeps her from envisioning her path. She does not contrast blackness and whiteness as opposing forces, but rather, she describes whiteness as a barrier to mindful thinking.

The trees of Plath's imagination often mark a point of excess on the mind's white landscape. Her mind's trees, in her journals and poetry, are sharp, pointed, piercing, and cutting. They do not usually blend in, nor do they provide soft and soothing motion, to the mind's landscape. Plath's trees signify a barbed ominousness and a noteworthy deviance. Frequently, the trees are black (*Journals* 12). In one excerpt, the trees partake in a landscape that threatens to take the vitality of life away (*Journals* 12). Further on in her journals, Plath records a moment when she looks out the window while pondering her relationship to perfection and superiority, and again, she focuses on a "white-and-blue" sky marked by "hairy black trees" (*Journals* 20). Feelings of inadequacy plainly provoke mental images of black trees.

When Plath learns that she will be going away to England, again her mind conjures representations of trees, but this time the trees are outlined in a whiteness cast from the domestic light of her kitchen. From within the confines of a well-lit and familiar space, Plath can imagine the blackness of trees as darkly seductive signifiers of release (*Journals* 58). On yet another night, Plath records an epiphany that occurs while she looks at stars through "black bare trees." This epiphany reveals to her that she must spend more time noticing and capturing "sudden veerings of direction" (*Journals* 64). The black trees of Plath's imagination represent the need to attend to deviation.

As she travels on a train toward France, she again notes the blackness of the trees (*Journals* 95). In this imaginative configuration, both whiteness and blackness are "weird" and "strange." The whiteness is "broken" and abandoned, and the blackness is distinctively maimed suggesting Plath's figurative (and only occasional) recognition that both white and black forces are uniquely disfigured by racial animosity.

The moon in "The Moon and the Yew Tree" provides no "door," no enlightenment. Its typical white light offers no guidance in this poem and no softening affect on the yew tree. Instead Plath describes this moon as "quiet / With the O-gape of complete despair." According to Wagner-Martin, Plath also uses "O-gape" "to describe the elongated mouths seen in African sculpture and painting—figures in pain or abandonment" (195). Plath thus superimposes African pain onto the white face of the moon in "The Moon and the Yew Tree," suggesting that the despair dragging behind the moon like a "dark crime" is the relationship between the white Western world and Africa. In this poem Plath expresses disgust for the impotent hands of the saints whose faces are "stiff with holiness"; in short, she experiences an extreme distaste for her own inert imagination and for her own (and others') uncompromising spirit(s). The yew tree does not respond to the white-knuckled moon, to the unseeing mind, nor to the rigidly pious spirit; it simply sends as its message an assemblage of blackness and cessation. Although the images of blackness and whiteness do fold into one another throughout the poem, Plath concludes the poem with a figurative stand-off between white denial—"The moon sees nothing of this"—and black placidity.

Plath continues this sense of mutual stand-offs and mutual culpability among victims and victimizers in "Bee Meeting." Broe contends that Plath fully understands the power presented in "Bee Meeting" as "paradoxical, relative, and, at best, suspect" (148). Van Dyne suggests that the poem houses "fantasies of oppression" as well as "wishes for vengeance" ("More Terrible" 156). Van Dyne further argues that Plath envisions herself in this poem as both "willing accomplice and unsuspecting victim" (*Revising Life* 105). The imagery associated with these antithetical, yet indelibly bound, roles emerges again through representations of blackness and whiteness.

The poem begins with villagers dressed in "square black head[s]" arriving at the bridge to meet the "I" of the poem. The "I" feels "nude as a chicken neck" because she has failed to dress in coverings appropriate to working with bees. The appropriately dressed people are wearing black. However, the one woman who touches the "I" and who prepares her to meet the bees is dressed in a "white shop smock." The villagers offer the speaker a "white Italian hat" and "a black veil" to wear for the meeting. The speaker assumes that the black veil makes her "one of them." However, the villagers are dressed more fully in black than she is; the speaker flaunts headgear both black and white suggesting that she is a contradictory personage occupying a dualistic position. Annas reads this duality as both a powerful identification with the queen bee as well as a "living sacrifice" to the bees (*A Disturbance* 148–149). The speaker's "white crown" (Annas, *A Disturbance* 149) represents her power and her vulnerability.

The villagers and speaker walk through hawthorn, small Old World trees with thorns and the occasional white and pink blossoms. Plath delivers a question to the poem at this point regarding whether the hawthorn emits the stench that is "etherizing its children," thus implying that Old World whiteness (and its associated infant color: pinkness) has the power to cast a gaseous envelope of foulness over its offspring. The poem warns that the power of whiteness has ancient sources and that the negative aspects of white power may figuratively be inherited through the air that one breathes. Annas poignantly reads the outcome of the poem as hinging on images of whiteness:

The white straw Italian hat and the white hive earlier in the poem, the magician's girl and the knife thrower's assistant who is a white pillar, and the white box in the last line which is both the beehive and the speaker's coffin, pull together the set of identifications in the poem. (*A Disturbance* 149)

However, Annas interprets these identifications as Plath's obsessions with the cycle of death and rebirth (*A Disturbance* 149). I read the whiteness in this poem as reflective of Plath's sense that a racially marked whiteness is an exhausting skin to be in and that the pressures of existing inside it ultimately lead to an untimely and unforeseen figurative death. The speaker in "Bee Meeting" faintheartedly utters, "I am exhausted, I am exhausted—," and imagines herself as a "pillar of white in a blackout of knives." She reluctantly understands that the black-veiled villagers have accomplished their task and that the task has been to drain her of power and to bury her in a suitable coffin, "a long white box in the grove." In "Bee Meeting," Plath highlights the enmity between blackness and whiteness, but she clearly points out that whiteness willingly participates in its own demise by failing to understand that the "white crown" adorning its head signifies both authority and target.

In "The Arrival of the Bee Box," Plath writes an omnisciently authorial and colonizing "I." The poem begins with the claim "I ordered this, this clean wood box." With this line, Plath introduces us to the speaker as commander and requistioner. The speaker imparts that the box is "locked" and "dangerous" and that she cannot see into it. In the third stanza, when she puts her "eye to the grid," the speaker discerns layers of blackness and darkness that she associates with "the swarmy feeling of African hands." At this moment in the poem, the box metaphorically becomes a vessel carrying slavelike creatures from Africa, "Black on black, angrily clambering." In the following stanza, the speaker, having somewhat adjusted to the visual aspects of the black on black creatures, proclaims that the noise they make appalls her. She describes their language as "unintelligible syllables" and expresses fear of them as a mass. In this role as white spectator of the Other, Plath's speaker expresses utter disgust with Otherness. She diminishes her fear of this threatening collective by assuring herself that "they can be sent back." After all, she asserts, these creatures are her commodities: "They can die, I need feed them nothing, I am the owner." Annas reads this poem as one in which Plath explores the tensions that exist regarding one's fit in society (*A Disturbance* 145). I read the poem as one in which Plath experiments with the various roles endowed upon white peoples and thereby explores how she, as a white woman, best fits the various molds of whiteness.

Immediately upon having soothed herself by proclaiming her ownership of and, therefore, power over the black creatures in the box, she permits herself a moment of compassion in which she "wonders how hungry they are." In this white role, the speaker envisions herself as provider for Others. The next line swiftly undercuts her moment of tenderness by shifting the white role from that of caretaker to that of self-preservation. In this new role, the speaker wonders whether the black creatures would forget her should she set them free. Concern about their forgetting her suggests that she might want credit and homage for freeing them, and as well, she might want them to overlook her mistreatment of them. Upon wondering about their ability to disremember her, she suggests that they might be far more attracted to a laburnum, which she personifies as blond and female. In this white role, she vacillates between wanting credit for her liberal compassion and wanting the security of knowing that other, more superlative white women, the exotic blondes, exist to distract the black creatures away from desiring her.

In the last stanza, the speaker explores the ultimate white role, that of God: "Tomorrow I will be sweet God, I will set them free." Van Dyne suggests that in "Arrival of the Bee Box," Plath is "mimicking male hierarchies" and "toying with the freedom that male authority might bring" (*Revising Life* 151). Broe, too, recognizes Plath's play with power, but she claims that ultimately the speaker concedes to the power of the creatures when she promises in the last line that the box will be temporary (150). To my mind, the fact that the poem ends with the creatures still boxed and with freedom rescheduled for tomorrow does not signify a concession nor mere mimicry of male authority. The white female speaker in "Arrival of the Bee Box" displays a determined complicity of her own in prolonging the enslavement of black creatures.

Blackness connotes enslavement, entrapment, and suffocation in yet another poem from *Ariel*. In "Wintering," Plath describes a room that she cannot breathe in because a blackness infiltrates the space "like a bat." This room, again a metaphor for her imagination, also houses "no light" but a dim "Chinese yellow" that makes objects look "appalling." In a realization that occurs out of the depths of threat, the speaker comprehends through "black asininity," "decay," and "possession" that "they"—the bees—own her. Literally, the poem discusses the speaker's relationship to wintering bees; however, the bees signify a species of life quite diminished in size and yet quite forceful in their ability to sting. Plath's bees, especially when correlated with black asininity, appalling Chinese light, and decay, may easily be read as metaphorically referencing racial Others, who historically have been viewed by some whites as belonging to another species.

In "Wintering," Plath explores a reversal in power structure whereby the racial Others might possess her. She characterizes these Others as "Neither cruel nor indifferent, / Only ignorant." By classifying the Other species as all women, Plath also identifies with them. Once again she experiences herself as both colonizer and colonized. Broe rightly argues that in this poem, the speaker confronts her growing horror about power (153). Annas suggests that Plath fears her own role as exploiter in this poem and that her ultimate identification with the bees flying in spring releases her from this exploitation (*A Disturbance* 156). However, I want to draw attention to a rarely discussed stanza in "Wintering" which undercuts Plath's complete identification with the bees and the racial Others and which reinvigorates the power of dominant whiteness.

In the seventh stanza of "Wintering," Plath's speaker specifies that to ward off the cold, the "they" have balled together in a mass. She likens them to a "Black / Mind against all that white." In this metaphor, Plath constructs a mass of blackness as being of one mind, and in the word "against," Plath locates an enmity between blackness and whiteness. Although the seasonal structure of the poem leads us to believe that the black mind will triumph because in spring the white snow will melt, Plath characterizes the snow as wearing an extremely particular white smile. Plath marks the smile as notable not only because of its whiteness, but because of the metaphor she employs to describe the smile's reach: "The smile of the snow is white, / It spreads itself out, a mile-long body of Meissen." Meissen is an East German city located on the Elbe River, which travels through East and West Germany. It is predominantly famous for its Messein-ware porcelain, a creamy, rather than a pure, white porcelain. A German ceramist, Johann Friedrich Böttiger, developed this highly artistic and ornately decorated pottery in 1708 or 1709. This porcelain was the preferred porcelain in

Europe until about 1756. The white smile of "Wintering" is a Messein smile. It is German; it has associations with a river as well as with an elaborately embellished and exquisite aerated whiteness. Plath's use of this particular whiteness undercuts any reading that assumes an ultimate freedom for the flying black bee Others in the poem. Messein whiteness has significant European roots; it is a whiteness elevated to and cherished as an art form. Significant also is the fact that Plath associates this pottery in the poem as containers of dead bee bodies: In stanza 8, she writes that the "mile-long body of Meissen" is a vessel "Into which, on warm days, / They can carry their own dead." Messein whiteness smiles as it accommodates the dead black Others. I read the white Messein smile of Plath's snow in this poem as a sardonic smirk that stretches far beyond the mere taste of freedom that the black bee Others may experience in a single spring.

Plath's interest in Germany and its relationship to exterminating and far-reaching power, particularly its consanguinity with nazism, emanates most forcefully in "Daddy." The vast majority of scholars who study Plath's poetry examine this poem and discuss the poem's (mis)use of Holocaust imagery as well as the black descriptors that permeate the work. Although Plath situates issues of racial dominance and Otherness at the forefront of this poem's literary tropes, scholars to date do not read this poem as evidence of Plath's white authorial position.

Annas reads "Daddy" as a poem whose landscape constructs social and political boundaries partially signified by blackness (*A Disturbance* 140). In addition, Annas claims that the purpose of "Daddy" is to exorcise "the various avatars of the other" (*A Disturbance* 143). Broe, however, finds Plath again locating an interchanegeability among self and Other especially in the roles of victim and victimizer (175). Guinevara A. Nance and Judith P. Jones argue that the word "black" provides the significant spark in the poem that "ignite[s] powerful associations among culturally significant symbols" (125). Axelrod finds the father-as-black-shoe representative of a force "capable of stamping on his victim" (53). Furthermore, Axelrod suggests that Plath ironically designs her "aboriginal speaker" as only capable of "black-and-white thinking" (56). Clearly, the poem invites racially marked readings concerned with issues of Otherness; however, the scholarship does not effectively address the white authorship and imagination that creates this Otherness in the poem.

Axelrod ventures close to marking the poet's whiteness when he addresses Plath's interest in things German. He describes the emotional year that Plath experienced previous to writing "Daddy," and then he summarizes her psychological state:

She was again contemplating things German: a trip to the Austrian Alps, a renewed effort to learn the language. If "German" was Randall Jarrell's "favorite country," it was not hers, yet it returned to her discourse like clock work at times of psychic distress. Clearly Plath was attempting to find and to evoke in her art what she could not find or communicate in her life. (52)

Dyer explains that Germany, along with the Anglo-Saxons and Scandinavians, evokes the "apex of whiteness" to the white imagination (19). What Plath desires at moments of psychic stress is a return to the purity she associates with whiteness as well as a return to her particular ancestral background which she claimed as German and Austrian (Rose, *The Haunting* 225). Yet any such return to or contemplation of things German, especially after World War II, ignited images of nazism for Plath and influenced an imaginative conflation of purity, personal ancestry, and the Holocaust. The language of "Daddy" reflects this conflation.

Jacqueline Rose insinuates that Plath's connection between her own father and nazism in "Daddy" is not the profound and ghastly stretch that other critics have claimed. Rose prompts us to entertain the idea that nazism relied heavily on the dominance of the symbolic father: "For doesn't Nazism itself also turn on the image of the father, a father enshrined in the place of the symbolic, all-powerful to the extent that he is so utterly out of reach?" (232). Clearly, Plath answers "yes" to this question by writing "Daddy." The poem opens with a metaphoric complaint issued by a "poor and white" foot that her "black shoe" will no longer do. The "black shoe," associated with Daddy, and associated with nazism, has become too constricting. In wanting to separate from her father and regain her purity—her white foot—she must blacken the father and remove herself from his taint. She must become Jew to his Nazi:

> An engine, an engine
> Chudding me off like a Jew.
> A Jew to Dachau, Auschwitz, Belsen.
> I began to talk like a Jew.
> I think I may well be a Jew.
>   (*Collected Poems* 223)

By taking on the markings of a Jew in the poem, she highlights the heart of whiteness debates: who exactly can claim to be white? In the context of the poem, Plath attempts to separate from her father, whose power she associates with blackness and nazism. As her father's victim, she takes on the role of persecuted Jew. Dyer explains that the Jews' relationship to whiteness has not been at all fixed in time. During World War II, the Jews, as compared to Aryans, were definitively not-white. However, like the Irish and the Mexicans, the Jews have been both included and excluded from whiteness throughout time. In particular, their special whiteness has been used as a "'buffer' between the white and the black or indigenous" (Dyer 19). The Jew that Plath becomes in "Daddy" is a "buffer" Jew in the sense that it permits her multiple associations with and protections from whiteness. As a

Jewish victim of Nazis, she is non-Aryan. As a Jewish victim of Otto Plath, whom she describes as black in the poem, she is white. As a white woman claiming identification with Jews, she proclaims separation from the domineering whiteness of nazism. In "Daddy," Plath particularizes and multiplies her whiteness in relationship to and variance from the negative forces threatening her. Occupation of a Jewish persona permits her just such vacillation.

Rose argues that these vacillations provide Plath opportunities to experiment with varying psychic positions:

Plath . . . moves from one position to the other, implicating them in each other, forcing the reader to enter into something which she or he is often willing to consider only on condition of seeing it as something in which, psychically no less than historically, she or he plays absolutely no part. (*The Haunting* 236)

In Rose's reading, Plath exhibits a willingness to sacrifice her own claim to white stability, inheritance, and purity of position in order to hold up an incriminating mirror to readers. Yet, as Rose points out, there is the problem embedded in stanza ten—"every woman adores a Fascist." In this line, the incriminating mirror ricochets back from the reader upon yet another of Plath's interesting identifications; she changes from affinity with the victimized Jew to adoration of the Fascist victimizer. She claims this particular adoration as emerging from her womanliness rather than from her Jewishness. Rose reads this line and the following "boot in the face" line as housing such ambivalent agency that they suggest that women adore being violated and they worship opportunities to violate Others. This reading poses "the question of women's implication in the ideology of Nazism more fundamentally than has normally been supposed" (Rose, *The Haunting* 233). Plath has toyed before with this idea of white women as potentially culpable in oppression of Others in "Moon and the Yew Tree," "Bee Meeting," and "Wintering"; however, as in most other circumstances, she ultimately recuperates the white woman from significant blame by concluding the poem with an image of the more responsible white male. "Daddy" thus ends with a visit from the villagers, similar to those of "Bee Meeting," who, this time, have come to kill the white man rather than the white woman:

> And the villagers never liked you.
> They are dancing and stamping on you.
> They always *knew* it was you.
> Daddy, daddy, you bastard, I'm through.
>   (*Collected Poems* 224)

In Plath's white imagination, white men's responsibility for oppression far outweighs that of white women.

The validity of purity's connection to whiteness, particularly to the whiteness of women, poses a concern for Plath throughout the last poems of her life. In "Daddy," the speaker comments, "The snows of the Tyrol [an Austrian alpine community] / Are not very pure or true." "Fever 103 Degrees" opens with this concern: "Pure? What does it mean?" Later in the poem, Plath identifies the meaning of purity with her own body: "I am too pure for you or anyone." She thus projects the female white body as excessively superior. Van Dyne discusses Plath's representation of Christ-like perfection in "Fever 103 Degrees." She suggests that Plath appropriates "conventional scripts of religious purification" (*Revising Life* 118) and infuses them with sexuality. Dyer's work on whiteness particularizes Christ, God, and the Virgin Mary in terms of whiteness. Although Dyer is careful to assign Christianity its Judaic and North African origins, he also reminds us that Christianity has been one of the major European exports to the larger world. He argues that icons and activities related to Christianity have been "felt in distinctly white ways for most of its history, seen in relation to . . . Manichean dualism of black:white; . . . the role of the Crusades in racializing the idea of Christendom; . . . the gentilizing and whitening of the image of Christ and the Virgin in painting" (17). In terms of Plath's "Fever 103 Degrees," the ascending female body mimics the white Christian ideal of virginity, purity, and perfection:

> I think I am going up,
> I think I may rise—
> The beads of hot metal fly, and I, love, I
>
> Am a pure acetylene
> Virgin
>   (*Collected Poems* 232)

The virginal, white, shape-shifting, and ascendant body of Plath's speaker answers the poem's opening questions about the meaning of purity with a resounding, "Not you, nor him," but a visual representation of the female white "I" as purity. Hughes insists, in his poem "Being Christlike," that Plath did not want to be Christ-like, but rather, she simply wanted to be with her father (*Birthday Letters* 153). The ascendance in her poem, therefore, becomes in Hughes's eyes a humble mode of transport toward connection. In order to make this assent, she knew she had to shed her body and its fleshy heritage.

In "Cut," Plath toys with methods of shedding skin. In this poem, in which the "I" cuts her finger, Plath situates a "little pilgrim," an "Indian" replete with a scalping ax, and the "Ku Klux Klan." The image of the "dead white" flapping piece of skin conjures from her imagination an association with a pilgrim being scalped by an Indian:

> What a thrill—
> My thumb instead of an onion.
> The top quite gone
> Except for a sort of hinge
>
> Of skin,
> A flap like a hat,
> Dead white.
> Then that red plush.
>
> Little pilgrim,
> The Indian's axed your scalp.
>   (*Collected Poems* 235)

Van Dyne suggests that this particular metaphor may be off-putting in that it reduces American history to a "campy soap opera" (*Revising Life* 147), but I suggest that what is off-putting about this particular metaphor is the encoded ideology that permits it to arise in the white poetic imagination. For Plath, the sensation of seeing a white flap of skin being unhinged to reveal its own "red plush" insides uncannily releases an embedded threat to white superiority posed by American Indian Otherness.

Plath notices whiteness when it is under threat of annihilation. Annas argues that throughout her poetry, Plath becomes cognizant of identity issues through "crisis points" (*A Disturbance* 119). I suggest that Plath's whiteness remains invisible to her until it becomes figuratively attacked. Recognition of her bodily whiteness turns, in the poem, into an ominous identification of the white female body as an enrobed Ku Klux Klan member, whose garments are darkening and tarnishing.

Dyer informs us that Ku Klux Klan discourse most acutely exhibits the reified white woman and the simultaneous impossibility of white women to maintain the pure connotations assigned to their whiteness:

> [T]he Klan invested so strongly in a mode of representation that etherealized white women to the point that to imagine them having sex and being delivered of children is scandalous and virtually sacrilegious. It is white women's duty but it is what white women are least able to do and still be white. Klan imagery only pushes to its crazed logical conclusion an instability long implicit in normative imagery of white women's sexuality. (29)

"Cut" ends with the revelation that a white female, too, can be responsible. She, too, can be a "dirty girl" both in Ku Klux Klan terms—to be sexually marked—and in terms of white female as dirtied with the role of racial oppressor.

Although Plath occasionally experiences and reveals the domineering inheritance encoded in white skin, she also relishes and fears the perceived sexual power encoded in female white skin. In "Ariel," Plath displays a "white Godiva" body, which Van Dyne designates as the moment when the poem shifts to "intelligible, complete sentences" (*Revising Life* 126). The white female sexual body thus strengthens Plath's sense of form and structure. Stevenson and Broe read "Ariel" as Plath's quintessential "color" poem (*Bitter Fame* 272; 165). Indeed the colors do drift one into another as if to suggest that a ride aback of the horse Ariel permits the world's colors to stream across the landscape. However, the flow of colors does not simply reflect variations in peoples or in landscape. The accumulation of images is particularly encoded with threatening racial implications. As the horse moves, the speaker notes "Nigger-eye / Berries" that "cast dark / Hooks." The powerful, yet vulnerable, naked white Godiva body perceives a plethora of menacing black figures aiming their hooks at her. Likewise, the world that whirls past Godiva's body also houses shadows of "black sweet blood mouthfuls." Plath depicts the white female body of "Ariel" as particularly susceptible to ensnaring and consuming black desire.

A complex skin emerges in "Lady Lazarus." To describe the persona's skin, Plath uses the twentieth century's most infamous binary representation of white racial superiority, nazism. The "I" describes her skin as a "walking miracle," "bright as a Nazi lampshade" in stanza 2, but then in stanza 3, she immediately describes her face as a "featureless, fine / Jew linen." This enactment of racial multiplicity permits Plath to speak to the contradictory victim/victimizer issues explored in "Fever 103 Degrees" and in "Ariel." In this poem, the white female body is encoded with both Nazi oppression and Jewish vulnerability. Annas rightly analyzes this poem as Plath's sense of women's condition as being "trapped in herself and her society" (*A Disturbance* 139). I suggest that the poem can further be read as revealing white women's entrapment in the contradictory roles of racial oppressor and engendered oppression.

CONCLUSION

In his last love poem to her, Hughes proclaims, "Everything you painted you painted white" (*Birthday Letters* 197). It is evident throughout her entire *oeuvre* that Plath both avows the existence of and equivocates about the imperviousness of whiteness and white privilege. She understands whiteness as both pure and lacking. Her poetry enacts a tenacious white preeminence over Others. The accretion of color imagery in her work, especially the numerous usages of black and white evidences her perception of the world as racially arranged. Plath's poetry enables us to identify, although it does not always clarify, the white urge to categorize peoples racially.

Plath's poetry exhibits whiteness in the forms of godlike command, worldly durability, and female virginal purity. The white world of her poetry is also profoundly threatened by black and by ominous dark shadows. While Plath either maintains or revives authorial whiteness in most of her poems, she also suggests the importance of whites coming to terms with their roles as oppressors. She particularly haggles with the divided position of white woman as oppressor and victim of oppression although ultimately Plath's primary subject matter is that of the white female self buckling in on itself.

Conclusion

Michael Omi and Howard Winant envision the task for racial theorizing as that of avoiding the "utopian framework" that purports ways in which we can "get beyond" skin color and the "essentialist formulation" that fixes skin as objectively and biologically marked (55). The journal *Race Traitor* divines a different need: It proclaims the need to abolish the white race altogether (Ignatiev and Garvey 2). Paul Kival, author of *Uprooting Racism*, argues for understanding the ongoing and persistent refusal to mark whiteness as a symptom of racism:

We [whites] are understandably uncomfortable with the label "white." We feel boxed in and want to escape, just as people of color want to escape from the confines of their racial categories. Being white is an arbitrary category which overrides our individual personalities, devalues us, deprives us of the richness of our other identities, stereotypes us and yet has no scientific basis. However, in our society being white is also just as real, and governs our day-to-day lives just as much as being a person of color. To acknowledge this reality is not to create it nor to perpetuate it. In fact, it is the first step to uprooting racism. (12)

White Women Writing White labels poets H.D., Elizabeth Bishop, and Sylvia Plath as white writers who, both wittingly and unwittingly, construct images of white mastery, dominance, hierarchy, and privilege throughout their works. Although these poets are not the only participants in the white poetic institution, they are extremely significant members. As Kival reminds us,

White women have been held to be the purest realization of white values. They have been locked up within this symbolism, and tremendous violence has been done in their name for their "protection" and the protection of white civilization. White women have both colluded with and resisted their role and the violence it has justified. (25)

H.D.'s representations of whiteness reflect her sense of an inseparable connection between whiteness and mastery. She struggles with the implications of this connection, but her poetry ultimately recuperates whiteness as masterful even after she performs interrogations of its power. Likewise, Bishop's work expresses nostalgia for a more significant mastery wielded by whiteness in the past. Only Plath suggests the importance of white women dealing with what we now discuss as "white skin privilege politics" (Ignatiev and Garvey 1).

Throughout this work, poetic discourse has been examined in light of a larger project—critical white studies—which analyzes the ways whiteness has remained invisibly powerful. My argument is that poetic discourse has long participated in and facilitated the maintenance of whiteness as an unmarked and dominant force. Critical white studies proffers many suggestions for the analysis of whiteness ranging from redefinition of terms to political activism. The critical white studies journal *Race Traitor* asserts, "The key to solving the social problems of our age is to abolish the white race" (Ignatiev and Garvey 10). Writers included in this journal believe themselves capable of being washed clean of their whiteness (Gilbert 55); they believe that they do not have to be white nor to "converse in the language" of whiteness (Peeples 81); they espouse that "treason to whiteness is loyalty to humanity" (Ignatiev and Garvey 91); and they believe that deconstruction of whiteness is not enough: destruction is the only aim (Ignatiev and Garvey 279). H.D., Bishop, and Plath would not have understood the new abolitionist politics of *Race Traitor*, but as Omi and Winant contend, race relations and racial knowledge are "shaped by actually existing race relations in any given historical period" (11). The racial theories of these poets' various "times" afforded them a different "common sense" regarding race. They partook of ample opportunities to ignore and deny their own skin as racially marked. Likewise, they would not have comprehended their poetic imaginations as racially encoded.

White Women Writing White draws attention, for the first time, to the racial signifiers that locate whiteness in the poetry of H.D., Elizabeth Bishop, and Sylvia Plath. This book does not label these women as racists, although the occasional poem, journal entry, and/or letter does reveal clear moments of extreme racism; instead, this book demonstrates ways to read poetry written by white people as racial works that reflect white worlds and white imaginations.

Bibliography

Alexander, Paul. *Rough Magic: A Biography of Sylvia Plath.* New York: Viking, 1991.

Alexander, Paul, ed. *Ariel Ascending: Writings about Sylvia Plath.* New York: Harper & Row Publishers, 1985.

Allen, Theodore W. *The Invention of the White Race: Racial Oppression and Social Control.* Vol. I. London: Verso, 1994.

Alvarez, A. "Poetry in Extremis." In Linda W. Wagner, ed. *Sylvia Plath: The Critical Heritage.* New York: Routledge, 1988.

Annas, Pamela J. *A Disturbance in Mirrors: The Poetry of Sylvia Plath.* Westport, CT: Greenwood Press, 1988.

———. "The Self in the World: The Social Context of Sylvia Plath's Late Poems." In Linda W. Wagner, ed. *Critical Essays on Sylvia Plath.* Boston: G. K. Hall, 1984.

Arthur, Marilyn. "Psychomythology: The Case of H.D." *Bucknell Review* 28 (2): 65–79 (1983).

Awkward, Michael. *Negotiating Difference: Race, Gender, and the Politics of Positionality.* Chicago: University of Chicago Press, 1995.

Axelrod, Steven Gould. *Sylvia Plath: The Wound and the Cure of Words.* Baltimore, MD: Johns Hopkins University Press, 1990.

Bartini, Arnold G. "Whiteness in Robert Frost's Poetry." *The Massachusetts Review* 26: 351–356 (summer/autumn 1985).

Benstock, Shari. *Textualizing the Feminine: On the Limits of Genre.* Norman: University of Oklahoma Press, 1991.

Bernal, Martin. *Black Athena: The Afroasiatic Roots of Classical Civilization.* Vol. 1, *The Fabrication of Ancient Greece 1785–1985.* New Brunswick, NJ: Rutgers University Press, 1987.

Besner, Neil. "Bishop in Brazil: A Review, Interview and Memoir." *The Elizabeth Bishop Bulletin* 6 (1): 2 (summer 1997).
Bhabha, Homi K. "Signs Taken for Wonders: Questions of Ambivalence and Authority Under a Tree Outside Delhi, May 1817." *Critical Inquiry* 12 (1): 144–165 (autumn 1985).
Bishop, Elizabeth. *The Complete Poems 1927–1979.* New York: Farrar, Straus, & Giroux, 1984.
———. *One Art: Letters.* Robert Giroux, ed. New York: Farrar, Straus, & Giroux, 1994.
Bloom, Harold, ed. *H.D.* New York: Chelsea House Publishers, 1989.
Boose, Lynda E. "The Getting of a Lawful Race: Racial Discourse in Early Modern England and the Unrepresentable Black Woman." In Margo Hendricks and Patricia Parker, eds. *Women, "Race," & Writing in the Early Modern Period.* New York: Routledge, 1994.
Borderline. Produced and directed by Bryher, H.D., and Kenneth McPherson. Starring H.D., Eslanda Robeson, and Paul Robeson. 1930.
Bowser, Benjamin P., and Raymond G. Hunt, eds. *Impacts of Racism on White Americans.* 2d ed. Thousand Oaks, CA: Sage, 1996.
Boynton, Robert S. "The Bernaliad: A Scholar Warrior's Long Journey to Ithaca." *Lingua Franca* (November 1996): 43–50.
Broe, Mary Lynn. *Protean Poetic: The Poetry of Sylvia Plath.* Columbia: University of Missouri Press, 1980.
Bruzzi, Zara. "'The Fiery Moment': H.D. and the Eleusinian Landscape of English Modernism." *Agenda* 25 (3/4): 97–112 (autumn/winter 1987–1988).
Burnett, Gary. "A Poetics Out of War: H.D.'s Response to the First World War." *Agenda* 25 (3/4): 54–63 (autumn/winter 1987–1988).
Carter, Ronald, and Deirdre Burton, eds. *Literary Text and Language Study.* London: Edward Arnold Publishers, 1982.
Chisholm, Dianne. "H.D.'s Autoheterography." *Tulsa Studies in Women's Literature* 9 (1): 79–106 (spring 1990).
———. *H.D.'s Freudian Poetics: Psychoanalysis in Translation.* Ithaca, NY: Cornell University Press, 1992.
Christian, Barbara T. "Response to 'Black Women's Texts.'" *NWSA Journal* 1 (1): 21–36 (1988).
Colwell, Anne. *Inscrutable Houses: Metaphors of the Body in the Poems of Elizabeth Bishop.* Tuscaloosa: University of Alabama Press, 1997.
Costello, Bonnie. *Elizabeth Bishop: Questions of Mastery.* Cambridge, MA: Harvard University Press, 1991.
Crowfoot, James E., and Mark A. Chesler. "White Men's Roles in Multicultural Coalitions." In Benjamin P. Bowser and Raymond G. Hunt, eds. *Impacts of Racism on White Americans.* 2d ed. Thousand Oaks, CA: Sage, 1996.
Dale, Peter. "'O Honey Bees Come Build.'" In Linda W. Wagner, ed. *Sylvia Plath: The Critical Heritage.* New York: Routledge, 1988.
Dana, Richard Henry. *Two Years Before the Mast: A Personal Narrative of Life at Sea.* Thomas Philbrick, ed. New York: Penguin, 1986.
Dembo, L. S. "H.D., *Imagiste* and Her Octopus Intelligence." In Michael King, ed. *H.D.: Woman and Poet.* Orono, ME: National Poetry Foundation, 1986.

DeShazer, Mary K. "'A Primary Intensity Between Women': H.D. and the Female Muse." In Michael King, ed. *H.D.: Woman and Poet*. Orono, ME: National Poetry Foundation, 1986.

Dickie, Margaret. *Stein, Bishop, & Rich: Lyrics of Love, War, & Place*. Chapel Hill: University of North Carolina Press, 1997.

Dimock, Wai Chee. "A Theory of Resonance." *PMLA* 112 (5): 1060–1071 (October 1997).

DiPace Fritz, Angela. *Thought and Vision: A Critical Reading of H.D.'s Poetry*. Washington, DC: Catholic University of America Press, 1988.

Dodd, Elizabeth. *The Veiled Mirror and the Woman Poet: H.D., Louise Bogan, Elizabeth Bishop, and Louise Gluck*. Columbia: University of Missouri Press, 1992.

Doreski, C. K. *Elizabeth Bishop: The Restraints of Language*. New York: Oxford University Press, 1993.

DuPlessis, Rachel Blau. *H.D.: The Career of That Struggle*. Bloomington: Indiana University Press, 1986.

———. "'HOO HOO HOO': Some Episodes in the Construction of Modern Whiteness." *American Literature: A Journal of Literary History, Criticism and Bibliography* 67 (4): 667–700 (December 1995).

Dyer, Richard. *White*. New York: Routledge, 1997.

Edmunds, Susan. *Out of Line: History, Psychoanalysis & Montage in H.D.'s Long Poems*. Stanford, CA: Stanford University Press, 1994.

Erkkila, Betsy. "Elizabeth Bishop, Modernism, and the Left." *American Literary History* 8: 284–310 (summer 1996).

———. *The Wicked Sisters: Women Poets, Literary History and Discord*. New York: Oxford University Press, 1992.

Fernandez, John P. "The Impact of Racism on Whites in Corporate America." In Benjamin P. Bowser and Raymond G. Hunt, eds. *Impacts of Racism on White Americans*. 2d ed. Thousand Oaks, CA: Sage, 1996.

Fiedler, Leslie. *Love and Death in the American Novel*. 1960. Reprint. New York: Stein & Day, 1966.

Fountain, Gary, and Peter Brazeau, eds. *Remembering Elizabeth Bishop: An Oral Biography*. Amherst: University of Massachusetts Press, 1994.

Fowlkes, Diane. *White Political Women: Paths from Privilege to Empowerment*. Knoxville: University of Tennessee Press, 1992.

Fraistat, Neil. *Poems in Their Place: The Intertextuality and Order of Poetic Collections*. Chapel Hill: University of North Carolina Press, 1986.

Frankenberg, Ruth. *The Social Construction of Whiteness: White Women, Race Matters*. Minneapolis: University of Minnesota Press, 1993.

Fredrickson, G. M. *White Supremacy: A Comparative Study of American and South African History*. New York: Oxford University Press, 1981.

Friedman, Susan Stanford. "Creating a Women's Mythology: H.D.'s *Helen in Egypt*." In Susan Stanford Friedman and Rachel Blau DuPlessis, eds. *Signets: Reading H.D.* Madison: University of Wisconsin Press, 1990.

———. "Exile in the American Grain: H.D.'s Diaspora." *Agenda* 25 (3/4): 27–50 (autumn/winter 1987–1988).

———. "Modernism of the 'Scattered Remnant': Race and Politics in the Development of H.D.'s Modernist Vision." In Michael King, ed. *H.D.: Woman and Poet*. Orono, ME: National Poetry Foundation, 1986.

Friedman, Susan Stanford, and Rachel Blau DuPlessis, eds. *Signets: Reading H.D.* Madison: University of Wisconsin Press, 1990.

Gelpi, Albert. "Re-membering the Mother: A Reading of H.D.'s *Trilogy*." In Susan Stanford Friedman and Rachel Blau DuPlessis, eds. *Signets: Reading H.D.* Madison: University of Wisconsin Press, 1990.

Gilbert, Joel. "Who Lost an American?" In Noel Ignatiev and John Garvey, eds. *Race Traitor*. New York: Routledge, 1996.

Gilroy, Paul. *The Black Atlantic: Modernity and Double Consciousness*. Cambridge, MA: Harvard University Press, 1993.

Goldensohn, Lorrie. *The Biography of a Poetry*. New York: Columbia University Press, 1984.

———. "The Body's Roses: Race, Sex, and Gender in Elizabeth Bishop's Representations of the Self." In Marilyn May Lombardi, ed. *Elizabeth Bishop: The Geography of Gender*. Charlottesville: University Press of Virginia, 1993.

Graves, Robert. *The White Goddess: A Historical Grammar of Poetic Myth*. New York: Farrar, Straus, & Giroux, 1948.

Gubar, Susan. "The Echoing Spell of H.D.'s *Trilogy*." In Harold Bloom, ed. *H.D.* New York: Chelsea House Publishers, 1989.

———. *Racechanges: White Skin, Black Face in American Culture*. New York: Oxford University Press, 1997.

Guest, Barbara. *Herself Defined: The Poet H.D. and Her World*. Garden City, NY: Doubleday, 1984.

Gwin, Minrose C. *Black and White Women of the Old South*. Knoxville: University of Tennessee Press, 1985.

———. "A Theory of Black Women's Texts and White Women's Readings, or . . . The Necessity of Being Other." *NWSA Journal* 1 (1): 21–31 (1988).

Hardwick, Elizabeth. "On Sylvia Plath." In Paul Alexander, ed. *Ariel Ascending: Writings about Sylvia Plath*. New York: Harper & Row Publishers, 1985.

Harrison, Victoria. *Elizabeth Bishop's Poetics of Intimacy*. New York: Cambridge University Press, 1993.

Hatlen, Burton. "Recovering the Human Equation: H.D.'s 'Hermetic Definition.'" *Sagetrieb* 6 (2): 141–169 (fall 1987).

Hayman, Ronald. *The Death and Life of Sylvia Plath*. Secaucus, NJ: Birch Lane Press, 1991.

H.D. "The Cinema and the Classics I." *Close-Up* 1 (1): 22–33 (July 1927).

———. *Collected Poems: 1912–1944*. Louis L. Martz, ed. New York: New Directions, 1983.

———. *Helen in Egypt*. New York: New Directions, 1961.

———. *Hermetic Definition*. New York: New Directions, 1972.

———. *Notes on Thought and Vision & The Wise Sappho*. San Francisco: City Lights Books, 1982.

———. *Trilogy*. New York: New Directions, 1973.

Helms, Janet E., ed. "Toward a Model of White Racial Identity Development." In *Black and White Racial Identity: Theory, Research and Practice*. Westport, CT: Greenwood Press, 1990.

Hendricks, Margo, and Patricia Parker, eds. *Women, "Race," & Writing in the Early Modern Period*. New York: Routledge, 1994.

Holbrook, David. *Sylvia Plath: Poetry and Existence*. London: The Athlone Press, 1976.
Holland, Norman. "*Tribute to Freud* and the H.D. Myth." In Harold Bloom, ed. *H.D.* New York: Chelsea House Publishers, 1989.
Hollenberg, Donna Krolik. *The Poetics of Childbirth and Creativity*. Boston: Northeastern University Press, 1991.
Hotz, Robert Lee. "Official Racial Definitions Have Shifted Sharply and Often." *Los Angeles Times*, April 15, 1995, A14.
Hughes, Glenn. *Imagism and the Imagists: A Study in Modern Poetry*. Stanford, CA: Stanford University Press, 1931.
Hughes, Ted. *Birthday Letters*. New York: Farrar, Straus, & Giroux, 1998.
Ignatiev, Noel, and John Garvey, eds. *Race Traitor*. New York: Routledge, 1996.
Jeffries, Lesley. *The Language of Twentieth-Century Poetry*. New York: St. Martin's Press, 1993.
Jones, James M., and Robert T. Carter. "Racism and White Racial Identity." In Benjamin P. Bowser and Raymond G. Hunt, eds. *Impacts of Racism on White Americans*. 2d ed. Thousand Oaks, CA: Sage, 1996.
Kermode, Frank. *The Genesis of Secrecy: On the Interpretation of Narrative*. Cambridge, MA: Harvard University Press, 1979.
Kime, Bonnie Scott, ed. *The Gender of Modernism: A Critical Anthology*. Bloomington: Indiana University Press, 1990.
King, Michael, ed. *H.D.: Woman and Poet*. Orono, ME: National Poetry Foundation, 1986.
Kirkham, Michael. "Sylvia Plath." In Linda W. Wagner, ed. *Sylvia Plath: The Critical Heritage*. New York: Routledge, 1988.
Kival, Paul. *Uprooting Racism: How White People Can Work for Racial Justice*. Gabriola Island, British Columbia: New Society Publishers, 1996.
Kloepfer, Deborah Kelly. "Fishing the Murex Up: Sense and Resonance in H.D.'s *Palimpsest*." In Susan Stanford Friedman and Rachel Blau DuPlessis, eds. *Signets: Reading H.D.* Madison: University of Wisconsin Press, 1990.
Laity, Cassandra. "H.D.'s Romantic Landscapes: The Sexual Politics of the Garden." *Sagetrieb* 6: 57–75 (fall 1987).
Lake, David J. "The Whiteness of Griffin and H. G. Wells's Images of Death, 1897–1914." *Science Fiction Studies* 8 (1): 12–18 (March 1981).
Lefkowitz, Mary. *Not Out of Africa: How Afrocentrism Became an Excuse to Teach Myth as History*. New York: Basic Books, 1996.
Lensing, George S. "The Subtraction of Emotion in the Poetry of Elizabeth Bishop." *The Gettysburg Review* 5 (1): 48–61 (1992).
Lindberg-Seyersted, Brita. "Sylvia Plath's Psychic Landscapes." *English Studies* 71 (6): 511–523 (December 1990).
Lombardi, Marilyn May. *The Body and the Song: Elizabeth Bishop's Poetics*. Carbondale: Southern Illinois University Press, 1995.
Lombardi, Marilyn May, ed. *Elizabeth Bishop: The Geography of Gender*. Charlottesville: University Press of Virginia, 1993.
Loomba, Ania. "The Color of Patriarchy: Critical Difference, Cultural Difference, and Renaissance Drama." In Margo Hendricks and Patricia Parker, eds. *Women, "Race," & Writing in the Early Modern Period*. New York: Routledge, 1994.

Lopez, Ian F. Haney. *White by Law: The Legal Construction of Race*. New York: New York University Press, 1996.

Malcolm, Janet. *The Silent Woman: Sylvia Plath & Ted Hughes*. New York: Alfred A. Knopf, 1994.

Martz, Louis L. "Introduction to *The Collected Poems*." In Harold Bloom, ed. *H.D.* New York: Chelsea House Publishers, 1989.

Matovich, Richard M. *A Concordance to the Collected Poems of Sylvia Plath*. New York: Garland Publishing, 1986.

Mazie, Margery, Phyllis Palmer, Mayuris Pimentel, Sharon Rogers, Stuart Ruderfer, and Melissa Sokolowski. "To Deconstruct Race, Deconstruct Whiteness." *American Quarterly* 45 (2): 281–294 (June 1993).

McCabe, Susan. *Elizabeth Bishop: Her Poetics of Loss*. University Park: Pennsylvania State University Press, 1994.

McCorkle, James. *The Still Performance: Writing, Self, and Interconnection in Five Postmodern American Poets*. Charlottesville: University Press of Virginia, 1989.

McIntosh, Peggy. "White Privilege and Male Privilege: A Personal Account of Coming to See Correspondences Through Work in Women's Studies." Center for Research on Women: Working Paper Series. Wellesley, MA: Center for Research on Women, 1988.

McNeil, Helen. "Sylvia Plath." In Helen Vendler, ed. *Voices and Visions: The Poet in America*. New York: Random House, 1987.

Merrin, Jeredith. *An Enabling Humility: Marianne Moore, Elizabeth Bishop, and the Uses of Tradition*. New Brunswick, NJ: Rutgers University Press, 1990.

Miller, Christanne. *Emily Dickinson: A Poet's Grammar*. Cambridge, MA: Harvard University Press, 1987.

Minh-ha, Trinh T. *Woman, Native, Other: Writing Postcoloniality and Feminism*. Bloomington: Indiana University Press, 1989.

Montefiore, Jan. *Feminism and Poetry: Language, Experience, Identity in Women's Writing*. New York: Pandora, 1987.

Monteiro, George, ed. *Conversations with Elizabeth Bishop*. Jackson: University Press of Mississippi, 1996.

Morris, Adelaide. "The Concept of Projection: H.D.'s Visionary Powers." In Susan Stanford Friedman and Rachel Blau DuPlessis, eds. *Signets: Reading H.D.* Madison: University of Wisconsin Press, 1990.

Morrison, Toni. *The Bluest Eye*. 1970. Reprint. New York: Plume, 1993.

——— . *Playing in the Dark: Whiteness and the Literary Imagination*. Cambridge, MA: Harvard University Press, 1992.

——— . "Unspeakable Things Unspoken: The Afro-American Presence in American Literature." *Michigan Quarterly Review* 28 (1): 1–34 (winter 1989).

Morrison, Toni, ed. "Introduction: Friday on the Potomac." In *Rac-ing Justice, En-gendering Power: Essays on Anita Hill, Clarence Thomas, and the Construction of Social Reality*. New York: Pantheon Books, 1992.

Nance, Guinevara A., and Judith P. Jones. "Doing Away with Daddy: Exorcism and Sympathetic Magic in Plath's Poetry." In Linda W. Wagner, ed. *Critical Essays on Sylvia Plath*. Boston: G. K. Hall, 1984.

Nelson, Dana D. *The Word in Black and White: Reading "Race" in American Literature 1638–1867*. New York: Oxford University Press, 1993.

Newitz, Annalee. "White Savagery and Humiliation." In Matt Wray and Annalee Newitz, eds. *White Trash: Race and Class in America*. New York: Routledge, 1997.
Nielsen, Aldon Lynn. *Reading Race: White American Poets and the Racial Discourse in the Twentieth Century*. Athens: University of Georgia Press, 1988.
Nims, John Frederick. "The Poetry of Sylvia Plath." In Paul Alexander, ed. *Ariel Ascending: Writings about Sylvia Plath*. New York: Harper & Row, 1985.
Oates, Joyce Carol. "The Death Throes of Romanticism." In Paul Alexander, ed. *Ariel Ascending: Writings about Sylvia Plath*. New York: Harper & Row, 1985.
Olney, James. *The Language(s) of Poetry: Walt Whitman, Emily Dickinson, Gerard Manley Hopkins*. Athens: University of Georgia Press, 1993.
Omi, Michael, and Howard Winant, eds. *Racial Formation in the United States: From the 1960s to the 1990s*. 2d ed. New York: Routledge, 1994.
Ostriker, Alicia. "No Rule of Procedure: The Open Poetics of H.D." In Susan Stanford Friedman and Rachel Blau DuPlessis, eds. *Signets: Reading H.D.* Madison: University of Wisconsin Press, 1990.
——— . *Stealing the Language: The Emergence of Women's Poetry in America*. Boston: Beacon Press, 1986.
Pearce, Roy Harvey. *The Continuity of American Poetry*. Middletown, CT: Wesleyan University Press, 1987.
Peeples, Edward H. "Richmond Journal: Thirty Years in Black and White." In Noel Ignatiev and John Garvey, eds. *Race Traitor*. New York: Routledge, 1996.
Perkins, David. *A History of Modern Poetry: Modernism and After*. Cambridge, MA: Harvard University Press, 1987.
Perloff, Marjorie. "*Angst* and Animism in the Poetry of Sylvia Plath." In Linda W. Wagner, ed. *Critical Essays on Sylvia Plath*. Boston: G. K. Hall, 1984.
Pettigrew, T. F. "The Mental Health Impact." In Benjamin P. Bowser and Raymond G. Hunt, eds. *Impacts of Racism on White Americans*. Thousand Oaks, CA: Sage, 1981.
Pieterse, Jan Nederveen. *White on Black: Images of Africa and Blacks in Western Popular Culture*. New Haven, CT: Yale University Press, 1992.
Pinker, Steven. *The Language Instinct: How the Mind Creates Language*. New York: HarperCollins, 1994.
Plath, Sylvia. *The Collected Poems*. New York: Harper & Row, 1981.
——— . *The It-Doesn't-Matter-Suit*. New York: St. Martin's Press, 1996.
——— . *The Journals of Sylvia Plath*. Ted Hughes and Frances McCullough, eds. New York: Dial, 1982.
Pollitt, Katha. "A Note of Triumph." Review of *The Collected Poems*. In Linda W. Wagner, ed. *Critical Essays on Sylvia Plath*. Boston: G. K. Hall, 1984.
Reid, Mark A. "Dialogic Modes of Representing Africa(s): Womanist Film." *Black American Literature Forum* 25 (2): 38–52 (summer 1991).
Roessel, David. "H.D.'s Troy: Some Bearings." *H.D. Newsletter* 3 (2): 38–42 (1990).
Rose, Jacqueline. *The Haunting of Sylvia Plath*. Cambridge, MA: Harvard University Press, 1992.
Rose, Lillian Roybal. "White Identity and Counseling White Allies about Racism." In Benjamin P. Bowser and Raymond G. Hunt, eds. *Impacts of Racism on White Americans*. 2d ed. Thousand Oaks, CA: Sage, 1996.

Salvidar, Toni. *Sylvia Plath: Confessing the Fictive Self.* New York: Peter Lang, 1992.
Sedgwick, Eve Kosofsky. "Privilege of Unknowing." *Genders* 1: 102–124 (spring 1988).
Sisney, Mary F. "The Power and Horror of Whiteness: Wright and Ellison Respond to Poe." *CLA Journal* 29: 82–90 (September 1985).
Smedley, Audrey. *Race in North America: Origin and Evolution of a Worldview.* Boulder, CO: Westview Press, 1993.
Smith, Barbara. "Toward a Black Feminist Criticism." In Elaine Showalter, ed. *The New Feminist Criticism: Essays on Women, Literature and Theory.* New York: Pantheon Books, 1985.
Snowden, Frank M., Jr. *Before Color Prejudice: The Ancient View of Blacks.* Cambridge, MA: Harvard University Press, 1983.
Stafford, Walter W. "If We Live in a 'Post' Era, Is There a Post-Racism?" In Benjamin P. Bowser and Raymond G. Hunt, eds. *Impacts of Racism on White Americans.* 2d ed. Thousand Oaks, CA: Sage, 1996.
Stevenson, Anne. *Bitter Fame: A Life of Sylvia Plath.* Boston: Houghton Mifflin, 1989.
——— . "The Iceberg and the Ship." *Michigan Quarterly Review* 35 (1): 704–719 (fall 1996).
Travisano, Thomas. "The Elizabeth Bishop Phenomenon." *New Literary History* 26: 903–930 (1995).
——— . "Emerging Genius: Elizabeth Bishop and the Blue Pencil, 1927–1930." *The Gettysburg Review* 5 (1): 32–47 (1992).
Uroff, Margaret Dickie. *Sylvia Plath and Ted Hughes.* Urbana: University of Illinois Press, 1979.
Van Dyne, Susan R. "'More Terrible than She Ever Was': The Manuscripts of Sylvia Plath's Bee Poems." In Linda W. Wagner, ed. *Critical Essays on Sylvia Plath.* Boston: G. K. Hall, 1984.
——— . *Revising Life: Sylvia Plath's Ariel Poems.* Chapel Hill: University of North Carolina Press, 1993.
Wagner, Linda W., ed. *Critical Essays on Sylvia Plath.* Boston: G. K. Hall, 1984.
Wagner-Martin, Linda W. *Sylvia Plath: A Biography.* New York: St. Martin's Press, 1987.
Ware, Vron. *Beyond the Pale: White Women, Racism and History.* New York: Verso, 1992.
Warren, Kenneth W. *Black and White Strangers: Race and American Literary Realism.* Chicago: University of Chicago Press, 1993.
Weatherhead, A. Kingsley. "Style in H.D.'s Novels." In Harold Bloom, ed. *H.D.* New York: Chelsea House Publishers, 1989.
Wiegman, Robyn. *American Anatomies: Theorizing Race and Gender.* Durham, NC: Duke University Press, 1995.
Winsbro, Bonnie. *Supernatural Forces: Belief, Difference and Power in Contemporary Works by Ethnic Women.* Amherst: University of Massachusetts, 1993.
Wolosky, Shira. "Representing Other Voices: Rhetorical Perspective in Elizabeth Bishop." *Style* 29 (1): 1–17 (spring 1995).
Wordsworth, William. "Prelude." In J. C. Maxwell, ed. *Lyrical Ballads.* New York: Penguin, 1971.
Wray, Matt, and Annalee Newitz, eds. *White Trash: Race and Class in America.* New York: Routledge, 1997.

Index

Aesthetics, 16, 23, 97, 103, 109, 114, 119, 120
Africa, 157–58, 160
African, 16, 19n, 60, 90, 124–25, 139, 160; cat, 157; ethics, 90. *See also* Black; Blackness; Negro
African American, 16, 18, 21, 78, 84. *See also* Black; Blackness; Negro
Afroasiatic, 24, 27, 57–61, 68, 70, 74. *See also* Bernal, Martin; Lefkowitz, Mary
Aldington, Richard, 33
Allen, Theodore, 3, 16, 19
Alvarez, A., 134
America, 4, 5, 139; Hispanic, 4; North, 84; South, 84, 113
American, 2, 99, 112, 125, 131; borders, 7; Latin, 80; poets, 128; skin, 5; white woman, 134
Annas, Pamela J., 135–36, 138, 140, 142, 144, 150, 152, 155, 159, 160–62, 166–67
Arab, 99–100
Arthur, Marilyn, 41
Asian, 15
Awkward, Michael, 1, 7

Axelrod, Steven Gould, 77, 126, 131, 146, 162–63

Baker, Houston, 6
Balzac, Honoré de: *Seraphita*, 28, 31; Venus, 30
Bartini, Arnold G., 87
Benstock, Shari, 57, 59
Bernal, Martin, 25, 38, 59–62, 68, 70. *See also* Afroasiatic; Lefkowitz, Mary
Bhabha, Homi, 16–17
Binary opposition, 6, 8, 92–93, 101–2, 110, 121, 126, 129, 133. *See also* Black; White
Bishop, Elizabeth, 7, 169–70; "Anaphora," 95–96; "Armadillo, The," 110; "Arrival at Santos," 105–6; and Blough (Muser), Frani, 78–79, 80–82; and Brazil, 75–76, 80, 82, 86, 105–6, 108, 112–15, 121; "Brazil, January 1, 1502," 105; "Burglar of Babylon," 114; "Cape Breton," 87, 100–101; and Carr, Marjorie, 79; "Cirque d'Hiver," 91–95; *Cold Spring, A*, 96–105; "Cold Spring, A," 96–99; "Cootchie," 94; and de

Macedo Soares, Lota, 75, 80–81, 96, 112, 115; *Diary of Helena Morley, The*, 108; "Electrical Storm," 106; "End of March, The," 120–21; and essentialist racism, 12; "Faustina, or Rock Roses," 101–2; "Filling Station, The," 114–15; "First Death in Nova Scotia," 106–7; "Five Flights Up," 87; *Geography III*, 117–22; "Giant Snail," 116; as ignorant, 8; "Imaginary Iceberg," 83, 85, 87–90, 108, 118, 122; "In the Waiting Room," 87, 117–18; "Invitation to Miss Marianne Moore," 102–5; "Large Bad Picture," 87, 107; "Letter to N.Y.," 87; "Love Lies Sleeping," 89–91, 93; "Manuelzhino," 108–10; "Moose, The," 118; *North & South*, 83–96; "Over 2,000 Illustrations and a Complete Concordance," 99; "Poem," 119–20; *Questions of Travel*, 105–16; "Questions of Travel," 106; "Riverman, The," 111–12; "Sandpiper, The," 115–16; "Santarém," 121; and self-reflection on whiteness, 75–122; "Song for the Rainy Season," 109; "Songs for a Colored Singer," 17, 94–95; "Twelfth Morning," 12; "View of the Capitol from the Library of Congress," 87; white writer, 1

Black, 5, 17, 19–20n, 22, 87, 94, 102–3, 107–8, 116, 118, 126–27, 129, 134, 152–53, 157, 161, 167; Africans, 19n, 38, 90; body, 41; boy, 12; community, 16; figure in art, 40; Greece, 25; heritage, 58, 62; men, 8, 49, 69, 79; as negative, 5, 10; Other, 18; people, 8, 17–18, 24; slave, 16, 19n; as unconstrained libido, 12; women, 23, 117–18. *See also* African; African American; Negro

Blackness, 4–5, 16, 32, 41, 62, 76, 94, 103–4, 106–7, 110, 114–15, 118, 126, 130, 132, 145, 156, 158, 161–62. *See also* African; African American; Negro

Boose, Lynda, 6–7
Boynton, Robert S., 60

Broe, Mary Lynn, 135, 146, 149–50, 155, 160, 167
Brown, 11, 19n, 119
Bruzzi, Zara, 28, 30–31
Bryher, 21–22, 33, 61
Burnett, Gary, 25, 56

Chinese, 98–99, 125, 143, 146, 150, 161
Chisholm, Dianne, 49, 59
Christ, 165; and whiteness, 27. *See also* Christianity; God
Christian, Barbara, 18
Christianity, 4, 16, 26–27, 90, 99–100, 105, 165. *See also* Christ; God
Colonial discourse, 5
Colonial expansion, 19n
Colonialism, 7–8, 15, 25
Color evasion, 10, 14
Colwell, Anne, 76–77, 82–83, 85–86, 88, 92, 97
Community, 2
Critical white studies, 170
Crowfoot, James E., 11
Cunard, Nancy, 26

Dembo, L. S., 71
Dialect, 10, 16–17
Dickie, Margaret, 82, 83, 84, 103, 125
Difference, 5, 17, 19n, 75
Dimock, Wai Chee, 21–22, 26, 29, 125
DiPace Fritz, Angela, 38–39, 47, 54, 56, 65
Dodd, Elizabeth, 24, 39, 98, 105
Doreski, C. K., 83, 95
DuPlessis, Rachel Blau, 24, 27–29, 52–54, 68, 90, 135
Durand, Lionel, 68–70, 72–73
Dyer, Richard, 7, 23, 27, 30, 41, 43, 49, 63, 86–87, 89, 91–92, 95, 97, 104, 107, 112, 118, 121, 129, 131, 133, 137, 140–41, 143, 156, 163, 165–66

Edmunds, Susan, 49–50, 58, 61–62, 68
Ellis, Havelock, 122n
Elusive mastery signifiers, 10, 13–14
England, 139, 157
Englishmen, 4
Englishness, 3–4, 17, 139
Erkkila, Betsy, 59, 83, 89, 91, 95, 113
Essential difference, 5

Essentialism, 5; and language, 10
Essentialist racism, 11–12, 31–32. *See also* Race; Racial; Racism; Racist; Romantic racism
Exoticism, 12, 17, 23, 26

Feminism, 8, 18; and disloyalty to, 9, 10
Fernandez, John P., 11
Fountain, Gary, 81
Fowlkes, Diane, 6
Frankenberg, Ruth, 5–6, 8, 11–15, 19, 31, 54, 64
Freud, Sigmund, 21, 58
Friedman, Susan Stanford, 22, 24, 26–28, 33, 40, 57, 65, 74n.1

Gelpi, Albert, 23
Gilroy, Paul, 19
God, 4, 107, 115, 152–53, 165. *See also* Christ; Christianity
Gold, Arthur, 80
Goldensohn, Lorrie, 76–77, 80–81, 112
Graves, Robert, 58–59
Greece, 22–25. *See also* Afroasiatic; Bernal, Martin; H.D., and Greece; Lefkowitz, Mary
Gubar, Susan, 33, 52–54
Guest, Barbara, 27
Gwin, Minrose, 18

Hardwick, Elizabeth, 142–43, 150–51, 174
Harrison, Victoria, 89, 94
Hatlen, Burton, 68
H.D. (Hilda Doolittle), 1, 7, 15, 169–70; "All Mountains," 40, 46–47; and body, 27; *Borderline*, 22, 39; "Calliope," 46; "Chronos Sequence," 40, 42–44; "Cinema and the Classics," 58; "Cliff Temple," 28, 31; "Contest, The," 29–30; "Egypt," 38, 48; "Epitaph," 40, 48; "Flowering of the Rod," 49, 56, 65; and Greece, 23–26, 38–39, 42, 48; "Halcyon," 40, 43–44; *Helen in Egypt*, 26, 38–39, 57–68; *Hermetic Definition*, 39, 68–73; "Hermetic Definition," 22; *HERmione*, 22; *Hymen*, 33–36; as ignorant, 8; and Imagist movement, 21, 27–28; and masterful whiteness, 21–74; and Moravianism, 25–27, 74n.1; "Myrtle Bough," 40, 42; *Notes on Thought and Vision*, 22, 27; "Red Rose and a Beggar," 13, 68–71; *Red Roses for Bronze*, 39–50, 61, 56, 58; "Red Roses for Bronze," 22, 39–40, 57; and sacredness, 25; *Sea Garden*, 27–33, 42, 73; "Sea Gods," 31; "Sea Violet," 30, 54; "Songs from Cypress," 44, 46; "Storm," 32; *Tribute to the Angels*, 23; "Tribute to the Angels," 49, 52, 54; *Trilogy*, 49–58; "Triplex," 40, 48; "Walls Do Not Fall," 49–50; "White Rose," 40, 45–46; "White World," 36–37; white writer, 1; *Wise Sappho, The*, 22, 37
Helms, Janet E., 1
Holiday, Billie, 78
Hollenberg, Donna, 36, 38–39, 54
Homeric Hymns, 28
Hopkins, Gerard Manley, 96
Hotz, Robert Lee, 4
Hughes, Glenn, 24
Hughes, Ted, 123–24, 131, 135, 137–39, 142, 150–51, 154, 165, 167; "Being Christlike," 165; *Birthday Letters*, 124, 165, 167; "18 Rugby Street," 124; "Fulbright Scholars," 124; "Perfect Light," 133; "You Hated Spain," 124, 139. *See also* Plath, Sylvia, and Hughes, Ted

Ideology, 3, 5, 11, 19, 22, 80, 87, 94, 99, 103, 115, 118, 120. *See also* White, ideology
Ignorance, 2, 8, 14–16; and collusion in oppression, 18; and inheritance of colonialism, 7
Imagination, 3, 13, 22–23, 28–30, 32, 42, 73, 77, 93, 99–100, 104, 114–15, 120–21, 131, 133, 135, 144, 163–65. *See also* White, imagination
Indian, 99, 105, 125, 165–66
Invisibility, 6, 9, 76, 92
Isis, 24, 62, 67, 70

Jeffries, Lesley, 2

Kloepfer, Deborah Kelly, 68

Laity, Cassandra, 24, 28
Lake, David J., 86
Lefkowitz, Mary, 60. *See also* Afroasiatic; Bernal, Martin
Lensing, George S., 2
Lesbian, 21; and love, 36, 75
Lindberg-Seyersted, Brita, 131
Lombardi, Marilyn May, 75, 77–78, 83, 85, 87–88, 93, 95, 101, 106, 116, 121
Loomba, Ania, 6–7
Lopez, Ian F. Haney, 33
Lowell, Robert, 112

Malcolm, Janet, 125
Martz, Louis, 39, 49, 54
Mastery, 12–14, 16, 18, 21–22, 29, 37, 40, 55, 65, 77, 82, 132–33, 136, 150–51. *See also* White, mastery
McCabe, Susan, 83, 85, 88, 90, 92, 96–99, 104, 112, 115
McCorkle, James, 83
Merrin, Jeredith, 83, 88
Montefiore, Jan, 2
Moore, Marianne, 94, 102–5
Morris, Adelaide, 23, 49, 56
Morrison, Toni, 17–18, 28, 80, 84, 124, 135

Native Americans, 19–20n, 124
Negro, 16, 125, 137, 153–54; cook, 78; namesake, 81; Portuguese, 79; race, 20n, 90, 137; servant, 78–79; singer, 78; voices, 76, 78. *See also* African; African American; Black; Blackness
Nelson, Dana, 6
Newitz, Annalee, 47, 91, 93, 95, 135, 141. *See also* White, trash
Nielsen, Aldon Lynn, 12, 14, 16–17, 19, 22

Oates, Joyce Carol, 125, 128, 139, 151
Odetta, 78
Olney, James, 2
Omi, Michael, 169–70
Ostriker, Alicia, 2, 52, 56, 84
Other, 5–6, 16–18, 26–27, 45, 48, 50, 53, 68, 71–72, 76, 101–2, 112, 114–15, 119, 126, 133, 135, 137, 141, 146–47, 151, 161, 164, 167
Otherness, 10, 17–18, 26–27, 45, 54, 64, 71, 79, 84, 94, 104, 119, 124, 136, 148, 151, 157, 160, 162

Pearce, Roy Harvey, 2
"Peculiar Institution," 3
Perloff, Marjorie, 152, 157
Pieterse, Jan Nederveen, 60
Plath, Sylvia, 7, 169–70; *Ariel*, 154–68; "Ariel," 138, 166–67; "Arrival of the Bee Box," 159–61; "Bee Meeting," 158–59, 164; *Bell Jar, The*, 77; *Colossus, The*, 134–42; "Conversation Among the Ruins," 129, 132; *Crossing the Water*, 142–50; "Cut," 165–66; "Daddy," 163–65; and early poems, 129–34; "Eavesdropper," 146; "Electra on Azalea Path," 133–34; and enactment of whiteness, 123–67; "Face Lift," 144–45; "Fever 103 Degrees," 165, 167; "Full Fathom Five," 138; and Hughes, Ted, 123–24, 131; as ignorant, 8; "In Plaster," 145–46; *It Doesn't-Matter-Suit, The*, 148–49; "Lady Lazarus," 167; "Little Fugue," 156; "Love Letter," 143; "Magi," 143; "Moon and the Yew Tree," 157–58, 164; "Moonrise," 139–42; "Morning Song," 155; "Mushrooms," 138; "Night Shift," 135–36; "Other, The," 151–52; "Pursuit," 130; "Rival, The," 155; "Soliloquy of the Solipsist," 132–33; "Stings," 155; "Stopped Dead," 146; "Surgeon at 2:00 A.M.," 143, 149–50; "Swarm, The," 152–53; "Tale of a Tub," 131; "Thalidomide," 153–54; "Thin People, The," 136; "Tulips," 156–57; "Whiteness I Remember," 14, 138–39; white writer, 1; "Wintering," 146, 161–62, 164; "Winter Landscape, With Rooks," 130; *Winter Trees*, 150–54
Positionality, 1, 7, 10–11, 13, 22, 27, 82, 88
Pound, Ezra, 21, 28

Presumption, 1, 2, 22; poetics of, 10–18; white, 10
Privilege, 6, 18, 64, 96, 151; white, 8, 49, 68, 76, 80, 84, 91, 95, 113–14, 123–24, 135, 137, 167, 169

Race, 8, 11–13, 19, 19–20n, 24, 39, 111, 118, 169; biological, 20n; classification of, 4; construction of, 4; and difference, 26; identity, 3; ideology of, 5, 19; innateness of, 4; research of, 4; sociological, 20n. *See also* Essentialist racism; Racial; Racism; Racist; Romantic racism
Race Traitor, 169–70
Racial: ancestry, 67; animosity, 158; conversion, 62; difference, 5, 51; discourse, 75; furies, 154; inheritance, 58; markings, 84–85, 92, 95, 125–26, 129, 132, 135, 145, 159, 162; outsider, 83; politics, 124; signifiers, 156; superiority, 124; understanding, 32. *See also* Essentialist racism; Race; Racism; Racist; Romantic racism
Racism, 3, 6, 8–9, 12–14, 19n, 26, 126; effect on white people, 10; as evil, 20n; heritage of, 3; maintenance of, 7; white guilt regarding, 11. *See also* Essentialist racism; Race; Racial; Racist; Romantic racism
Racist, 25, 75, 154; attitudes, 11; classification, 5; discourse, 5, 15–16; implications of ignoring whiteness, 9; languages, 5; restructuring of community, 12. *See also* Essentialist racism; Race; Racial; Racism; Romantic racism
Red, 11, 19–20n, 126
Reid, Mark, 18
Rich, Adrienne, 84
Robeson, Essie, 21, 23
Robeson, Paul, 21–22, 39, 41, 45, 69–70
Roessel, David, 57
Romantic racism, 10, 12, 77, 105. *See also* Essentialist racism; Race; Racial; Racism; Racist
Rose, Jacqueline, 163–64

Sandburg, Carl, 17

Sappho, 22, 37, 57; and whiteness, 22–23
Sedgwick, Eve Kosofsky, 15
Sisney, Mary F., 87
Skin, 39, 70, 132, 144–45, 167; color, 25, 29, 33, 69, 101, 125, 169
Slavery, 5, 14, 16, 160
Smedley, Audrey, 4, 5, 14, 16, 19, 51–52
Smith, Barbara, 18
Smith, Bessie, 78
Snowden, Frank M., Jr., 24–25, 60, 70
Stafford, Walter W., 3
Stereotypes, 10, 17–18
Stevenson, Anne, 1, 83, 126, 133, 135, 138, 140, 144–45, 149, 167
Swenson, May, 79
Swinburne, Algernon Charles, 28

Travisano, Thomas, 2, 84, 96, 112

Uroff, Margaret Dickie, 82, 83, 84, 103, 125

Van Dyne, Susan, R., 125, 153, 156, 158, 160, 165–66
Van Vechten, Carl, 26

Wagner-Martin, Linda, 133, 154, 157–58
Ware, Vron, 8
Warren, Kenneth W., 12
Weatherhead, A. Kingsley, 33
White, 19–20n, 23, 29–31, 75, 77, 83, 86–87, 94, 96, 98, 116, 119, 121, 123, 126–27, 148, 151–52, 154, 157, 161, 165; Americans, 4, 5; apologies, 6; assimilative paradigms, 53; authorship, 68, 83; beauty, 22; body, 49, 58–59, 60, 76, 85, 107–8, 141, 146; bones, 64; characters, 16; conscience, 6; culture, 6; as desirable, 30; discourse, 5, 10, 14–17; and excellence, 85; failure, 91; fear, 12; feminism, 8–9; feminist criticism, 6; as hierarchically desirable, 10; "I," 129, 132, 155; identity, 19; ideology, 115; imagination, 115; life, 111; love, 46: male ideology, 6; markers of difference, 7; mastery, 29, 40, 46, 65; mythologies, 5; people, 1, 4, 5–7,

16, 18, 23, 33, 76, 86, 93, 97, 104, 129; poetics, 22–23, 41; poets, 10, 105; Portuguese emigrants, 4; positionality, 10–11, 13, 68, 114; power, 41, 68, 131, 137, 143; presumption, 10; privilege, 8; psyche, 54; race, 3, 5, 6, 23; racial dominance, 88; racial politics, 2; readings, 18; scholars, 6, 18; self, 14; story of racism, 6; supremacy, 9; synonymous with freedom, 16; as tradition of civility, 16; trash, 47, 102, 135; treatment of Other, 6; unmarked, 5; virtue, 30; Western self, 5; women, 1, 3, 6–9, 14, 18–19, 40, 57, 81, 94, 101, 105–6, 113, 117, 130, 134, 146, 156; women poets, 7, 9; women scholars, 6–7; working class, 91; writers, 10, 12, 16, 19, 87, 107, 169. *See also* Essentialist racism; Mastery; Race; Racial; Racism; Racist; Romantic racism

Whitening, 4

White writing, 1–2, 10, 14, 83, 169; definition of, 2

Wiegman, Robyn, 5, 7, 9–10

Williams, William Carlos, 16, 21

Winant, Howard, 169–70

Wolosky, Shira, 113

Wordsworth, William, 2

Yellow, 11, 108, 111, 119, 142, 145–49, 161

About the Author

RENÉE R. CURRY is Professor of Literature and Writing at California State University, San Marcos. She is the editor of *Perspectives on Woody Allen* (1996) and coeditor of *States of Rage: Emotional Eruption, Violence, and Social Change* (1996).